CREATING
RAINMAKERS

CREATING RAINMAKERS

The Manager's Guide to Training
Professionals to Attract New Clients

FORD HARDING, CMC

WILEY

John Wiley & Sons, Inc.

Published by John Wiley & Sons, Inc., Hoboken, New Jersey
Published simultaneously in Canada

For general information on our other products and services or for technical support, please contact our Customer Care Department within the United States at (800) 762-2974, outside the United States at (317) 572-3993 or fax (317) 572-4002.

Wiley also publishes its books in a variety of electronic formats. Some content that appears in print may not be available in electronic books. For more information about Wiley products, visit our Web site at www.wiley.com.

Library of Congress Cataloging-in-Publication Data:
Harding, Ford.
  Creating rain makers : the manager's guide to training professionals to attract new
  clients / Ford Harding.
       p.   cm.
  Includes index.
  Originally published: Holbrook, Mass: Adams Media, 1998.
  ISBN-13: 978-0-471-92073-1 (cloth)
  ISBN-10: 0-471-92073-8 (cloth)
  1. Professions — Marketing.   I. Harding, Ford. Creating rainmakers. 1998.
  II. Title.
  HD8038.A1H368   2006
  658.8 — dc22

                                                            2006042645

Printed in the United States of America

10 9 8 7 6 5 4 3 2 1

Contents

Acknowledgments

My first book was based heavily on my own experiences. This one is based largely on the experiences of others. I could not have written it without the help of hundreds of people who were willing to share their experiences, describe rainmakers that they have known, and help me when my thinking became tangled. Gathering the information needed for this book helped me to learn many things that I had not known about old friends and to make many new ones. I hope reading *Creating Rainmakers* is as beneficial and enjoyable for the reader as researching it was for me.

Many of the rainmakers interviewed for this book are mentioned in the following chapters by name. Thanks to all of you. Those who described rainmakers they have known were equally helpful but are not named in the text. Rich Cobin, Ben DiSylvester, Richard Finkelstein, Duncan Finlayson, Charles Galloway, Tracy Gerlitz, Steven Gray, Carol Greenwald, Cheryl Grek-Chalifoux, Pat Heaney, Ed Hendricks, Ellen Jackson, Frank Jacoby, Missie Johnson, Bill Kaffer, Jim Kielley, George Kolodka, Bob Maher, Tom O'Neill, Mike Paris, Stephen Parkoff, Kim Perrett, Jerry Perricone, Joe Pine, Dory Raposa, Michael Reilly, Mark Santiago, Mike Schell, Mike Seltzer, Ralph Smith, Karen Stuckey, Kirk Tyson, Lionel Wishneff, and Loren Wittner all provided introductions to rainmakers or information about them. In some cases, they did both. Also providing valuable information were Alan Andolsen, Karl Bartscht, Cliff Earls, Stuart Emanuel, Steve Fein, John Ferraro, Charles Green, Martin McElroy, and Greg Steinberg.

Ira Herman introduced me to investment principles that stimulated my thinking for Chapter 2. Barbara Andolsen, Ed Kennedy, and

John Bliss all critiqued an early version of Chapter 12. Because it deals with a difficult subject, their comments were particularly valuable. All opinions in that chapter are my own. That chapter and Chapter 7 both appeared originally in *Journal of Management Consulting*, which has kindly permitted me to use them here. Many of the ideas in Chapter 7 are those of its coauthor, Annette Felzani Dwyer.

Ed Walters, my editor, provided much helpful guidance. I thank my agent, Jeff Herman, for taking the book on. Joe Reilly's sharp eyes and feel for the language have improved all of what follows.

Without the help of my wife and son, I doubt whether I would have had the will or freedom from distraction to write this book. They have been supportive and tolerant throughout the process. I dedicate this book to my mother, Patricia B. Harding. Her kindness, energy, determination, and resilience have been the formative forces in my life.

Introduction

Every professional firm needs more people who develop new business. Accountants, actuaries, architects, attorneys, engineers, and management consultants are all familiar with this problem. Bright, young, technical talent is always available. Seasoned project managers are usually so. But never are there enough rainmakers.

The shortage has profound results. Competitors win business that could have been sold had the talent been available. New offices go unopened. Firm revenues and profits fall below what they could have been. Growth is retarded in a booming market. A practice or sometimes a whole firm wanes because it cannot replace rainmakers who have retired. Subtle consequences may be invisible to firm management. The partners at one $40-million-a-year professional firm I am familiar with have estimated that the firm must reach $100 million in fees over the next fifteen years to support their future retirement. To achieve that goal, they will need more people skilled at bringing in business. How many firms have conducted a similar evaluation?

At professional firms, such people have been called rainmakers since the late 1970s.[1] The term avoids the word *selling*, found distasteful by many professionals, and expresses the awe often felt for successful business-getters. Like the powers of one who can conjure up rain, their powers can seem almost magical. Listen to these quotes from seasoned professionals about rainmakers they have known:

- He is the best rainmaker I ever saw. He has brought in huge amounts of work. He walks down the street and a big case drops in his lap. [a lawyer]

- He was the only person I ever knew who could just pick up the phone and call people and get an engagement. Whenever we had a shortfall in revenue, he would do this. [a consultant]

- Whenever we were in a really tight spot, he seemed to bring in a big project out of nowhere. [an architect]

- His success ratio was much better than anyone else's in the firm. He had the appearance of having a 50 percent success rate [of getting business] from the people he contacted. [a consultant]

Rainmakers generate lots of revenue and profits and create opportunities for others in the firm to do important work. A few rare people have generated hundreds of millions of dollars of business during their careers. In many large consulting firms today, every partner is expected to generate at least $3 million worth of business each year. The true rainmakers will bring in more than $5 million. At a major law firm, figures are comparable. The most effective rainmaker that I know in the architectural industry develops about $10 million worth of fees or more each year. In many of the professions, even in small firms, a rainmaker brings in well over $1 million a year.

It is hardly surprising that such people are so much in demand. Yet management at most firms is unclear how to get them. Most wrestle with two competing views on the subject, nature or nurture. Some believe that rainmakers are born, not made. They believe it is impossible to develop them. Who among us has not felt this way, at least occasionally? This is the Nature Theory. It results in the "shakeout" or "prayer" approach to obtaining rainmakers: Firm management hires technically competent young people for entry-level jobs, seasons them over several years, and prays that a few will shake out as rainmakers.

This theory implies that management has little control over the creation of its most critical asset. It becomes a numbers game, pure and simple. If a firm hires enough junior people, with a little luck, a few will emerge as rainmakers. For large organizations, this may be true. A smaller firm or practice may simply not hire enough junior people for this shake-out approach to work. Some large firms have sought to increase control by looking for the personality traits of future rainmakers in the young people they hire. This wise procedure often gets scrapped when surges in business create an urgent need for new hires to do the work.

When too few rainmakers shake out from the process, those who believe in the Nature Theory can do little but try to hire proven business-getters away from other firms. This can work well, but has drawbacks. The law of supply and demand ensures that recruiting rainmakers will be expensive in both head-hunting fees and starting salaries. And it assumes the firm can find the right person in the first place. The narrower the niche a firm is recruiting for, the more difficult it will be to find someone with the right background. Hired guns know little about their new firm's past work, which dampens their effectiveness until they learn. A person who makes rain at one firm sometimes is unable to do so at another, making the approach risky. Long-tenured employees at a firm may resent a rainmaker recently hired at a salary much higher than their own. If they withhold cooperation, his chances of success drop. (Recruiting rainmakers is not the major focus of this book, but Appendix A provides guidance for those who need to do it.)

The Nurture Theory holds that rainmakers can be developed through proper training, mentoring, and financial incentives. Firms where management holds this view invest in training and formal mentoring programs. They structure compensation systems to encourage business development. Unfortunately, this approach has not always been effective either. Formal training programs may enhance a professional's reactive selling skill, but they seldom turn him or her into an aggressive hunter for new business. All too often, classroom learning is forgotten once the professional returns to the pressures of engagement deadlines and billing time. Mentors and the mentored seldom find the time for mentoring.

Firm managements tend to swing between these two theories. At times, they will say, "You can't give people the fire" that they need to track down business. Worse, they may say, "You can't teach people to be like us," as partners at one big firm said to the head of executive development. They are particularly likely to say these things during good times, when the need for rainmakers is less pressing and every available hour is needed to produce work. When business is bad, they may revert to the Nurture Theory and try a few programs to see if this time it will work. Trying to develop rainmakers in a recession is like planting crops in the middle of a drought, a thought that seems not to occur to some management teams. In short, the efforts of professional firms to end the shortage of rainmakers have been largely ineffective.

I have been troubled by this problem. When I ran a regional office and served on the executive committee of one firm and when I served as director of marketing at another, I felt the impact of the shortage of rainmakers firsthand. I have also seen many fine professionals' careers stymied when they failed to make the transition from doing and managing engagements to marketing and selling them. The words of the head of training at a big firm still ring in my ears: "We promote people to partner on the basis of their technical abilities. They get to keep their jobs on the basis of their marketing abilities. It causes a lot of turnover." This is wasteful. And, I believe, unnecessary.

I am optimistic enough to have a deep faith in most people's ability to learn, though old enough to know that not everyone can or wants to. Most professionals are smart. Most are motivated by a desire to serve, by the need for intellectual stimulation, by money, or by a desire for recognition by their peers. In other words, they are good raw material for someone interested in developing people. I believe most professional firms simply don't know how to do it. Good at developing people's technical skills, most firms are terrible at developing their marketing and sales skills.

To start with, firms are often confused about what they are trying to do. The message that younger people must bring in business is seldom reinforced by the compensation system or the day-to-day discussions those younger people have with partners, which, instead, center on client work. Though exhorted to bring in new clients, young professionals are seldom shown how to do it. Firm rainmakers often work alone or with other rainmakers, obscuring how they bring in business from those who need to learn about it. Young professionals most often work with peers in client organizations, and these peers are seldom in a position to decide about what firm to hire. In this circumstance, no one seems to know exactly what the young professionals should be doing to market the firm.

I had to face this problem when I became the head of a management consulting firm's regional office that was losing twenty-five cents on every dollar it took in. Most of the problems could be traced to inadequate business development. I realized that I could not solve the problems without the active participation of the other professionals in the office, but my first efforts to involve them were ineffectual.

One day I met with a client, the head of research for a large pharmaceutical company that was renowned in the industry for inventing new drugs. The company's researchers weren't any smarter than others in the industry, so I asked this man what he did to get so much out of them. "Half my time," he said, "is spent making sure they are solving the right problem. We have very smart and motivated people who are very good at solving problems, but they are apt to focus on the problems that capture their interest rather than the ones that most need solving."

This simple and powerful insight helped me realize that I had not developed a clear idea of what I wanted from others in the firm. First, I needed to fully understand what rainmakers do so that I could develop the professionals in the firm to do the same things. Second, I needed to know what kind of support I needed to put in place to help them perform like rainmakers. These were the problems I had to solve.

I have found that the answers to these questions are far more complicated than I originally expected. They vary from professional to professional and from firm to firm. From all the possible ways to develop new business, each professional and firm must select a handful and make them work. It is my objective in this book to help you find the right answers to these problems for the people in your firm. At the same time, I believe this book helps explain how rainmakers who cannot really perform magic sometimes seem to. I hope *Creating Rainmakers* will clarify what it takes to succeed at bringing business into a professional firm.

This book is written for the people who manage professional firms and who want to create rainmakers. It will help them create the environment necessary for the development of rainmakers and show what specific things can be done to develop those rainmaking skills. At base, it is a book about sales and marketing management, a poorly developed field in the professions.

The book will also provide guidance for those who want to learn to be rainmakers. It complements my first book, *Rain Making: The Professional's Guide to Attracting New Clients*, which was written for the professional who must make the transition from managing and doing client work to marketing and selling it, but the approach and most of the material are different.

This book has two parts. Part I defines what rainmakers are and do. It is based on interviews with more than a hundred rainmakers and with people who have watched them in action. Part II covers specific elements of the rainmaking process, such as lead generation and selling, in greater detail. Both are written with an understanding that professional firms must balance client work with client development while maintaining profitability. The appendices cover important issues that others are more qualified to write about than I am.

Part I

The Rainmaker Model

1

What Is a Rainmaker?

To create rainmakers, you must first have a clear idea of what a rainmaker is and does. Yet, there is little information about this special group of people. What exists is largely impressionistic or based on the experiences of one or two people rather than on research.

To remedy this, I studied rainmakers, people who have been phenomenally successful at bringing in work to their firms and who keep many other professionals employed by doing so. I interviewed both rainmakers and people who know them well. More than 100 rainmakers were included in the survey from the fields of management consulting, benefits consulting, accounting, law, consulting engineering, and architecture. In many cases, I was able to gather information on the same rainmaker from two or more sources. I have supplemented this original research with a review of biographies, autobiographies, articles, and other published sources that describe how rainmakers generate business.

For the purposes of this work, I define rainmakers as professionals who do two things well. First, they generate leads for new business. That is, they go out and create opportunities to talk with prospective clients about problems they can help solve. True rainmakers don't just wait for the phone to ring; they go out and find business. Second, they turn a portion of these leads into new business with their selling skills. To be true rainmakers, they must generate enough business to keep many others in their firms employed. Other professionals may do one or the other of these things, but they don't do both. They are best at minding clients and grinding out work.

From the rainmaker interviews and reading, this is what I have learned:

Rainmakers Don't Fit a Single Personality Type

People who run professional firms are apt to make judgments on the basis of personality types about who has potential to develop as a rainmaker. Although some of these judgments are probably correct, most are made without any real understanding of what it takes to be successful at developing business. Some professionals fall into the "are-they-like-us" trap, epitomized by the head of a midsize accounting firm who told one of his aspiring marketers, "you need to be more like me. You're about 80 percent like me, but you need to be exactly like me." Though few people have so simplistic or arrogant a view, there is a tendency to compare young professionals to current rainmakers to decide whether they have potential.

Those who run firms are not the only ones who make these comparisons. Over the years, many young professionals have told me that they don't really consider themselves to be "the selling type." By this they usually mean they are not aggressive extroverts. Alternatively, they compare themselves to one or two highly successful rainmakers and, not surprisingly, given differences in age and experience, find they come up short.

Anyone who holds such views needs to know that people of many different personality types can succeed at client development. Listen to these descriptions of different rainmakers:

- He was impressive, well-tailored, and when he walked into a room everybody looked up. There was an immediate magnetism and attractiveness.[1]

- He was unimpressive. He was very ordinary. People's heads didn't turn when he entered the room.

- He is extremely personable and charming. He is lively and cheerful. People feel a lift after being with him.

- He had a gray personality. He looked like the archetypical industrial engineer with a pocket protector.

- At first she seems mature and serious, but when she laughs, you would think she was twelve years old.

- He was a gambler and always heavily leveraged.
- He was cautious and never did anything he wasn't comfortable with.
- He reminded me of a used car salesman.
- Above all else, he was a gentleman.

I could go on and on with contrasting statements:

- He was very articulate with an acerbic wit. He had the ability to be totally charming. But he could be totally cold when he rebuffed someone. He was extremely volatile. He was mercurial.
- He had a gentle manner. If he was angry, it was always expressed in his face and not in what he said. He was admired by everyone who knew him.
- Money wasn't the primary driver for him.
- He likes to surround himself with nice things. He has fresh flowers every day in his office and wants top-quality things around him all the time and takes it for granted that he should have them. He is generous. If he thinks you're worth x, he will give you $x + 1$.
- He knows how to pinch a penny.

Listen to these quotes about two partners at the same firm, each of whom brings in about $6 million of business a year:

- He is an old-line WASP; very organized, very quiet, and very thoughtful.
- He's a cowboy. He goes out and sells. No matter what he does, he is always laughing. Something funny always comes out. He has a talent for that. He's a good talker. He speaks very fast and always has an answer for everything, though it isn't always the right answer.

Perhaps not surprisingly, these two rainmakers are reported to not get along with each other.

Here are three final quotes that I want you to remember. The first is from Roland Berger, perhaps the most successful rainmaker in the consulting industry today; the second about an extremely successful attorney at a western firm; and the third from a big accounting firm:

- Everyone in the firm says I am so extroverted. But I have always thought of myself as an introvert. I was very much so in my early years.

- He is not a born rainmaker. He doesn't have the gift of gab and is unprepossessing. He is soft-spoken....He is not comfortable with groups, but has disciplined himself to be good at it.

- Early on, I had a lot of difficulty with [client development]. I am very shy, though most people who know me would laugh if you told them this. I had a lot of difficulty going to those lunches, but I forced myself to do it.

Not much here will help us identify or train future rainmakers, but there is an important message, nonetheless. We need to exercise great caution about making judgments on the basis of superficial personality types about who has potential to make it as a rainmaker. Specifically, contrary to popular sentiments, extroversion is not a prerequisite to successful rainmaking.

There Is No One Way That Rainmakers Make Rain

If there is no single personality type that makes a good rainmaker, you might ask, do rainmakers share a common way of getting business? Is there a best way to make rain?

A lot has been written about how to bring business into a professional firm, much of it recommending one approach over another. Attitudes toward cold calling provide a good example of the differences of opinions about how a firm should develop clients. David Maister, for example, classifies marketing tactics into three groups with cold calling falling into the "Clutching at Straws" category.[2] Another anti–cold caller, Alan Weiss, says "...your marketing thrust should *not* be... — heaven forfend — making cold calls"[3] (italics in original). Contrast these opinions with those of Richard Connor and Jeffrey Davidson,[4] or of Stephan Schiffman,[5] all of whom promote what are essentially cold-calling systems. Although cold calling seems to attract especially strong and divergent opinions, similar differences can be found in other ways of getting business.

The survey of rainmakers that was conducted for this book shows that there is no single right way of getting business. Here are descriptions of a few of the ways that rainmakers attract new clients:

- He would gather names from speaking engagements and enter them on his list. He had a clipping service and two secretaries who would look for articles mentioning any company on the list. He would send these articles to his contacts with a personal note asking what they thought about the situation or asking how it would affect compensation [his consulting specialty]. Twenty to twenty-five or more of these letters went out every week, and they generated a flow of calls back to him. That's where his business came from.

- Basically, he got his business through cold calling. He would decide to make a business development trip four or five weeks in advance. He would then send a letter and call people and let them know he was coming. He would organize his trip to tie into affirmative responses he received. He was not a campaign-oriented salesman. His approach was to go out and close a sale and he could do it, often in one meeting. He was the best closer I ever saw.

- When he had an engagement, he would make a point of meeting second-level people, like the chief financial officers, and develop a relationship with them. When they moved on to another company, as some of them always did, he would stay in touch and eventually get work. He never lost touch and had a real knack for cultivating these second- and third-level people. He had a skill for picking out people on the way up. He liked the sharks and got on well with them. He would only have half a dozen to a dozen of these relationships at any one time, but they were remarkably fruitful.

- His business comes almost exclusively from his personal network. He has been at it for forty years now and is at the top of the heap. He pays a lot of attention to getting to know people, and wants to know them at a lot of levels. He has always done a lot of charity work and meets people there. He then establishes a personal relationship. He [sees people socially and] often takes his wife along and likes to meet [his contacts'] spouses. He consciously sits down each morning and goes through a mental Rolodex of who he hasn't seen for awhile and then calls to see if someone can have lunch. He makes a list each day and makes a series of calls from it. He stays in touch with every major client every six to eight weeks. He sends them opera tickets or buys them lunch or calls just to say hi. When he hears about a possible piece of business, he will call around to find someone who can make an introduction for him. He always can. It never fails.

- He didn't have an awful lot of leads. Most of them came from past clients, who he kept in close contact with. His skill was turning [a small opportunity] into a substantial account. He was able to surround an account. He was good at moving up the food chain. Our firm always came in at the middle and moved up. It was sort of insidious. He always made a point of going to the next level up and touching base.

As you can see, there are many ways to make rain. Within a few professions, there is a tendency for many rainmakers to rely on one approach. Engineers, for example, are likely to rely on networks. But this is only a tendency, and different approaches are chosen by different professionals, depending upon their circumstances and personalities. Most rainmakers combine several methods.

Having highlighted the different opinions that several authors hold about cold calling, I should note that cold calling is far from uncommon and is used by rainmakers in every profession covered in the survey. Contrary to what some people believe, cold calling can be used to sell many types of professional services. But it is not necessarily the best way for everyone.

Given this finding, I looked for tactics that all aspiring rainmakers should employ, if only as an adjunct to their main business development efforts. The most obvious candidate was public speaking. Almost all the literature recommends this activity. Reviewing the interview summaries, you might at first think they would confirm this common knowledge:

- He built his stature by writing prolifically for law reviews and journals and speaking often on panels.
- He had an aggressive speaking and writing schedule.
- She built her business by speaking. For years she spoke to every group she could get in front of.
- He loved to give speeches and was excellent at it. He was a brilliant speaker.
- He built his reputation on the platform. He was a terrific platform guy. Everyone wanted to hear him speak.
- Public speaking is like falling off a log for him. He likes to get up in front of people and speak extemporaneously so he can charm them.

But a substantial minority of the rainmakers are poor public speakers or speak infrequently, if at all:

- He didn't give speeches because he was terrible at it. He would mumble.

- I'm not a big speaker. In my field, giving away secrets in speeches doesn't help you.

- He did no public speaking or publishing.

One can only conclude that public speaking is often helpful, but is not a prerequisite, to becoming a rainmaker.

The quotes repeated here should caution all of us from making any simple assumptions about what rainmakers are like or what they do. To understand what truly distinguishes rainmakers from other people, one has to look deeper. Let us start with personality traits, as opposed to personality types.

Others have done work in this area, most notably James Weitzul.[6] He identifies seven behavioral traits that are common among this group (overachiever, entrepreneur, active, passive, aggressive, sensitized, and compulsive) using the SKAP (Skill, Knowledge, Ability, Personal characteristics) profiling technique. His work generally supports the conclusion that those successful at selling professional services can have widely varying personality types; they can, for example, be active or passive, aggressive or sensitized. He offers useful insights into how to deal with the different types of individuals when recruiting, training, and giving performance appraisals. His work benefits from applying disciplined psychological research to the subject.

Though the results of my study do not disagree with his — and I would recommend his book to anyone interested in the subject of managing rainmakers — they are quite different. This may partially result from populations studied; he doesn't say what professions were covered in his survey. We have very likely been looking for different things. For whatever reasons, he does not discuss what, in the study done for his book, were the defining attributes of rainmakers.

Rainmakers Are Optimists

The first and most striking of these defining attributes is optimism. Almost all rainmakers see the positive side of life. Listen to these quotes:

- He would always see opportunity in every situation. This isn't often true of auditors who are trained to be skeptics, but he wasn't a skeptic. [Other people] can often see fifty reasons why something won't work, but he always saw fifty reasons why it would.

- He was an optimist in the extreme, an eleven or a twelve on a scale of one to ten. We couldn't analyze our historical backlog for a long time because he was always putting work on the books after a good meeting and some of it never materialized.

- I've never heard him saying anything negative. The glass is always half full. No matter how disheartening the loss of a project, there is always another one out there.

- He was very positive about his own abilities. He approached everything on this basis and would say, "What could possibly go wrong?" when talking about things within his own control.

- He was extremely optimistic. Things were always looking up. We were always about to get the next big job — and *he was usually right!* [emphasis added]

- He was very optimistic always. He always thought we would do well and that the business would thrive *and, generally speaking, when he paid attention to it, it did.* [emphasis added]

- He is an optimist and *is generally right about being optimistic* about sales opportunities. [emphasis added]

- One distinct attribute was his positive thinking. It could overwhelm people at times. He couldn't stand to be around negative thinkers, and once even fired a baby-sitter because she sounded too negative. He was optimistic to a fault, though *often his optimism turned out to be justified.* He never saw any rejection. To him it was never rejection. He could convert anything into a positive. [emphasis added]

These are only a handful of the comments on this extremely common trait among the rainmakers I studied. Reviewing the interview summaries, this characteristic stands out so clearly that it cannot be ignored by anyone who wants to create client developers. It leads directly to the question: Knowing this, what action should I take?

The action that we should take depends on what we think optimism is. There are three possible interpretations: Optimism can be seen as a character trait, as a result of knowledge, or as a skill.

If a character trait, it is either genetic or instilled so early in life that it is hard to change later. If that is true, it becomes critical to select people we hire for this trait, if we want them to develop into rainmakers. In other words, the Nature Theory, described in the introduction to this book, is right. Many professionals I have spoken with feel this is the case. If you feel this way, too, you are not alone. And in some cases and to some degree, you are right. Some people *are* inherently more optimistic than others. Rainmakers may have something that the rest of us simply don't.

Yet, our level of optimism is also affected by knowledge. Anyone who has children realizes this. We have all seen children who believe they can do the impossible or who become afraid of an event, such as an airplane crash or the death of a parent, that is extremely unlikely to occur. Children don't have enough knowledge and experience to weigh an event's probability and so are often mistaken in their optimism or pessimism.

Knowledge also affects outlook later in our lives. You can easily manipulate an adult's optimism — and I have done so — by giving him or her a simple task. First, offer a reward if the person can complete it within a specific time frame. Then try manipulating his or her assessment of probability of succeeding by increasing or lowering the perceived difficulty of the task. For example, sit a person in a chair, give her a ball, and tell her that she has three seconds after you say go to get the ball into a wastebasket that you hold in front of her. Her optimism is likely to decrease as you move the wastebasket farther away, and to increase if you point out that she is not required to remain seated in her chair. Only when you have enough experience to assess probabilities can you make realistic judgments about outcomes. And when it comes to client development, rainmakers simply know things that the rest of us don't.

So optimism is, in part, a deep-seated personality trait. It is, in part, a result of having the knowledge to make realistic assessments about what will happen in the future. But it is also something else. Optimism has been studied extensively by psychologists, who have gathered compelling evidence that it is a skill that people can learn. An intriguing book by Martin Seligman explores the subject in detail[7] and shows a strong link between optimism and success in many fields, including sales. Seligman is a professor at the University of Pennsylvania, where most of the leading research into cognitive therapy has been done. This approach to treatment helps people improve their lives by teaching them to replace destructive thought patterns with constructive ones. The approach has been particularly successful at helping people fight depression, which is closely linked to pessimism, the opposite of optimism. In short, it is used to teach people to be more optimistic. To the extent that optimism is a skill, we can train professionals to have it.

We now have three things we can do to make sure that our prospective rainmakers are more optimistic. We can recruit optimistic people, we can educate them to show them what rainmakers know about rainmaking that others don't, and we can teach them how to think optimistically. We deal with each of these subjects later in this book.

Before leaving (temporarily) the subject of optimism, I want to point out how frequently the respondents in my survey commented that the rainmakers' optimism turned out to be justified. Once the pattern of optimism emerged, I asked about it specifically, but the comments about the justifiableness of the optimism were all unsolicited and always spoken in a tone of disbelief, as if they had been preceded with the phrase, "I have to admit that...." Rainmakers, it seems, have good reason to be optimistic. This finding, too, will warrant additional consideration. As I have said, sometimes what rainmakers do almost seems like magic.

Rainmakers Are Driven People

Having the optimism to expect good results from their efforts, rainmakers are driven to make things happen and to build their companies:

- He works at bringing in business every hour of every day. He's dogged and relentless. Every Sunday I can count on getting two or three voice mail messages from him.

- When I took a job at the firm, a partner told me that [the rainmaker] was insatiable, and he is. He always wants more and believes he can get it and usually does. His company is his life.

- On one occasion [he] went into the office on Christmas Day to dictate a report....The client came first.[8]

- He was a driven guy. He lived, slept, and breathed his business. It was clearly the most important thing for him and caused his divorce. Business was everything to him.

- He's like a kid and can't pace himself, but goes all out until he crashes from exhaustion.

Yet many retained balance in their lives:

- I have a lot of breakfast and lunches with people, but not many dinners. I find that if you go to dinner, you say everything you've got to say in the first half-hour and blow the whole evening. I've got a family [I need to spend time with].

- He was better than anyone else I ever knew at separating his business from his personal life. When he went home, he left the office behind him.

- There have been a lot of times when, at the end of the day, a client would want to go to dinner and I needed a break from that and said I couldn't go. I never felt bad about that.

These quotes suggest that success as a rainmaker and a private life are not mutually incompatible, though many rainmakers have so thoroughly mixed their professional and personal lives that it is impossible to say where one leaves off and the other begins.

Optimism and a relentless drive are two personality traits that the overwhelming majority of rainmakers seem to have. There are also similarities about what they do to get business.

Rainmakers Have a System for Finding New Business

Most respondents described a system that the rainmakers use week in and week out to get business. Business development is a part of their daily routine. The words *system*, *meticulous*, and *relentless* were spoken often when describing the rainmakers. I have already presented brief quotes that capture elements of these systems in the description of the diversity of methods used to get new clients. The specific approach may depend on the rainmaker's personality and the nature of his practice, but whatever it is, the rainmaker pursues it systematically and tenaciously. Listen to these quotes:

- [Turnaround consultant, Jay Alix] maintains [his network of contacts], staying in touch with hundreds of people via an elaborate index-card system. He totes around 3-by-5 cards, which he orders in batches of 10,000, and jots down an idea or name of a task on each, organized by date. A time-management zealot, he stockpiles the cards in his car, next to his bed, and even in the bathroom.[9]

- [A friend who refers me business] once asked why I keep sending him thank-you letters. He said that I don't need to thank him anymore. I said not to try to stop me, because as soon as I started making exceptions in my system, it would break down.

- He would carve out a period of time every day — well, not every day, but many days — when he would do nothing but be on the phone.

- He used to schedule two hours every morning, between 8:00 A.M. and 10:00 A.M., five days a week for marketing and sales work. This is the time he made his calls, worked on proposals, and prepared presentations. He did it whether he was in the office or on the road. If he was traveling, he would do it from his hotel room. The only thing he would let interfere with this work was a call from a client who had had difficulty reaching him.

- He used what we called his "Blue Card System," on which he kept track of all his contacts, though we never really understood how it worked and he didn't show it to us.

Once this pattern emerged, I began to ask my informants directly about systems and usually received a clear, though not always complete, description of the system the rainmaker in question used. A few people denied that the rainmaker they were describing used a system, and in some cases this was probably true. But even when they denied the existence of a system, later descriptions of how the rainmaker worked made it clear that there was one. For example, one informant insisted that the electrical engineer she was describing disliked structure and didn't use a system, but later she noted the following:

> He operates out of spiral notebooks, like college notebooks. He has them going back thirty years. Every conversation and every lead is recorded in the books. He will put people's [business] cards in them with tape. He saves them all and can always go back and look things up. The notes are pretty scratchy, but it works for him. They're his chronicle, and he is proud of them.

Another informant stated that the accountant he was describing "wasn't a systems kind of a guy; I don't remember a particular system." Later, he observed that:

> He...would bump into some idea and then work it with his clients. He was great at selling new product to an existing client that way. Once, he read an article about breakeven analysis and decided that he would do one for each one of his firm's top fifty clients. He did and then visited them to talk about the implications of what he had found. He used to talk about how much business he got from this.

The informant described several campaigns that followed almost the same pattern.

The great majority of the rainmakers in the database have a system. Systems are so critical to a rainmaker's success that much of this book is devoted to their design and operation.

Rainmakers Are Good Listeners and Synthesizers

Almost all the rainmakers are superb listeners and able to synthesize what they hear and then provide a valuable response. This is a key to selling success:

- Above all else, he was a good listener. He became your partner in the problem real quick.

- He would wait patiently at a meeting until he got to the point where he knew what he wanted to say. He would sometimes talk only during the last five minutes, but then would talk clearly about solutions.

These quotes, and many similar ones made by the respondents during the interviews, show that rainmakers possess classic selling skills combined with the problem-solving skills essential to a good professional.

Rainmakers Never Lose Track of a Client

The rainmakers never lost track of a client or prospective client or other important contact. Once they develop a relationship with someone, they never let go:

- A lot of her [client development] time is spent just keeping up with people she has known for years. She has several thousand people on her mailing list. She takes time to sit face to face and call many of them.

- He kept the names of everyone who attended a seminar in a notebook and would keep in touch with them year after year. He would always send a note when they moved companies or got promotions.

- He kept in constant contact....Everyone received at least four pieces of mail a year. He would call at least twice a year.

- He never lost touch with a client. He had his little book and, if he had ten minutes in an airport, always had a call to make. He would follow them from account to account. He followed one person into five different companies over twenty years.

The rainmakers realize that the cost of obtaining a new client is much higher than that of keeping an old one. Many affirm that their relationships mean something to them beyond the possibility of future work. Whatever the reason, they never lose touch.

These core elements are what make rainmakers different from other people. Optimism helps push them through the first tough years of building a client base. As we will see, this is an extremely difficult period for most professionals. It is the time when many professionals become discouraged and turn away from client development. Optimism also helps rainmakers through the inevitable selling slumps that occur. It is the foundation for their drive.

Their drive and systems ensure the consistent effort that is essential to getting business. Even when distracted by client work, they know exactly what marketing they must do and can do it quickly and efficiently when they can grab time during the day. The systems ensure that their marketing time isn't squandered among an array of unrelated activities.

The rainmakers' listening and problem-solving skills ensure that when they do have an opportunity to make a sale, their chances of succeeding are relatively high. By never letting go of a client, they maximize the return on their lead generation and selling efforts.

These are the things that rainmakers do, and these are the things we must teach our professionals to do. The rest of this book will describe ways to help them.

Most Rainmakers Are Poor Mentors

Before turning to that subject, I want to comment on one other characteristic of the rainmakers that explains, in part, why they are so difficult to develop. Though a few of the rainmakers covered in the survey are good mentors, and train others in their organizations to bring in business, the great majority aren't. Listen to these quotes:

- He didn't mentor much. I never went to a sales meeting with him.

- Nobody went on many sales calls with him. He had a fetish about that. He felt it distracted the prospect and made the call more difficult. He was not a good mentor.

- He was a terrible mentor. We even tried hiring a couple of MBAs to follow him around and learn what he did, so we could clone him. They would leave in frustration. He never found time for them. He wanted to mentor but didn't know how to do it. He just couldn't teach. He could tell you what you did wrong until he was a pain in the neck, but he couldn't teach you.

- He was a terrible mentor. He would walk up your back with spiked shoes on if he needed to. He always viewed life as a zero-sum game with no room at the top for everyone.

- He was an excellent mentor for technical work but not in marketing. He put my drafting board right outside his office and would stop and show an interest in what I was doing and make suggestions. But he did business development very much on his own. He didn't offer to teach it to others.

- He wasn't much of a mentor. In his mind, he probably had better things to do than to mentor people.

- It was always a bit of a mystery about how he [brought in business].

- [Mentoring] isn't a terribly strong interest of his. He is available to answer questions, but doesn't take the initiative to shepherd people along.

- He has acknowledged that he is not a good mentor. He is too outwardly focused. He is very impatient with those that work with him and very judgmental, especially with those who work in marketing. He is quick to criticize and always wants more from them. He can be exhausting to work for. He often second-guesses you. You always feel you are disappointing him. He keeps a tickler file and constantly sends notes reminding you to do even small things and asking for a progress report. He micromanages.

- His people don't develop into practice managers; they are minions who do what he tells them to.

- He wasn't interested in sharing his style and technique with others. He moved fast and was more of a loner. It was hard to follow what he did.

- I don't know why he can't just show us what he does, but he can't.

That rainmakers are often such bad mentors means that we can seldom rely on them to pass on their abilities to the next generation. At best, this will throw a firm or a practice into difficult times when a rainmaker retires. At worst, it exposes the firm to immediate suffering, for some rainmakers have a darker side:

- His style and success caused problems at [the large accounting and consulting firm where he was a partner]. His success rate was so much higher than everyone else's that he felt he deserved a bigger share of the pie. Disagreement over this issue ultimately caused him to leave the firm and start another company. It happened after he landed a big contract [with a large aerospace company], the biggest one he had ever sold. It had a lot of consultants on the job which was to run two and a half to three years. That's when he began drinking too much of his own Kool Aid. When he left, he took the account and seventy people with him.

- All he wanted was control and didn't care much about the welfare and development of the firm. He was hired by the firm along with three others as rainmakers, and they did what they were hired to do; they grew the firm. But none of these people shared the loyalty and heritage of the firm that those who had come up in it had. [One day the four rainmakers] announced that they were appointing themselves the management committee and that if we didn't accept that, they would leave. We caved into their demands, and they took over total control of allocating profits and the operation of the firm. [At first, the firm did well, but after about a year they] had a falling-out among themselves. Two of them left the firm, taking a lot of business with them, and it closed after being in business since 1842.

If rainmakers do not mentor, firms must find other means of developing their successors. This book shows ways to do that. This will help you avoid dependence on a few rainmakers. This, in turn, makes it difficult for any individual to damage the firm in the ways I have just described.

2

What Rainmakers Know
or the Mathematics of Selling

In the previous chapter, I showed that virtually all rainmakers are optimists and that one source of their optimism appears to be knowledge that others don't have. They appear to know (or they assume) things about bringing in business that make them optimistic about their chances of success. If this is true, we can help others become more effective at business development simply by teaching them these things. In this chapter, I describe what I believe rainmakers know that other people don't. We can improve our chances of developing rainmakers by educating them on these things (increasing their knowledge and understanding), as opposed to training them (increasing their skills), which we will address elsewhere.

Business development is not a science, but it does operate by a logic that is subject to analysis and that dictates how we should behave and what we should expect. This logic can be described as the mathematics of selling, and somehow rainmakers understand it. Rainmakers employ at least some of six basic principles, all of which have mathematical implications. These principles may be simple, but their combined implications are profound.

The Investment Principle
When, in his interview, architect A. Eugene Kohn, the founder of Kohn Pedersen Fox Associates PC, said, "The more people you know, the more opportunities you get," he was giving his version of the

Investment Principle. This principle explains a lot about how marketing works and shows why mature rainmakers' powers to bring in business seem almost magical. It also explains why developing business is much harder early on. It is one of the most fundamental principles of selling and can be stated as follows:

> *The value of a network of market contacts is worth more than the sum of its parts, and that value grows geometrically with the size of the network.*

This is true because investments in client development behave, in some ways, much like financial investments. An investor who deposits $2,000 annually from her salary in a fund with a 10 percent return will have more than $360,000 at the end of thirty years because of the compounding effect of the interest (see Exhibit 2.1). Compounding greatly increases the value of investing: In the first year, interest adds

Exhibit 2.1

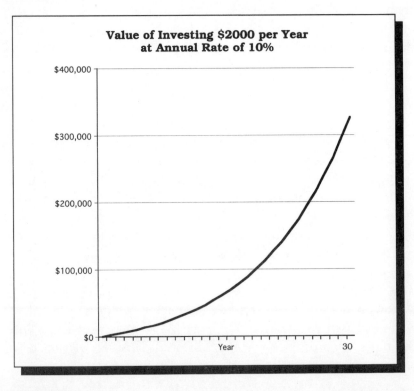

but $200 to the fund; in the thirtieth, it adds more than $34,000 (or seventeen times the $2,000 contribution from salary in the same year).

Whether it is through classic networking, cold calls, or client work, rainmakers invest in the creation of large networks of contacts. Networkers get business because they help other people with their business ventures, and a percentage of those they help return the favor by hiring them or by referring them to still others who do. Imagine moving to a city where you know no one and where you plan to build your practice by networking. You must meet people and find ways to help them. In this simplified example, the only thing that your contacts want is introductions to others they would benefit from knowing. You go out and meet two people and now can introduce them to each other. We will call this one match. When you meet a third, you will be able to make a total of three potential matches. With a fourth, you can make six. With a fifth, ten (see Exhibit 2.2). The number of possible matches grows geometrically as people are added to the network. A professional who has been doing the same thing for several years and has 500 people in her network can make 124,750 possible

Exhibit 2.2

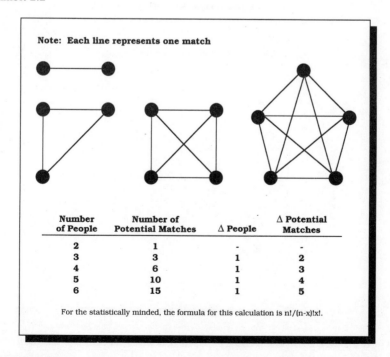

Note: Each line represents one match

Number of People	Number of Potential Matches	Δ People	Δ Potential Matches
2	1	-	-
3	3	1	2
4	6	1	3
5	10	1	4
6	15	1	5

For the statistically minded, the formula for this calculation is n!/(n-x)!x!.

matches. As a real example, an accountant interviewed for this book who is an amazingly successful rainmaker obtains his business opportunities through his network. He once told me that he has 1,375 names in his database, which means he has 944,625 potential matches that he can make. No wonder he is so fantastically successful at finding ways to help people. No wonder he sees a higher return from his effort than the neophyte does.[1]

Now compare Exhibit 2.3, which shows the growth of a network graphically, to Exhibit 2.1, which shows the growth of a steady investment of $2,000 at 10 percent per year. They have the same J-shape curve. It is a shape that explains why young investors often fail to make the steady investments needed to plan for retirement and also why young professionals often fail at marketing.

The young investor is likely to have other demands for her money, perhaps for a new car or a down payment on a house. After, say, three years, when she has put away $6,000 from her salary, she will have an investment worth $7,282. This is not a lot of money and hardly a substantial contribution toward retirement. Unaware of the

Exhibit 2.3

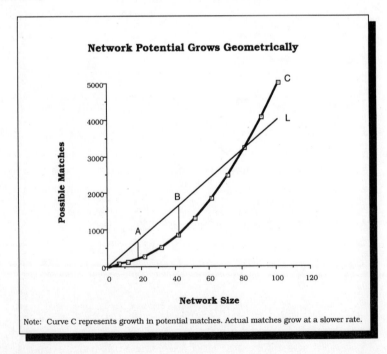

Note: Curve C represents growth in potential matches. Actual matches grow at a slower rate.

shape of the curve, she is likely to pull out her savings to take care of immediate needs, at which point she has to start investing all over again at the bottom of the curve.

Similarly, the young professional interested in developing clients goes out and starts networking. After a short time he has other demands on his time, most likely to do client work. Not seeing the return on his initial networking effort as very large and unaware of the shape of the curve, he gives up networking to focus on an activity where returns on his time seem greater (usually client work). His relationships go cold, and later he has to start networking all over again.

Even if he is persistent at first, he is likely to give up later. This is because most human beings think about changes over time as if they were linear.[2] In other words our expectations about the return on our client development effort are likely to look like line L in Exhibit 2.3. At point A, a professional new to client development will be disappointed because the actual amount of matches he can make falls below the number he feels he should be able to make based on the amount of effort he has put in. Not being a quitter, he keeps trying. At point B, he reassesses his effort. Though he is modestly more successful than at point A, he is even farther behind where he feels he should be based on effort (that is, the distance between line L and curve C at point B is even greater than at point A). At this point, he is at risk of giving up, deciding that networking just doesn't work for him and that perhaps he isn't a good client developer, even though in reality he has been doing the right things and is making good progress. The risk of giving up will be greatly increased if his supervisor fails to understand what is happening and also shows disappointment at the results of his efforts. His best move, of course, would be to work even harder and push himself up curve C as fast as he can.

I have heard many young professionals express disappointment at the results of their efforts after working at client development for a few months, showing that they don't understand the J-shape curve of business development. Somehow rainmakers do. Listen to these quotes from two young lawyers, one a litigator and one a real estate attorney, and both recently emerged rainmakers who have developed business by networking:

- I read as many books on sales and marketing as I could and would listen to tapes. I realized from these that it would be a long-term approach, but I figured I was young and I had time.

- When I started practicing, I was twenty-five years old, and so were all of my peers. I realized that we would all be power brokers later, so I cultivated these relationships both for business and for friendship. Now a lot of my work comes from this group.

Although it is more difficult to demonstrate mathematically, I believe all market development efforts build in the same curvilinear way. For example, the increased results from cold calling over many years result from:

1. Having more people that you meet with periodically. If, on average, 10 percent of the people you call on have a need for your services at any one time, the fees resulting from your effort will almost certainly increase if you are calling on one hundred people rather than ten.

2. Having a better chance to learn about a need from a prospect. The more you visit a person, the more you learn about him or her and the company, and the greater the chance that an additional piece of information will give you enough knowledge to position a sale. Further, the prospective client becomes increasingly comfortable with you and is likely to volunteer more or to decide to take a chance on you. This means that your chances of making a sale after your tenth visit are greater than during your first, all other things being equal.

3. Knowing several people at a company. Information you obtain from one person may help you sell a piece of business to another.

4. Gaining a reputation as a person knowledgeable about an industry or a specific kind of problem. By reminding prospects of your expertise, your reputation is enhanced, which increases the number of referrals received.

A rainmaker who has called on many people and kept in touch by mail, phone, and periodic face-to-face visits over the years is likely to be extremely successful for this reason.

As redoubtable a rainmaker as Joe Flom, of Skadden, Arps, Slate, Meagher and Flom, shows that he recognizes the investment nature of growing a business, even when depending on clients for referrals. During his interview for the survey he stated: "People don't understand the impact of compounding. One person talks to two, two talk to four, and so on. Word gets out when you do a good job. There is a hell of a grapevine out there on who can do a good job for you."

Let us return to our investor to understand another critical implication of this curve. If the young investor has a thirty-year working life as our example suggests and fails to invest for the first fifteen years of that working life, she will have to put more than $10,000 away in each of the remaining fifteen years to reach the same $360,000 total value at the end of the thirty years that she would have had by investing $2,000 each year for all thirty years. The cash contribution will be $150,000 instead of $60,000, or two and a half times greater. In other words, investing a little money consistently early in one's career can greatly reduce the amount of investment that must be made later to arrive at a desired result.

It is the same with client development. The professional who consistently finds a modest amount of time for client development and invests it wisely will have a much easier time later in his career when he must bring in business to get promoted than one who waits. The head of a large consulting firm provides a good example of this. He became CEO, in part, because he controlled the firm's largest client. Early in his career, he had completed a project at this client and struck up a friendship with his counterpart there. Both were just beginning their careers and had little influence in their organizations, but the consultant never lost touch with this new friend. Sometimes it was easy because he worked on other engagements for the client and could stop in and say hello. At other times, he had to go out of his way to keep in touch, but it really didn't take that long to make a phone call or a brief visit a couple of times a year. Today, the friend is the chairman of the client company and the consultant has a relationship with him developed over twenty years. This relationship creates a strong entry barrier for other firms that want the client's business. How hard would it have been to develop so close a relationship if the consultant had let the friendship go cold for ten years at some time during his career.

The survey surfaced many similar examples. Environmental attorney Dixie L. Laswell, of the Chicago-based firm of Seyforth, Shaw, Fairweather & Geraldson, said:

> I began to develop business early when I was an associate. I learned that the best source of business was existing clients. I developed relationships with people at my level at companies where we were already doing work. As they moved up the corporate ladder and as I moved up the firm ladder, I developed the trust and relationship that resulted in them

calling me when they had legal matters. Some moved to other companies and would call me, and this brought in new clients. After ten years, I had a strong base of business from this source.

Marvin Mass, the president of Cosentini Associates as described by one person who knows him well, provides another example:

> He probably realized early on that there was value in knowing all the real estate people in New York. That's how he began. Early on, he centered on relationships with his peers and built a practice as a building engineer for the major real estate entrepreneurs in New York. He and they moved up and, through work as well as shared philanthropic and charitable causes, have forged a strong relationship that spans two or three generations within the top real estate families.

The young marketer would be wise to reflect upon these examples. The more seasoned professional who has not invested in marketing early in his or her career will have to accept the need to make larger investments now. Though it is best to start early, late is better than never. When I began my current practice, much of the network I had developed for a different kind of consulting ceased to produce business for me. I had to build a new one relevant to my new business. It took three years of intense discipline, but it worked.

The implications of the curve for managers of professional firms are also clear: If they can get young professionals to make small but consistent investments in relationship building early in their careers, the task of creating rainmakers will be much easier than if they work only with senior associates and partners. During these early years, input measures — such as the number of contacts made with past clients and the number of articles written — are more important than output measures because it is unrealistic to expect much business to result from the time spent. If the investments are small, they should not be too disruptive to the firm's bottom line. But they must be consistent.

At some level, rainmakers understand this client development curve. I was particularly struck by the description a civil engineer, Emad Youssef, gave me of conversations he has had with Tony Sartor, the rainmaker who encouraged him to market. Here is a rainmaker who does know how to mentor. (Think about Exhibit 2.3 as you read this quote.)

When I first took this job [as a client developer, a shift from the project manager position he had held], I had a time schedule in my mind when I had to succeed or be a failure. I wasn't feeling good about how it was going, [he is at point *A* on the curve] and Tony told me, "I know you can do it. It's innate in you. Take all the time you want."

At the end of last year, I had brought in about $2 million worth of business, but wasn't feeling like that was much compared to what Tony had done and told him so. [He is at point *B* on the curve.] He said, "Are you kidding? I've been at this for seventeen years. My base is much bigger than yours. Anyway, you've planted a lot of seeds this year — wait, you'll see. It will happen next year." He was right; the first few months of this year were gangbusters. I don't know how he knows these things.

As we have seen in the quotes from the survey, rainmakers are always optimistic that they will bring in new business if they work at it. They know that client development is an investment. Chapter 9 describes how these investments are made.

The Affinity Principle

A network made up of people who share business concerns will produce higher returns than a less focused one.

This seems both logical and self-evident, but rainmakers work much harder than others to increase the richness of their networks. Principally, this is done by focusing on people who can hire them or on people who have influence with those who can hire them. As the founder of one large international consulting firm said:

People are reluctant to talk with CEOs. I tell our people that they can spend time talking to someone on the shop floor or to the CEO, and the CEO is probably more interesting and may even give you some work. But for some reason, people are reluctant to talk to CEOs.

There are many ways to increase the richness of your network. Focused networks may include:

Many people in one company. The information you have about a company where you know many people allows you to make suggestions for improvement because you can piece together information in ways that other people can't. Large accounting and consulting firms have partners who work close to full time as relationship managers at major clients. They get to know people in key positions throughout the company and have responsibility for sniffing out opportunities to help the client. One such person that I know has a relationship with the president as well as with many other people at a large telecommunications company. He studies the client with an objective outsider's eye and gathers information during his conversations with people at many levels. From time to time, he sends the president a facsimile that opens with the line "I am worried about. . ." and spells out an issue that needs attention. One of every four or five of these facsimiles results in an engagement.

Many people in one industry. Knowing many people in an industry allows you to get more out of a network. Bob Nolan, the founder of Robert E. Nolan Company, consulted to the insurance industry and developed a rich network of insurance executives. A colleague described how he used that richness to good purpose:

> I remember that one night we went to dinner with [a senior person from an insurance company]. For two and a half hours, Bob and he matched industry war stories. Both could track people two or three jobs back from the ones they held now. All the time, Bob was putting [the client's] stories into his mental database. Afterwards, he said, "Hey, didn't we learn a lot?" He had the ability to bring up one of these stories in a gracious way with someone in the story later. It was an easy way to get a meeting.

Clients and the people who sell to them. Many accountants network with their clients and the people who provide them advice in financial areas, bankers and lawyers. Architects and engineers network with each other and with clients. In networks constructed this way, the professional provides value to the client by introducing him or her to people who can help solve problems. At the same time, the professional helps professionals in other fields by providing them introductions to and information about prospective clients.

People within a geographic market. It is also possible to build a network based on geographic affinity. Maurice Olivier, Managing Director for Europe and the Middle East for Arthur D. Little, Inc., and a man who has built several networks in his career, described how he built one in just eighteen months based in one country where he wanted to expand the firm's business:

> I now have seven or eight top CEOs in [that country] that I can call and receive a return call within thirty minutes. To a degree, there is a nomenklatura in most countries. Maybe 5 percent of the people there can influence who gets retained for consulting work. To identify these people, you have to think in systemic terms. What is the system in which the companies you want to work for operate and who in the system influences others? I both identified a local network and built it by being systematic about meeting people and responding to their needs. I now have good relationships, not just with corporate executives, but also with lawyers, investment bankers, and other people who give me a lot of advice and are not competitors. It is useful to have friends with whom you can share information and confidences. They can recommend you, and you can recommend them. However, there are many subnetworks, and it is dangerous to be linked only to one. You must make visits to people in each to get information and understand what is going on and slowly develop relationships. It is the same at the companies. Understanding a business community as an integrated network and then working within it from that perspective is the way to build a practice.

Rainmakers work hard building richness, as this quote from Richard Eisner, founder of the accounting firm, Richard A. Eisner and Company LLP, shows:

> For the past thirty-three years, I've had three or four lunches a week with different people. You have to be judicious about who you spend time with, but you never know where business will come from. I've enjoyed my lunches because I've been able to meet with friends and other interesting people. I'm not marketing so much to prospects as I am to referrers. For me, these are attorneys, investment bankers, accountants, commercial bankers, and venture capitalists. Rather than meet with businessmen, I prefer to meet with referrers because I want to create a sales force out there to bring our firm leads.

The subject of targeting your business development efforts will be addressed further in Chapter 6.

The Mindshare Principle

You must come to business contacts' minds when they face the kinds of problems you can solve.

Having a large network of business contacts who share an affinity with each other will not help you unless these people refer business to you. This means:

- The contacts must understand what it is you and your firm do.
- They must think of you when they face or hear about a need for what your firm does.

These, too, are simple statements with important implications. Our clients and other business contacts are busy and distracted. Each knows hundreds of people, many of whom have a more prominent position in their lives than we do and others of whom clamor for attention. During a year, our contacts deal with many different problems that do not come with a neatly labeled "Benefits Consulting Issue" or "Environmental Engineering Issue" or "Estate Planning Issue." Rather, they are seen as broader business or personal problems. An executive may have to integrate a newly acquired company into his own. He is likely to focus on reducing redundancies in overhead, soothing customers, and integrating manufacturing and distribution. Several critical weeks may pass before the executive must face the merger's employee benefits implications. A division manager may face a production shortage at one of her plants, not realizing that capacity can be increased if certain environmental problems are overcome. Instead, she may decide to build a branch plant or outsource a portion of her production. A client may serve as best man at a wealthy friend's wedding. He has a wonderful time without ever thinking about the tax and estate planning advice his friend needs because of the major change that has just occurred in his circumstances. In a complex world, most of our business contacts think of us little, if at all. Rainmakers are aware of this. As one accountant put it: "We all tend to think that the world is always thinking about us, and it's not."

When our contacts do think of us, their understanding of what we do is both incomplete and inaccurate. They are likely to identify us with the specific service they received from us in the past and forget others. They are almost certainly unaware of changes in our services, even if we have told them once or twice. This is true of even big, well-known firms. One consulting firm had an outsider conduct detailed interviews with all major clients at each of its regional offices. The message came back again and again that clients did not know about many of the services they offered.

Solving this problem requires clearly defining a position for yourself and your firm in the market and frequently making this position clear to your contacts in a way that is stimulating. These are issues of positioning, thought leadership, and frequent contact, which we address in Chapters 6, 7, and 9. Rainmakers understand them well. Roland Berger, founder of a large consulting firm based in Europe that bears his name, is well aware of this need:

> You have to be present in people's minds. It's like a mosaic with the pieces, including seeing you mentioned in an article, receiving a letter, or hearing a speech you give. Letters remind people of me and my services and my organization. They remind people that I am interested in them. But I only send them when I have something to say. I try not to inflate what we do, so that each communication retains its value. Speaking reinforces credibility. I'm fairly well-known in public now, and there are multiple layers of reminders.

The Numbers-Game Principle
You have to pursue many to win a few, and if you pursue enough, the chance of winning becomes high.

Selling is a numbers game, subject to the rules of probability as much as is a game of cards.

There are two kinds of games, those of chance and those of skill, and selling is a game of skill. This means that if we play with skill, our chances of winning increase, but luck (things that we cannot predict and that are beyond our control) also influences whether we win or lose. Let's take a look at these two aspects of selling: luck and skill.

There are many steps to developing a prospect into a client, and luck comes into play at each of them. Take, for example, an attorney who gives speeches to meet prospective clients. Luck, in part, determines how many potential prospects attend one of his speeches. Luck, in part, determines whether a prospective client takes his phone call when he calls to ask for a meeting after the speech. Luck, as we define it here (that which is unpredictable and beyond the attorney's control), determines whether the client's business situation makes her receptive to the attorney's message when they meet. Finally, if the prospective client asks the attorney to make a competitive proposal and presentation, luck determines how effective those of his competitors will be.

Such a sequence creates a series of contingencies, each with declining probability of success. That is, the probability of *a* and *b* both occurring is smaller than the probability of *a* occurring or of *b* occurring. The probability of *a* and *b* and *c* all occurring is smaller still. This same logic applies to an attorney who gives a speech. The chance of having someone hear the speech, who later agrees to a meeting, who asks for a proposal, *and* who hires him is, by definition, smaller than the chance of having someone hear the speech, who later agrees to a meeting and asks for a proposal.

This means, of course, that the probability of turning any single person who attends the speech into a client is very small. Understanding this at least intuitively, most professionals don't try very hard to do so. They prefer to focus on where they perceive the probabilities of winning are highest, that is, on those few prospective clients who have asked them about the firm's services. This will help bring in business in the short run. In the long run, it is likely to result in a shortage of good prospects.

The rainmaker reacts differently. Realizing that the probability of turning any single initial contact into new business is small, he or she makes more contacts and pursues all of them aggressively. The rainmaker knows that if he or she pursues enough contacts, a few will result in new business. Listen, for example, to this story about a Detroit-based accountant and successful rainmaker:

> I once gave a speech on the radio about finding an "angel," an investor to back a company. This resulted in a huge number of phone calls from people wanting to find angels. I turned all these names over to [the rainmaker], and he tracked each deal — *every one*, even some I wouldn't have pursued because they didn't seem promising. He didn't give up. He took relationships away from all of it.

A basic marketing rule, then, is that you must pursue many to win a few. As we will see, there are things you can do to decrease the number of prospects you have to pursue to win, but this results in a change of degree, not in a change of rule. It means that management must find a way to help its professionals pursue many with the understanding that the probability of any specific one of these targets becoming a new client in the short term is low.

A second characteristic of luck also has a major impact on marketing success: Any marketer will have streaks and slumps. Sometimes the marketer will win a lot of engagements in a row; at other times, he or she will have a string of losses. An unskilled marketer will have longer and more frequent slumps and shorter and less frequent streaks than a skilled one, but both will have streaks and slumps. That is how numbers games work. If you roll a die, a six will come up, on average, 16.67 percent of the time. But if you roll it often enough, six will occasionally come up three times in a row and occasionally not come up for ten rolls.

Especially in games of skill, human beings tend to attribute streaks to periods of especially great skill and slumps to losing one's edge. This has been studied in sports where, for example, basketball players talk about having hot hands during streaks and cold ones during slumps. The evidence shows there are no such things. A study of the Philadelphia 76ers by Gilovich and Tversky showed that after adjusting for a player's skill by considering his season-long shooting record, strings of baskets and strings of misses of a specific length occurred with no greater frequency than one would expect from a random prediction. Similar studies have been made of batting streaks and slumps in baseball with similar results.[3]

This means that a professional must work to develop his or her marketing and sales skills but must not be unduly distracted by short-term strings of wins and, especially, losses. Because optimists don't personalize failure, they avoid such distraction naturally. The rest of us must work at it.

Firm management must avoid being overjudgmental about short-term streaks and slumps for the same reason. It is extremely easy for management to feed a person's tendency to personalize failure by criticizing performance in a heavy-handed way. Instead, consistent emphasis is needed in good times and bad on fundamental skills that will increase a professional's chances of winning.

We discuss these skills in greater detail in later chapters. A quick review is important here. First, we consider effective targeting. A professional who focuses his or her efforts on those prospective clients most likely to hire him or her will win more often than one who wastes effort on prospective clients that are too small or too entrenched with a competitor. These people are worth the time only if the firm is prepared to take a long-term view of business development. Many firms are. A good example of a professional who targeted effectively is the consultant described in Chapter 1 who focused on upwardly mobile, second-tier executives at companies where he had engagements.

The questioning and listening skills that all rainmakers possess also increase the chances of making a sale. Claude Shannon, an engineer from Bell Laboratories who helped develop the branch of mathematics called information theory, described information as the reduction of uncertainty.[4] In other words, information takes some of the chance out of selling. It is obtained by questioning and listening, and a great deal of information can be obtained in a short time this way. In fact, it can be shown mathematically that a skilled questioner can identify the right answer from one million possibilities with but twenty yes-or-no questions.[5] This says a lot for the value of good questioning skills. Probably few rainmakers know this math, but they understand its implications and question and listen skillfully.

The professional who first begins to market will be much more subject to the whims of chance than the seasoned rainmaker because he or she has not yet developed these skills nor invested enough time to see a significant return. To this person, it can seem impossible to exert control over the results of marketing. The effort may seem so uncertain and unproductive as to be a waste of time. Firm management must help such people get through this difficult period by making sure that they understand the mathematics of selling.

Over the past year, I have worked with a young professional who was asked to obtain meetings for her firm's partners with prospective clients. During the first few months, the work proved unrewarding, and she found herself easily distracted, both because she found other work more rewarding and because management, seeing little return on her marketing time, provided little reinforcement and actually assigned her to other activities.

After I talked to her boss and to her about the mathematics of selling, she rededicated herself to her call program, and within a few months, she was obtaining an increasing number of meetings with prospective clients for the partners. Her skill at asking for meetings has increased — she can describe to me what she has learned that gets results. She is also able to see a return on the investment she has been making for months. Still, every time she picks up the phone, there is a high probability that she won't reach the person she is calling because he or she will be out or busy or unwilling to take a call from a stranger. She has learned to see the times she does not connect not as failures, but as necessary steps to getting a meeting. She is well on the way to becoming a rainmaker.

Time Allocation Principle
Selling won't happen unless you make time for it.

Easily understood, this principle is hard to implement, as any young professional will testify. With only twenty-four hours in a day, time made for selling usually means a decrease in time spent on something else.

Exhibit 2.4 models the time management problem that a professional faces. Circles represent the discrete activities on which a professional can spend time, and the arrows the effect that spending time in one activity has on the time required for others. The

Exhibit 2.4

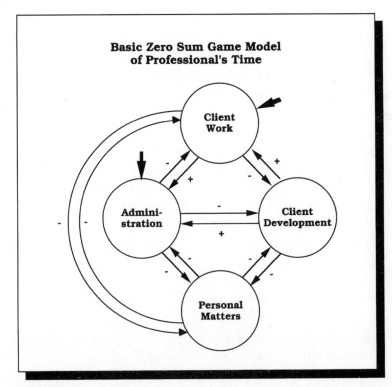

large arrow from outside leading into the client work circle represents the demands made on the professional's time by other people in the firm who sell work that the professional must do. Similarly, the bold arrow leading into the administration circle represents demands on the professional's time for firm administrative matters and administrative demands, such as interviewing prospective employees. A plus sign (+) indicates a positive relationship. That is, if more time is spent on the originating activity, more time will be required for the receiving activity, and if less time is spent on the originating activity, less will be required for the receiving one. A minus sign (−) represents a negative relationship. If more time is spent on the originating activity, less will be available for the receiving one, and if less time is spent on the originating activity, more will be available for the receiving one.

Thus, time spent on client development will ultimately result in sales, creating a demand for time for client and administrative work. Time spent on client and administrative work results in less time available for client development. Note that client development has a positive relationship to other work-related activities, but all other activities have a negative relationship to client development. Within the confines of the model, this means that spending time on client development today will make it difficult to do so in the future because client and administrative work will drive down the hours available for client development. This problem is compounded by the demands made on a young professional's time to do work sold by others and by the administrative demands of the firm. Many large law firms in New York, for example, now require associates to bill 2,000 hours per year or more. Assuming a two-week vacation, this means they must bill, on average, forty hours a week. On top of this, they must find time for administrative work and their personal lives. This creates a serious barrier to finding time for client development.

Though the model simplifies a more complex reality (good administration increases efficiency, increasing the time available for the most valuable activities), it captures the professional's problem with time. It shows how the imbalance between positive and negative relationships tends to drive out client development activity.

The model also shows that all work-related activities draw time away from personal matters, and vice versa. This explains the difficulty that many professionals have in maintaining balance in their lives.

Rainmakers find a way to succeed either within the confines of the model or by creatively adapting it to their personal situations. Helping young professionals learn to do the same is key to their emergence as rainmakers. The survey of rainmakers shows several approaches that can work.

Limit Personal Time

Some rainmakers simply let client development time cut deeply into their personal time. Take, for example, this description of what a young litigator did. Litigators face special problems when marketing because the need to avoid looking like ambulance chasers is even greater for them than it is for other professionals. Early in his career, this lawyer decided to solve the problem by putting himself in the way of getting business, recognizing that it would come to him if he got to know the right people and kept in front of them in appropriate ways:

> You can't be a nine-to-fiver if you want to bring in business. I began in 1992 when I was thirty-two by going to every business meeting I could. I went to chamber of commerce meetings, Institute of Packaging Professionals meetings, Business & Industry Association meetings — you name it and I was there. I wanted to meet everybody. I did it in the evening and largely at my own expense. The firm didn't provide much support for this effort. I realized pretty soon that I wouldn't meet end users at these events, but that I could hook people up with each other and build up chits. After about a year, I started to get [referred] some nice cases.

Some professionals who take this approach are single. Others have understanding spouses. Still others end up divorced. But it has worked for many professionals wanting to develop their own practices.

Combine Personal and Client Development Time

Some rainmakers have solved the problem by combining their personal and client development time. These people have, in essence, reconfigured the base model shown in Exhibit 2.4 to look like Exhibit 2.5 and thereby greatly simplified the competition for time.

This approach is well characterized by an accountant who sells his services to high-net-worth people:

> I am always on stage. Whoever I meet, be it socially or in a family setting or a more typical business environment, there is always the potential for business. Therefore, your lifestyle

Exhibit 2.5

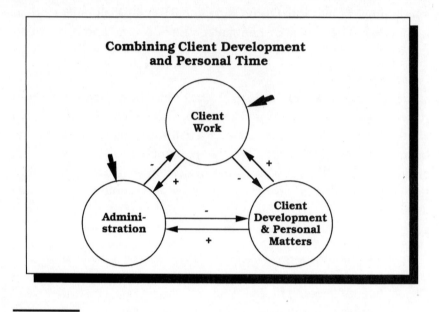

and self-image are a part of it. I spend a lot of money on clothes and dress for the occasion. That means I can dress casually, like today, or in a $1,500 suit with an Italian designer tie.

Having a lot of high-profile clients allows me to travel in very varied circles. I will eat in restaurants four times a week and have eaten in every name restaurant in [this city] at least once. This allows me to talk about where I have eaten. When I travel, I always stay at the best hotels for the same reason. This may cost $100 more a night, but if it leads to a $30,000 client, it's worth it. People talk about where they go. They say to themselves that if you stay at that kind of hotel or eat at that kind of restaurant, you must be successful and so must be good at what you do.

My wife is a big help. She dresses attractively and is able to socialize with the right groups and in her way promotes me. We have dinner parties and have a beautifully appointed apartment. We subscribe to the [symphony] and the ballet. We have a summer house in [an area where other affluent people have summer houses] and meet other people who go away on weekends, too, and tend to be affluent.

I always have conversations with people. For example, if I play tennis at one of my clubs, I always talk to the people I play with for five or six minutes and find out what they do. If they are the right kind of person, I will go to the desk and ask to be booked with them again in a couple of weeks. Usually, the person doesn't know this happened. We play again and we talk again. If you play with someone four times and talk for ten minutes each time, you've talked with them for forty minutes. They know what I do and ask for advice, which I give for free. I nurture this for two or three years sometimes and never suggest they use us. Eventually, I will get their business.

When I meet someone, it's a very soft sell. I don't hand out business cards easily. I don't sound as if I'm trying to sell them anything. The opportunities arise because of who I put myself on the line to meet. You get business by who you meet. This is all somewhat programmed, but it becomes natural. You must market by integrating your lifestyle into the natural world of business.

These words are from a rainmaker at the peak of his career and describe only one aspect of his client development, ignoring, for example, the quality of his service, which he works hard to maintain. But it exemplifies an approach that is also used by younger rainmakers, who do similar things in their own way. A young attorney who has become a successful rainmaker finds that much of his business comes from his cycling club, which gathers regularly for group rides. Referring to his personal life and to his personal and business network, he said:

We are expecting a child. Many of our friends have them now, so it is a part of our social growth as well as the growth of our family.

Though some aspiring rainmakers will accept such an outlook without difficulty, I know from conversations that many professionals find it distasteful. To them, I make the following points:

- It is not an all-or-nothing situation. You can mix parts of your business and personal lives, and not others.
- You will develop lasting friendships that go well beyond work with some of the people you meet this way. Many of the rainmakers mentioned the personal pleasure that the relationships they have developed while looking for business give them.

- You don't have to do it. Many have found another way, such as the management consultant who said, "There have been a lot of times when, at the end of the day, a client would want to go to dinner and I needed a break from that and said I couldn't go." If you choose not to do it, you must find some other way to build client development time into your schedule.

Combine Client Work and Client Development Time

Still other rainmakers solve the problem by combining client work and client development time. They modify the base model, shown in Exhibit 2.4, to look like Exhibit 2.6. Recognizing that much of their billable time also presents them with client development opportunities, they use the time for both purposes. Charles Emley, a successful consultant and now dean of the Peter F. Drucker Graduate Management Center at the Claremont Graduate School, described this approach:

> The way I viewed a successful career was to have a portfolio of clients. A manageable number is somewhere between three and seven. I tried to keep a level of face time with these clients even when I wasn't working with them full tilt.

Exhibit 2.6

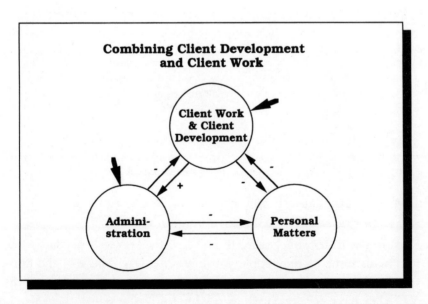

Whenever we began to see a decrease in the amount of work we received from client A, I always had a reservoir of work beginning with B, C, D, or E. The point was never to disengage, to always be working with the firms at least a little. I would know a lot of people in these organizations, but would have close contacts with three or four. I believe it is easier and more cost effective to maintain a constant portfolio of clients than to develop new ones.

Of course, some of the time spent is pure client development time, as Emley points out:

You must have a sufficient reservoir of time and money to keep contact going with a key client, even though you may not be earning anything from the client while you are doing it. We would sometimes be able to provide advisory services that also helped us maintain the relationship. But you must also be able to invest by giving the client some services for free. You must show the client that you are willing to make that kind of investment. It helps you keep a part of the client's mindshare.

Exhibit 2.7

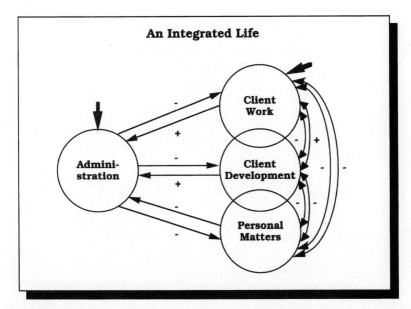

Fully Integrated Lives

Many rainmakers develop a combination of the preceding two approaches, diagrammed in Exhibit 2.7. These people integrate client development with client work and with personal time so that many of their activities overlap. As a rainmaker matures, this seems to become more common. Their success allows them to reduce billable time in favor of client development, and client development and personal time become well mixed.

Stepping (or Being Pushed) Off the Cliff

Some rainmakers solve the time problem by simply abandoning, temporarily, their commitments to activities other than client development. Most often, this is the case with those who started their own firms. This approach is exemplified by architect Ron Schmidt, founder of Ronald Schmidt & Associates:

> When I went out on my own, I didn't wait to have a project the way most people do. I thought I had a lot of contacts and I did. I got on the phone and called everyone I knew and said I was going into business. I ran ads and sent out flyers announcing the opening of my office. I had a cocktail party to open the office and a lot of people came. It worked out well.

This abandonment of other activities isn't always voluntary. The founder of an engineering firm described such a situation: "I never planned it. I started my own company because one client said he would give me all his business. A week later, he died. I had a wife, a kid, and a mortgage. That's how I became a marketer."

The approach that different rainmakers take to solving the zero-sum-game aspects of client development depends on the nature of their practices and on their personal proclivities. A geographically dispersed client base makes socializing with clients more difficult, though not impossible. A highly personal service will require more socializing than a more corporate one, almost by definition. Part of the job of management must be to help aspiring rainmakers understand the alternatives available to them and to select an approach that is appropriate to their circumstances.

The Accumulation Principle

If you can hang onto your current clients and add others, your business will grow faster than if you do just one or the other.

Exhibit 2.8

	Year 1	Year 2	Year 3
Retained (80%)*		$ 80	$ 98
New (35%)†		43	53
Total	**$100**	**$123**	**$151**

* 80% of previous year's revenues from old clients
† 35% of current year's revenues from new clients
These are percentages of different things and so
cannot be added.

This simple principle has major implications. Its logic is shown in Exhibit 2.8, which shows what happens when you keep 80 percent of the business you had in the previous year and 35 percent of your business each year comes from new clients. You end up with an annual growth rate of 23 percent. The rainmakers understand this logic and work aggressively at both keeping old clients and adding new ones. As simple as the principle is, it is fundamental to the success of many rainmakers and, of course, more easily stated than done.

I have already described what several rainmakers do to get new clients. These quotes will give you a sense of their dedication to keeping old ones:

- I am the kind of person who, if I get a call from a client at 10:00 P.M., will get back in my shoes and go see him. I am very much service driven. Relationships come second. [a strategy consultant]

- He is still active on projects and puts in about two hours a day doing engineering work. If there is a problem, he wants every client to know they can call him and get it solved. Internally, sometimes it drives people crazy, but he holds to it. When someone calls him who is unhappy, he doesn't rest until he gets it solved. [an electrical engineer]

- People say we treat them as if they were our only client, which is the way we want them to feel. [a management consultant]

- I always wanted clients to feel that they would get 100 percent of me and maybe something extra. I expect our attorneys to service the clients they have and that those clients will be happy with the work. I have always said to our people that the important thing is to get a client you are working with to do more and more with you rather than going out and finding someone new. The client knows about the level of service you have provided and will refer you to others. [an attorney]

Each of these six principles is quite simple by itself. Acting on all of them at once is like juggling a dozen eggs. You have to know just what you're doing, and be fast and focused. In the first chapter of this book, I noted that almost all rainmakers have a system that they work relentlessly. I believe these dynamic systems are necessary to deal with the complexity that acting on the six principles simultaneously over long periods results in. In Chapter 4, we look at the characteristics of these systems.

Before leaving this chapter, it would be fair for you to ask how aware the rainmakers are of these principles. As the quotes show, many talked in ways that suggested they are, yet few articulated any of the principles directly. Most behave as if they are aware of all or most of them. Some of the principles are simple enough that it would be surprising if the rainmakers were not aware of them. Many of the rest of us may also be aware of these principles, but how many of us act on them with the relentlessness of the rainmakers?

Following all the principles is not absolutely necessary to success. A few rainmakers clearly did not. One did a poor job of hanging on to existing clients. One or two had networks that were surprisingly small. But that should not be surprising. The survey encompasses a diverse group of people facing vastly different selling situations. We are unlikely to find universal rules among them. That so many acted and spoke as if they were aware of the six principles should provide confidence in their value.

3

How Rainmakers Think or the Skill of Optimism

Understanding the mathematics of marketing and acting on that knowledge over many months in the face of repeated inability to win new clients are, of course, two quite different things. The first is a function of intellect; the second requires faith. It requires the ability to bounce back again and again from what many would see as failure. In short, it requires optimism. Most of the rainmakers are optimists.

There is a joke about a man who has identical twin sons. On their birthday, they are visited by an aunt who asks their father how he can tell them apart. The father says, "It's easy, Tim is a pessimist and Tom an optimist." The aunt doesn't see how that helps tell one from the other, so the father suggests she visit their rooms. The first is filled high with new toys. In their midst sits a crying child. "What's the matter, Tim?" she asks. "I have so many toys, I don't know which to play with. I'm afraid if I do, I'll break one or lose all the parts." The aunt soothes him and goes to the next room. This one is filled almost to the ceiling with horse manure, in which a boy is joyously flailing around. "What are you doing, Tom?" asks the aunt. The boy responds, "I figure with all this manure, there has to be a pony in here somewhere."

Knowing this joke, you can imagine my surprise during my interview with Bob Gaida, a partner at BDO Seidman LLP, when he said, "I approach every event I go to with the attitude, 'I know there's a new client in here somewhere and I'm going to find him.' " He had never heard the joke.

That rainmakers have faith and bounce-back ability was readily apparent in many interviews:

- I've never heard him say anything negative. The glass is always half full. No matter how disheartening the loss of a project, there is always another one out there. He can be very inspiring. [an engineer]

- Even during the early 1990s when we were going through a very hard time and earning perhaps half the revenue we had before and have since, he remained upbeat and would say things would get better. I can't imagine him being down at all. [an architect]

- He doesn't get discouraged and constantly sees opportunities in what is happening. He feels there is always more business out there to be had. [a lawyer]

- The problem could always be solved, the contract would always be signed, and the schedule could always be met. He was always very positive. In the days when everyone recommended IBM products, he would recommend non-IBM products because of their new features. He was usually wrong, and it wouldn't work, but then he would sell another project to fix it. [a technology consultant]

- He always thinks we are going to win an engagement, always. Even though it's obvious to others that we can't win every time, he expects to. [an accounting partner at PricewaterhouseCoopers]

Many of the rainmakers recognize this trait in themselves and its importance to their success:

- I've been heavily influenced by positive-thinking people all my life. Marketing is about attitude. When you read books about great salespeople, it's all about attitude. They never give up. You have to put the fear aside and go ahead. [Ron Schmidt, architect, Ronald Schmidt & Associates]

- You can't get discouraged. If you do, you have to go back to scribbling papers, so you can't. [a lawyer]

- You have to accept the fact that sometimes you must fail in order to succeed at business development. [Guy Geier, architect, The Hillier Group]

This faith that things will get better and the ability to bounce back after defeat are characteristics of optimists.

Sometimes a native optimism seems to have been reinforced by early sales success that showed the young professional what was possible. In some cases, the rainmakers look back at these events with amusement:

- Six months into my first accounting job, I had a new client for the firm. My mother sold it for me. She went into a candy store that was opening up and asked if the owner had an accountant. When he said no, she said, "You should use my son, the accountant." I called on him, as green as I was, and sold the business. That started me off, and now I have a corporate practice of $3 million annually. [Roy Hoffman, accountant, Goldstein Golub, Kessler & Company]

- I had a friend who was a Chilean citizen who needed a witness at his naturalization and asked me to help him, and I did. Later, he joined a large soft drink company and would call and ask for small favors, and I would do what he asked, just to be helpful because he was a friend. One day he called and asked me to meet with someone at his company. I went to lunch with them and at the end of the lunch was asked to do some work for them. I came back with an order to put in a core financial system for the company. I was still a manager and received a very warm welcome back at the office. [Mel Bergstein, technology consultant, DiamondCluster International. At the time of the story, he worked at Andersen Consulting.]

- I got involved in client development as a first-year associate. I was at a party hosted by a neighbor who was a trustee of a college. At the party, I talked with the president of the college, who commented on some labor relations issues he was facing. When I got back to the office, I researched labor relations law at colleges and universities and sent him an article and asked him if he would like to meet a senior partner with our firm. The three of us had lunch, and he liked the senior partner. After that he hired me. [Carol Berlin Manzoni, lawyer, Ross & Hardies]

Though some may have had early luck or a little help, for most of the rainmakers, this optimism seems to be such a deep-seated personality trait that I believe they were born with it. That is not to say that their optimism is always well founded. One rainmaker in the survey went bankrupt, and several others came close to filing for bankruptcy due to overly optimistic assessments of their own abilities in areas where they lacked expertise, usually real estate investment. Yet optimism seems an element critical to their success as rainmakers.

Not all of us were born with such a buoyant outlook. And those who believe in the Nature Theory might argue that if we weren't, perhaps we should give up on our efforts to make rain. Fortunately for us, research into optimism shows that such a conclusion is too hasty. Many of us can become more optimistic because it is a skill. This does not mean that we may ever be as optimistic as someone who is naturally so, anymore than learning golf or tennis skills will give us the same ability as a natural athlete. But most people can learn enough about thinking optimistically to succeed in client development.

Research shows that optimism results, in part, from thought patterns that we can control with practice. A few examples will clarify what I mean.

> *Example One:*   A young accountant has lunch with a client, and the client says that she has passed the accountant's name to a friend who is thinking of changing auditors. She gives the accountant her friend's name and number and suggests that he follow up with a phone call. He has not worked with this client long and is surprised and pleased by the referral.
>
> When the accountant gets back to the office, he calls the prospect who is out, so he leaves a message mentioning the name of the client who gave the referral. After a week passes with no return call, the accountant calls again and leaves another message. Again there is no response. He finds this discouraging and says to himself, "I guess this wasn't such a hot lead." Nevertheless, he calls again and leaves a third message. As he hangs up the phone, he thinks to himself, "He doesn't really want to talk with me. My calls are becoming a nuisance, and that's no way to get business." He briefly considers calling the client who gave the referral, but says to himself, "I don't want to bother her. She's done what she can for me. Her friend has probably made up with his auditor or chosen someone else." After that he gives up trying to reach the prospect.
>
> *Example Two:*   During a period of slow business, a consultant is told by her boss that she needs to start developing business if she

wants to advance her career. She protests that she doesn't know how to develop business and that she is probably the best project manager in the firm. He agrees that she is an excellent project manager, but adds that only those who bring in business make partner. He advises her to work at business development while she has some time.

So, she goes to the annual, three-day conference of a trade association for human resource professionals, the market that her firm sells to. There are 1,500 people at the opening reception and dinner. Her immediate reaction on entering the ballroom is "What a zoo!" She gets a drink and tries to strike up conversations. The first group she tries to enter is engaged in a deep discussion of a recent reorganization at their company. Finding it difficult to add anything, she says to herself, "This is awful; I don't belong here," and moves on. She sees a man in a rumpled sports jacket standing by himself with a drink and considers introducing herself, but decides not to, saying to herself, "He certainly doesn't look like someone with authority to hire consultants." She tries a woman who is standing near the door. They have a brief conversation, during which the woman scans the room and then excuses herself, saying that she sees someone she has been looking for. "I hate this! This isn't the kind of thing I do well," says the consultant to herself. Later, she runs into an alumnus from her firm, who is obviously glad to see a friendly face. They sit next to each other at dinner, and she retires early. The remaining days follow a similar pattern.

When she gets back to the office, she looks at the business cards she has collected and starts to write letters to people she has met. She cannot remember anything about the person whose name is on the first card. She can't even remember when during the three days she met him. She thinks, "A letter wouldn't make any difference anyway," and puts the cards aside. A week later, she gets assigned to a new project and turns away from business development with relief, vowing never to attend another trade association meeting, if she can help it, and saying to herself, "I'm just not good at marketing."

Example Three: At an office meeting, the regional manager of an engineering firm passes out response cards that readers of the firm's newsletter have filled out and returned. Most of the cards simply note a change of address, but the ones on the twelve cards given to a young electrical engineer have a small X in the box in front of a line that reads, "My company plans to renovate air-conditioning systems this year." The office manager asks each professional to follow up on the leads he has been given.

As a first reaction, the engineer thinks, "What? This isn't my job. I'm not going to do this." But he says nothing. The cards sit on his desk for a long time. Each time he sees them, he thinks, "I shouldn't have to do this. I can't make this work."

One afternoon the regional manager stops by his workstation and asks about his progress on calling the names on the twelve cards. The engineer promises to get to it. The next morning, he picks up the phone and calls the person on the first card. A voice mail recording answers, and he leaves a message. The second person answers his own phone. The engineer introduces himself, somewhat clumsily, and explains the purpose of his call. The prospective client says that the company plans to do the renovation work in-house and that he will call if he needs help. Hanging up, the engineer says to himself, "This will never work. This isn't the way professional services are sold. It would take forever." Briefly, he also thinks, "I'm making a fool of myself. I'm a klutz at this." He turns to other things.

These examples are fictitious, but anyone who has run a professional practice will recognize them immediately as the kinds of things that happen all the time. All three situations have several points in common.

First, all happen to professionals inexperienced at selling who do not know about the mathematics of marketing and, therefore, don't know how to interpret what is happening. Second, all happen relatively early in the client development process, before the professional has a chance to talk with a prospect about a problem he or she might be able to help solve. As we have seen, at this point in the sales cycle, the probability of turning any single contact into new business is low. The time to conversion from contact to client is also likely to be long. The professionals realize these things, and they draw the erroneous conclusion that the effort is not worthwhile. Third, all the professionals think negative thoughts that are almost certainly inaccurate. For example, when the accountant in the first example says to himself, "I guess it wasn't such a hot lead," he is making two mistakes. First, he is implying that it seemed a hot lead in the first place, a dubious premise. Second, he is inferring that it is not a hot lead from the extremely limited evidence of two unreturned phone calls. There could be many reasons why the prospective client has not returned his calls other than lack of interest. The accountant might have said more accurately that this lead seems better than many and worse than some and that there is not enough evidence yet to determine how seriously to take it. However, the accountant's more negative thoughts discourage him from continued effort. In essence, the professionals in the examples defeat themselves by negative thinking. Anyone who runs a professional practice has seen that happen.

Cognitive therapists have shown that when people learn to recognize the inaccuracies in their negative thoughts and correct them, their behavior often changes, too. Before going into this subject, I want to clearly dissociate it from the positive-thinking concept, closely allied to the team-player concept, which has been popular with some corporate executives for many years and which Donald Smith so aptly describes as a brickbat used by executives against anyone who disagrees with them.[1] None of the rainmakers in the survey could be described as yes-men and only some were team players. In my experience, labeling people as negative thinkers and excoriating them for being so will not help them develop the thought patterns needed to succeed in client development.

Studies have shown that even coaches who have long worked closely with athletes have difficulty identifying the true optimists.[2] Categorizing professionals as optimists or pessimists on the basis of observation in day-to-day business activity can result in decisions that are harmful to both the individual professionals and the firm. Optimism has several parameters[3] and individuals can be optimistic on one parameter and pessimistic on another. There are also degrees of optimism on each parameter. Awareness of the need for optimism permits firm management to identify *potential* problems, but does not give them the skills needed to decide who is an optimist and who isn't.

Cognitive therapists treat pessimism by teaching people to identify inaccuracies in their own thought processes and to correct them.[4] Usually, they ask the people they treat to keep a log of their negative thoughts, like the one shown in Exhibit 3.1. This example shows the thought processes of the accountant in Example One. First, it identifies the situation in which the negative thought occurs. This will help the accountant identify the kinds of situations that stimulate negative thinking. In the second column, the accountant records the negative thought. In the third column, he analyzes it for inaccuracies, and in the fourth, he reinterprets the negative thought into a more accurate assessment of the situation. By doing this repeatedly, he can modify his thought processes.

Exhibit 3.2 provides a blank form for use in this kind of analysis. As an exercise, review Examples Two and Three, and fill out the form for the consultant and engineer, identifying the situation that stimulates negative thoughts, the negative thoughts, the inaccuracies in these thoughts, and a more accurate reinterpretation. For comparison, Exhibit 3.3 shows how I have completed this exercise.

Many efforts to develop rainmakers founder on the issue of attitude. Unwittingly, firm management may reinforce the self-defeating thinking of aspiring rainmakers. Someone may set goals that seem unrealistically high to young professionals, rather than letting them set their own goals at a level they feel is achievable. Someone may criticize aspiring rainmakers' efforts heavy-handedly and thereby contribute the weight of authority to their own self-doubts. Or a mentor may not be much of a rainmaker, and suffer from the same negative thought patterns as those he or she is trying to coach. As a result, the mentor may give up on them too quickly. This area warrants the closest attention of a firm that wants to create rainmakers.

Exhibit 3.1 Example One

Marketing/Selling Situation	Negative Thought	Inaccuracy	Reinterpretation
Third unreturned phone call to prospective client referred by Jane Morris.	I guess this wasn't such a hot lead.	Implies it was a hot lead in the first place. Infers that it is not a hot lead on the basis of insufficient evidence.	This lead seemed better than many and worse than some, but I don't have enough evidence to decide how seriously to take it.
	He doesn't really want to talk with me. My calls are becoming a nuisance.	Imputes disinterest and irritation to prospect from insufficient evidence. There could be many reasons why he hasn't called back.	I don't really know why he hasn't called back. It would therefore be premature to judge his level of interest, so I will try calling again or try to reach him by another means.
	I don't want to bother Jane Morris. She has done what she can for me.	Implies that Jane Morris would be bothered by a call and that she can't do anything more. There is no evidence for either belief.	I don't know how she would feel about my calling her, but a call bringing her up to date on my lack of progress and asking for advice on what to do would not bother most people.
	He (the prospective client) has probably made up with his auditor or chosen someone else.	There is no evidence to support this statement.	I don't know what has happened and need to talk with the prospective client to find out.

Exhibit 3.2

Marketing/Selling Situation	Negative Thought	Inaccuracy	Reinterpretation

Exhibit 3.2 (continued)

Marketing/Selling Situation	Negative Thought	Inaccuracy	Reinterpretation

Exhibit 3.2 (continued)

Marketing/Selling Situation	Negative Thought	Inaccuracy	Reinterpretation

Exhibit 3.3 Example Two

Marketing/Selling Situation	Negative Thought	Inaccuracy	Reinterpretation
Opening reception at a three-day trade association conference.	This is awful. I don't belong here.	Imputes awfulness to the conference on the basis of exposure which is too brief for an accurate assessment. Imputes outsider status to myself.	I am uncomfortable at this reception, which is a natural feeling when I don't know anyone. If I persevere and meet people, it may get better later. I belong here as much as anyone does, because I have paid my admission fee and so am entitled to attend. I may not belong in a specific conversation, but there are others.
	I hate this! This isn't the kind of thing I do well.	Implies I should be liking this or that something is wrong. Implies that I should be doing this well but am not.	We often have to do things we don't like and often they seem less onerous after working at them for a while. I haven't yet learned how to work a room like this, but I probably can learn to do it as well as many other people here, if I decide to work at it.
Preparing to send letters to people met at conference.	A letter wouldn't make much difference anyway.	Implies that the letter should make a substantial difference to be worth writing.	Selling is made up of many small acts which have a cumulative effect. A letter is probably worth writing for that reason.
Reflecting on conference.	I'm just not good at marketing.	Implies that my inability is innate and permanent. Imputes incompetence to me.	I don't have a lot of marketing experience. If I work at it I will probably get better. I am entitled to make some mistakes as I learn.

Exhibit 3.3 Example Three

Marketing/Selling Situation	Negative Thought	Inaccuracy	Reinterpretation
Being asked to call prospective clients who returned a response card.	This isn't my job. I'm not going to do this.	Implies assignment is being made unfairly and the withholding cooperation is justified.	I may not like having this assignment, but the work seems to be evenly spread. Sometimes I need to do things I don't want to do to support the office and because I am asked to.
Seeing cards lying on desk.	I shouldn't have to do this.	Ditto above.	Ditto above.
	I can't make this work.	Imputes incompetence to me. Implies an unclear standard of success.	Even if I don't like it, I can make calls to twelve people, which is what I was asked to do.
After being told by the second person I called that he had no interest in our services.	This will never work. It would take forever.	Insists that a desirable outcome could never happen, which is untrue. Implies that a long campaign has been requested.	The probability of any single call turning into business is low, but the people being called have noted a need and the time required to make the calls is small.
	This isn't the way professional services are sold.	Implies I know how professional services are sold, when I really don't know that much about it.	This may be one way to sell professional services. It doesn't require much time so I might as well try it.
	I'm making a fool out of myself. I'm a klutz at this.	Implies person I called feels that I am a fool, when I have no evidence of that. Imputes klutziness to me. Implies that I am expected to be good at this.	We all speak clumsily sometimes, and the prospect probably understands that. I will get better at making the calls with a little practice.

4

What Rainmakers Do or the Power of Systems

"I didn't have time." So runs the standard plaint for failing to market. It is the single most common excuse for failing to perform this vital activity and understandably so. Professional work tends to be all-consuming. It is urgent and deadline driven. It requires a commitment to client service that can easily push out other activities like client development. Yet, as we have seen, rainmakers find the time. If we are to develop rainmakers, we must show aspiring rainmakers how this is done.

The survey shows that most rainmakers have systems for obtaining new business and that they work those systems relentlessly. The precise nature of the system varies from rainmaker to rainmaker, but the great majority have one. These systems help the rainmakers build client development into their daily routines because they:

- Tie the many little activities required by the six principles into a coordinated whole.

- Increase the efficiency with which business development work gets done. When you know exactly what you must do, work takes less time. You don't have to stop and think about what you need to do next; you can simply get on with the work. Give most professionals fifteen unexpected minutes in which to market, and they wouldn't know what to do with the time. A true rainmaker would have a list of people he or she could call or a quick letter to write, mandated by his or her system.

- Increase consistency of effort. Knowing exactly what needs to be done and being able to do it efficiently helps you fit the work into what little time is available. It increases your ability to plan marketing into your day or fit it in during odd moments. So, for example, one rainmaker would block time every Tuesday morning to make forty marketing phone calls and wouldn't come out of his office until he had made them. Of course, he could not make these calls if he didn't have a list of forty people he wanted to reach each Tuesday and a reason for calling each one of them. His system efficiently provided him these things. Knowing exactly what has to be done allows you to schedule the effort more consistently.

- Increase the quality of the marketing effort. When you do something consistently and repeatedly, you get good at it.

- Make it easy to delegate or automate work. A system makes automation and delegation easier because it requires repetitive tasks that can be systematized. In Chapter 1, I described a rainmaker who used direct mail as the core of his system. Two secretaries would clip articles from newspapers and magazines mentioning targeted companies. The rainmaker would then send these articles with a cover letter to contacts at those companies. Early in his career, he undoubtedly clipped the articles and wrote all the letters himself. Because he had a system, he was later able to delegate all the article clipping and some of the letter writing to support staff. Repetitive tasks that systems require lend themselves to delegation or automation.

These are benefits for individuals. A firmwide system has additional benefits. It makes it easy to:

- Train professionals to market. It is much easier to train others when you know exactly what you want them to do than when you don't. Those few rainmakers who were excellent mentors often trained their successors to work a specific system.

- Monitor the marketing effort. When you know exactly what is supposed to happen, it is relatively easy to determine whether it is happening or not. So, for example, you can monitor whether firm members are making a designated number of phone calls

each week or capturing the names of people who attend the
speeches they give.

- Identify and fix problems. A system is constructed of a series of
linked processes. When it stops working, either a process or a
link has failed, and it is relatively easy to figure out where the
problem lies.

But what is a marketing system? A review of the database shows it
must comprise four major elements (see Exhibit 4.1), each of which
contains one or more processes. With minor adaptations, the chart can
be used to explain each of the systems created by rainmakers in the survey. The four major elements are:

- *Targeting:* There must be a method for selecting people to contact who have reasonable potential for becoming profitable
clients. By focusing on prospective clients offering reasonable

Exhibit 4.1

A Rainmaker's System

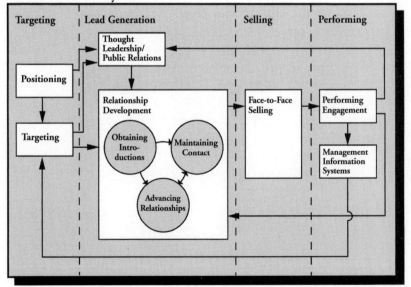

potential, you can make the best use of scarce marketing time. Some rainmakers, like the one with the direct mail campaign, focus on broad targets and contact many people. Others, like the rainmaker who developed relationships with the top four or five people at each client company, have narrow targets. But they all have a clear idea of who they are trying to get to.

- *Lead Generation:* The system must provide a mechanism for getting face to face with targeted people because unless you do so, there can be no sale. Thought leadership belongs in this portion of the system because speaking and publishing generate leads and because the name recognition they create makes it easier to obtain meetings with prospective clients by other means.

  Relationship development is a critical process within lead generation. Most professional sales require a relationship. The chances of winning are almost always enhanced if you have a relationship with the prospective client. This is particularly true for services with long selling cycles. The system must provide a method for developing a relationship with both former clients and prospective ones.

- *Selling:* You must be able to convert prospective clients into clients. If you don't, the rest of the system has no value. Rainmakers know how to persuade clients to hire them.

- *Performing:* This is where you earn your fee. It is, in many respects, beyond business development, but inextricably tied to it. While working on engagements, you can build the foundations of a relationship that can last for years. You also gain experience that helps you separate good prospects from bad ones in the future. You build the reputation for good work that is essential for getting more work.

Processes need not be complicated. In fact, many of those used by rainmakers are exceedingly simple. Some processes can be completely eliminated. Some rainmakers, as we have seen, do not give speeches or write articles or engage in other thought leadership activities. But most of the processes must exist, and they must be linked for a system to work.

Many of the systems have one process that serves as an engine — the main force that keeps the system working. In one we have described previously, this was an article-clipping and letter-writing process. In another, it was a lengthy relationship-building process with second-level executives at client companies. But *all* the processes must be interrelated for you to work a true system. That is, the outputs of one process become inputs of the next. Otherwise, instead of a system, you will be working a number of independent processes.

One firm I worked with had a newsletter. The practice heads within the firm also had personal networks of past clients and people they had met when giving speeches from which they developed most of their business. When I was asked to look over the firm's client development efforts, one professional brought me a stack of response cards that had been sent out with an issue of the newsletter and returned with a mark in a box that indicated the respondent might need the firm's services in the coming year. No one had contacted these people, even though the cards had been returned months before my arrival. The newsletter response cards represented a centralized process that wasn't linked to the firm's decentralized relationship development process. Without that link they were useless.

The schema shown in Exhibit 4.1 will hold few surprises for anyone who has developed business. Yet, it is flexible enough to explain most rainmaking systems. Listen, for example, to this description of how one partner at a large accounting and consulting firm worked:

> He used to schedule two hours every morning, between 8:00 A.M. and 10:00 A.M., five days a week for marketing and sales work. This is the time he made his calls, worked on proposals, and prepared presentations. He did it whether he was in the office or on the road. If he was traveling, he would do it from his hotel room. The only thing he would let interfere with this work was a call from a client who had had difficulty reaching him.
>
> He would call three groups of people. First, he had a list of everyone he ever met on an engagement. He would work through this list alphabetically. Second, he would call people he met at the many speeches he gave or make cold calls, trying to get a relationship started. Third, he would call people he was referred to by clients. Often these were people from a different part of the company the client worked for. A lot of these calls were spent letting those people know what was going on elsewhere in their own companies.
>
> He controlled his effort by time, not by number of calls. One day he would spend forty minutes on the phone

with one person, the next he would call several people in the same amount of time. He kept detailed records of all his calls and conversations on his laptop.

He was an excellent speaker and spoke at many conventions and seminars. He would usually do so without prepared notes. He had a huge knowledge base and had a strong presentation style with a sarcastic humor that people enjoyed. He also kept his speeches short and would encourage people to interrupt him with questions. Then the speech would go in whatever direction the question took him. He would often ask questioners to see him after the presentation to go into a subject in more depth. He would follow up with them immediately. Every time he received a business card anywhere, he recorded the information on it into his laptop within twenty-four hours. He probably did this every day of his life.

[He ran engagements at a high level and] would juggle several at once. He was never at any job site for more than a couple of hours. Clients learned to see him as a mover and a shaker and a "go-to" guy if they had any problems on the engagement. This stature increased the appeal of his phone calls when he followed up with people after an engagement was over.

All the major elements of the system are represented in this brief description of the most successful rainmaker in his firm. Note that all the separate processes are clearly linked. When he gives a speech, the names he gathers go into his call process, which is the engine of his system. When he works with a client, the names he gathers on the engagement go into his call process, too.

Exhibit 4.1 provides a basis for evaluating your own rainmaking systems. For example, you might analyze what successful rainmakers in your practice have done that makes them so successful. Several firms have developed successful marketing strategies by modeling what one successful person did and developing it for broad application across the firm. If you take this approach, you must identify and document the processes rainmakers use in each major component of the system. How do they select their targets? How do they get face to face with prospective clients? How do they develop relationships? How do they advance and close a sale? You must also identify the exact nature of the inputs and outputs to each process, and how the various processes are linked.

Professional firms vary in the level of support they provide to business development. This variation can also be described in terms of the schematic shown in Exhibit 4.1. Some firms leave almost every process to the individual partners. This has been particularly true among law firms, for example. I will call it the Rainmaker Model of a firm. Each partner is expected to bill a certain number of hours each year. No one is particularly concerned about how a partner does this as long as it is done. Speakers speak, writers publish, and networkers network. Some survive because they have established relationships with one or two good clients who provide them almost all of their work. They hardly market to anyone else. If a partner fails to bill at expected levels several years in a row, he or she may be asked to leave the firm.

Other firms provide dedicated resources for almost the entire system. I will call this the Product Model. They have dedicated marketing staffs who select the prospective clients the firm will pursue. The marketing staff also provides thought leadership material in the form of white papers and articles. Professional business developers generate leads, develop relationships with prospective clients, and begin the selling process. Only at this stage does the partner who will lead the engagement become involved.

United Research Corporation provides a good example of a firm that fully adopted the Product Model. This performance improvement consulting firm grew from roughly $20 million to more than $100 million in fees over three years, before it was bought by Gemini Consulting. Its system worked approximately as follows: The firm targeted major corporations that it segmented by industry. Though the firm had an organized public relations effort that worked to obtain favorable press coverage of successful engagements, the engine of the system was a sophisticated cold-calling process. Dedicated telemarketers obtained meetings with senior executives at targeted companies. These telemarketers were college-educated, and some had received MBAs. They researched the companies they were targeting and developed phone relationships with gatekeepers. Principal responsibilities included identifying an area where a target executive had a bias for action and obtaining a meeting to discuss it.

They obtained meetings for executive salespeople who were able to develop a peer relationship with senior executives. Using a carefully designed sales process, the executive salespeople would draw out the targeted executive's concerns and feelings, using a questioning methodology. The questions were designed to further build the prospective client's commitment to action. At a second meeting with this prospect, the executive salesperson would explore questions about how the two organizations could work together and what were the barriers to change.

Once an issue had been clearly identified and the broad outlines of an engagement established, the executive salesperson would suggest bringing into the discussions the likely point person from the client's company and a partner from United Research, introduced as a specialist in the problem to be solved, who would manage a diagnostic engagement. This was done in a way that would carefully preserve the peer-to-peer relationship of the executive salesperson and the target executive, and establish one between the partner who would be in charge of the diagnostic and his counterpart in the target company. The two representatives of the consulting firm would then work out a detailed diagnostic project with the two executives from the target company.

A diagnostic project typically ran for several weeks and was used to build momentum for the following engagement as well as to gather information that would be needed to scope and price it. While it was being conducted, the executive salesperson would remain in touch with the senior executive and negotiate the terms for the next phase of the work. Once this phase was sold, a new team came in to deliver the work.

The precision with which the various processes were linked and managed made this a highly sophisticated system. Firm management knew the number of times, on average, that the telemarketers had to dial the phone to obtain a meeting for the executive salesperson. They knew that for every four meetings that were scheduled, three would be held. And they knew how many meetings each executive salesperson had to have each week, again on average, to make annual revenue targets. The revenue targets themselves were based on the cost of maintaining this expensive system. Management knew what conversion rates to expect from first meetings to second ones and from diagnostic projects to full engagements. Each process was clearly defined and had explicit links to the next.

Most firms lie somewhere between the two extremes of the Rainmaker Model and the Product Model. The firm provides dedicated resources for some of the process but expects billable people to perform other parts of the process.

Movement from an approach that lies close to the Rainmaker Model to one closer to the Product Model has proved difficult for many firms. Many consulting firms, for example, have tried to duplicate the highly successful approach developed by United Research and failed. Several have introduced telemarketers to obtain meetings for partners the way the United Research telemarketers did. Though the telemarketers obtained the meetings, the partners often lacked sales skills that would have allowed them to convert initial meetings into a discussion about an issue of importance to the targeted executive. Furthermore, they often failed to take the meetings arranged by the telemarketer seriously, allowing client demands to take precedence and so forcing the telemarketer to reschedule sales meetings again and again. This burned out telemarketers and put off prospective clients. As a result, the partners landed few new engagements from the system.

Others have hired professional salespeople comparable to United Research's executive salespeople, but not given these individuals partner status. They resisted letting the executive salesperson maintain a peer-to-peer relationship with the top executives at targeted companies. This undercut the system in two ways. First, it made it almost impossible for the executive salesperson to do his or her job. Second, the best executive salespeople became frustrated and left the firm. A system must fit with the culture and values of a firm, or the firm must adapt to the culture and values required by a new system, if a firmwide system is to work.

Analyzing your own firm's system can be a worthwhile endeavor, and it will go a long way toward telling you how to improve your marketing success. Some questions to ask when you do it are:

1. *Who has responsibility for performing each process (or part of a process)?*

   Many client development failures can be traced to lack of clarity about who has responsibility and authority for each process.

2. *Do you have all the processes you need?*

   Many firms are missing a key process or two. For example, many lack a firmwide approach to handling a sales meeting with a prospective client, leaving the approach to each partner. This usually results in highly uneven sales effectiveness. Alternatively, a firm that has a lackluster image might ask how formalized its thought leadership process is.

3. Are processes clearly linked?

The links between processes are often vague or completely lacking in many firms. This is often because the expected inputs and outputs of a process are not clearly defined. So, for example, the firm devotes resources to obtaining speaking engagements for partners, but the partners are required neither to bring back names, addresses, and phone numbers of people they speak to nor to enter this information into a firmwide lead-tracking process.

4. Are the people responsible for performing each process adequately trained or compensated to do it?

Processes often fail because the people responsible for them are inadequately trained or compensated. A firm that expects most of its business to come from partners' personal and business networks, for example, might wisely invest a little money in training its partners how to network. One that wants partners to bring in more business would be wise to compensate them in a way that will encourage them to do so (see Appendix B).

We will address these issues in Part II. Before we do, we need to look at some of the limits to the Rainmaker Model.

5

Limits to the Rainmaker Model

The primary purpose of this book is to show how a firm can develop its people to bring in business. An essential element of my argument has been the creation of a model of how rainmakers develop clients under the belief that if we understand how rainmakers have succeeded, we can show others how to. I have called this the Rainmaker Model. Few firms that have struggled with getting their people to sell have devoted much attention to this model in the past. They have had good reasons for this lapse.

First, there has been an antisales mentality in the professions for many years, originally reinforced and, in part, created by industry proscriptions against aggressive client development. Anyone who has recently entered the professions may not realize how severe those proscriptions were. Ralph Smith, of Snow Becker Krauss, recalls that when he began to practice, some law firms refused to let their lawyers carry business cards because it was felt to be too commercial to do so. An attorney at one large, international firm remembered:

> When I started out in 1969 and well into the 1970s and early 1980s, the older New York firms weren't interested in rainmaking. Each had a stable of institutional clients that kept them busy. The man I worked for thought that it bordered on unethical even to take a client out to dinner. This attitude prevailed at the firm. We felt that being a first-rate lawyer in a first-rate firm would get people to call you and get you referrals.

Most notable among law firms, the same attitude prevailed among dominant firms in many professions. Marvin Bower, James O. McKinsey's successor at McKinsey & Company, and a man who had as much to do with the firm's success as anyone, was well known for his aversion to anything that might look the least commercial. He was certainly instrumental in getting consulting viewed as a true profession. A lawyer before he became a consultant, he modeled many of his ideas about professional firms on law firms. He reported to one academic studying McKinsey, "One of the best ways to establish management consulting as a profession is to emulate the older professions. Leading law and accounting firms do not solicit clients, nor do we."[1] Though he later changed his mind, he initially resisted publication of a firm brochure. "Because I viewed anything like that as promotional material, I did not consider it appropriate for the professional firm we wanted to be."[2]

One of the rainmakers in the survey recalls being invited to lunch at the Plaza Hotel along with other new hires by the managing partner of the New York office of the accounting firm that gave him his first professional job. Conversation was stilted by the imbalance of a mature, wealthy, and powerful professional entertaining the most junior people in the firm. To break the ice, the partner asked each of the young men (they were all men in those days) to tell what he thought was the key to success in accounting. Every young accountant wanted his answer to make him look good, and each answered accordingly. When the future rainmaker's turn came around, he answered, "Sales." The surprised partner answered vehemently, "Absolutely not!"

You can still find similar sentiments expressed today. In a recent book, one respected lawyer, Sol Linowitz, refers to "rainmaker" as a cynical term and generally deplores the current trend toward marketing and selling legal services and rewarding people for doing it.[3] Many of the practices he cites are, indeed, deplorable, such as one firm advertising its phone number, 1-800-EX-JUDGE. It is harder to understand why, in the next sentence after this example, he classifies a bar association conference on marketing legal services as the same kind of thing.[4]

Certainly, professionals have always worked hard to bring in business, sometimes going to extreme lengths to put themselves in the way of people they wanted to meet. James O. McKinsey reportedly rented an apartment so that he could meet the person living across the landing.[5] A rainmaker in my survey, a partner at a big-name accounting firm, bought and showed a dog of the same breed as the dog owned and showed by someone *he* wanted to meet. He also found out the tee-off time of a man he wanted to meet at the country club he had joined. He then showed up on Saturday morning, hoping that the man would need an extra to make up a foursome. It worked, and the man later became a client. Linowitz, himself, was advised to join civic groups where he could develop relationships that might later bring him business, and he acknowledges that this is what happened.[6] But it was considered unprofessional ever to ask for business.

In the antisolicitation climate that prevailed, it is hardly surprising that client development was not much talked about, written about, or studied. Professionals did not want to admit they actively pursued clients even though many of them did. Rainmakers developed clients pretty much alone and, in some cases, were looked down upon by their peers for their pains. This was not a context within which a body of knowledge on marketing and selling would grow. And it didn't.[7]

But the need to sell and the freedom to talk about it grew. In 1964, a Supreme Court ruling decided that the First Amendment protected lawyers' rights to solicit new business. In 1975, it struck down minimum fee schedules as price fixing, opening the doors to increased competition. Finally, in 1976, it struck down prohibitions against advertising. These rulings were generally felt to apply to all professions, many of which had been less constrained by professional association proscriptions on client development in the first place.

Since the 1960s, the rapid growth in the number of professionals has increased the pressure to market and sell. In the twenty-two years between 1972 and 1994, the number of lawyers in the United States grew by 156 percent, and the number of accountants by 107 percent. The number of management consultants has probably grown even faster though there are no hard numbers in so amorphous a field. Between 1983 and 1994, the number of architects grew by 37 percent.[8] In some areas, this growth simply reflects the increased demand for professional services as the world has become more complex. The growth of information technology has created a huge demand for consultants and engineers who can help companies capture its benefits. New laws are passed, and professionals thrive — accountants and lawyers on new tax laws, engineers and lawyers on new environmental laws, and so on. But the growth in the number of professionals has outstripped demand in many areas, increasing competition for clients. This competition intensifies during business downturns. The trend is likely to continue.

A final reason for the emergence of aggressive selling comes from the source most difficult to argue with: our clients. Faced with spiraling costs for professional services, they have learned that even in the professions, promoting competition helps control costs. When clients force professionals to compete, they also push them to become more sophisticated at selling. Because most institutional clients live by selling something, themselves, forcing professionals to compete this way bothers them not at all.

In the absence of an established body of knowledge on how to market and sell professional services, those professionals who wanted to learn how to bring in business had to turn to other sources. Many looked at their own experiences selling products earlier in their lives. There are many examples of this in the rainmaker database and in books about rainmakers. A consultant at a large firm told me:

> I've always sold things. I started selling newspaper subscriptions. They offered prizes for the most subscriptions sold, and I wanted them and won most of the months they were offered. I was ten years old and you were supposed to be twelve, so I lied. Later I sold pot holders to neighbors up and down the block. In high school I had a landscaping business.

An accountant said:

> I started out selling very young. In grammar school, I won an award for selling the most magazines. I must have been about twelve years old and still remember the euphoric feeling I had standing on the stage and having the principal give me an award while everyone applauded. That made me think that selling was something that felt good and wasn't hard to do.

A lawyer at a large Southwestern firm had worked in his parents' millinery shop and later sold clothes; James O. McKinsey, a former professor and author of books on accounting, compared selling professional services to selling textbooks;[9] and an architect spent time in his mother's florist shop. Another architect, Charles Luckman, sold newspapers as a boy and soap as a young man. The first chapter of his book, which describes these experiences, cites several lessons that Luckman learned about selling in his early years that too many professionals still don't know.[10]

One of the best stories of this kind was told to me by Steve Rush, a civil engineer and founder of Site Development Engineering in St. Louis:

As long as I can remember, I have sold things. I was the oldest of seven children, and although there was always enough money for necessities, pocket change was rare. So I created my own pocket change by selling mailing labels door to door and selling my services by cutting grass, caddying, and shoveling snow. As long as I can remember, I have sold things.

When I was ten and living in Ohio, I had a paper route for *The Plain Dealer,* and they had a contest for a trip to New York City. We had to get fifteen new customers in order to go. I remember that I had eleven signed up and time was running short. I went through three hours of rejection and wanted to give up. My mother said, "Let's try one more." Well, I signed the next four houses. I've never forgotten that. I learned that selling is a numbers game. I learned how to handle rejection, that it's a part of selling.

Selling products *can* teach lessons valuable in selling professional services. Compare the preceding story to Rush's description of how he started his own firm in 1986.

I went through the phone book and picked out eighty-six firms where I wanted to meet people. My goal was to visit all of the firms in one week. Most of them were architects and developers. I grouped them by location, so I could use my time efficiently.

On Monday morning, I started out to make cold calls. I was nervous as heck that I would get the door slammed in my face. I asked the receptionist for the person who made decisions about engineering services. I only wanted to talk with decision makers, and about 80 percent of the time I did. I told the receptionist that I only wanted seven minutes of the decision maker's time. When the meeting started, I would tell the person that he could throw me out after seven minutes, if he wanted to. In about two minutes, I knew if there was a chance for work and would act accordingly.

On the last day, Friday, I had no jobs and had three or four people say they might use me in the future. On my way to my last call, I ran into someone I knew who asked what I was doing. When I told him, he recommended I see a friend of his. After my call, I phoned that person and ended up going immediately to his office. He needed a small survey. I did it over the weekend and gave it to him first thing on Monday morning. That led to more small jobs from him

and kept me busy for two months. That's how I got my first
client. I was mentally and physically exhausted by the end
of that week.

Let's try one more is one of the most valuable lessons about selling that
anyone can learn.

Many rainmakers did little or no selling early in their lives. Some
turned to sales literature to learn how to do it. The books they read
were, of course, almost exclusively devoted to the sale of products.
This, too, they found valuable:

- I read as many books on sales and marketing as I could and would
  listen to tapes. I realized from these that it would be a long-term
  approach, but I figured I was young and I had time. [a lawyer]

- He did study sales techniques, though he said he didn't. I know
  because he would get excited about a new technique and talk
  about it. [a management consultant]

- When I had only been with the firm for two weeks, I went to a
  Society for the Marketing of Professional Services meeting where
  Nancy Cameron Egan was speaking on Trout's book on positioning. It was fascinating. I then read a lot about marketing and
  sales. [an engineer]

Thus, a Product Model has helped many rainmakers learn to sell
for three reasons:

- Many professionals had their first selling experiences selling
  products.

- There is abundant literature on the subject, created in the
  absence of an antiselling bias that existed in the professions.

- There was a lot of valuable information to be learned from it.
  Some recent works that address the sale of large, complex products are particularly worth reading.[11]

Like any model, the Product Model has its limitations, especially
in the sale of professional services. Specifically:

- It implies a full-time, dedicated sales force selected for attributes
  that make good salespeople in the first place. This is a condition
  that does not apply in most professional firms.

- It implies a distinction between marketing and sales that is much
  stronger in product companies than it is in most professional firms.

- It implies the presence of marketing and sales management to a greater degree than is present in most professional firms. The concept of sales management is, at best, weakly developed in the professions.

The Rainmaker Model addresses the first of these problems quite well. It is designed to reflect the experiences of people who must manage as well as sell. This is a major strength for professionals.

It addresses the second two problems less effectively. The model implies that the rainmaker must market as well as sell and is self-motivated enough to manage his or her own effort. In short, the Rainmaker Model largely reflects the efforts of Lone Rangers, who work their magic independently of others. Developing many such people in a firm may not be the most effective way to make it grow. Today, selling many large engagements requires teamwork. A firm often needs to support the marketing and sales effort in ways that, in varying degrees, run counter to this Lone-Ranger approach:

- Management can provide some marketing and selling activities on a centralized basis, relieving professionals of, and perhaps even excluding them from, these responsibilities. This can be as limited as providing centralized public relations or as extensive as providing dedicated marketing and sales forces with responsibility for a major portion of the total effort.

- It can manage the sales effort and thereby increase the chance that those who are less naturally predisposed to selling learn and make a contribution. The classic rainmaker does not much care to be managed.

Some firms have been particularly effective at doing these things. Among them are Hewitt Associates, International Profit Associates, and more recently, Ernst & Young. Part II of this book will describe the major processes in a rainmaking system with the objective of helping you decide what to do on a centralized basis and what to leave in the hands of individual professionals. It will also provide suggestions on how to develop your professionals to do these things for themselves.

Part II

The Elements of Rainmaking

6

Targeting and Positioning

We have already seen in Chapter 2 that rainmakers build big networks, that members of these networks are selected for their affinity, and that rainmakers strive to stay at the front of their network members' minds. This is true whether the rainmaker makes cold calls, develops a classic referral network, runs seminars, or employs some other means of finding new clients. Targeting assures the affinity of a network. Positioning helps you capture mindshare. Because these concepts are closely related, I address both of them in this chapter.

The services a firm offers and its history in the marketplace define a clientele. Targeting refines the definition to increase competitiveness and profits. Firms that don't target run several risks. On studying the issue, management at one firm I know learned that more than 200 percent of its profits came from its largest twelve clients. It was losing money on almost all of the others. Weak targeting also makes positioning difficult.

Based on the services a firm offers and its history, its clients and prospective clients have a perception of what it does, how well it does it, and at what price it does it. The position that clients ascribe to a firm is usually relative to its competitors. The firm is perceived as offering a broad or narrow mix of services, serving large or small clients, and having a high or low fee structure relative to others. A firm positions itself to refine that perception and so increase competitiveness. A good position creates a unifying vision of the firm, easily understood by firm members and the market.

A firm with a loosely defined target market will find it difficult to develop a sharp position relative to competitors because different portions of its market will want such different things. In these cases, a firm's own employees usually are unclear about what differentiates it from competitors. They then communicate their lack of clarity to the market.

Whether your firm is large or small, you will find it easier to create rainmakers if the firm itself is well targeted and positioned. Good targeting and positioning save aspiring rainmakers time figuring out who to pursue. They provide a structure within which professionals can take their own actions, much the way a game strategy helps individual athletes perform at their peak.

Targeting and positioning should be done at several levels. The firm needs to provide a clear message both to its market and to its professionals about whom it wants as clients and what it offers to them that differs from what competitors provide. This defines the field within which the practices or professionals are free to play, and provides them with the support of a clear firm definition of the firm, which, at best, becomes a brand identity. Practices or lines of business within a firm need to send a similar message to their professionals. Individual professionals must select their personal market targets and position themselves as experts and specialists within this field. Their targeting should come right down to the names of specific people they wish to meet and do business with. We will look at what a firm or practice should do, first.

Exhibit 6.1 provides a questionnaire to help select targets and develop a position for your firm or practice. The text explores the implications of each question. To ensure that many points of view are included, senior firm (or practice) management and others known for their creativity and market sensitivity should work through the questions as a group exercise. Reviewing the questions before the group meets will allow you to prepare historical information in advance, and so expedite discussion.

1. *In two sentences, describe what your firm does.*

First, you need to identify your current target market and position. Your view of these subjects is usually reflected in the way you describe your firm. You should be able to describe it concisely in a way that differentiates it from competitors. People won't remember much more than you can say in two

Exhibit 6.1
Firm Targeting and Positioning Questionnaire

1. In two sentences, describe what your firm does.

2. Whom do you sell to now?

3. What kinds of clients are most profitable for you? Are there markets or kinds of clients you are serving that are unprofitable or marginally profitable for you? If so, what are they?

4. How does your description of your firm compare to the way competitors describe themselves?

5. Who are your indirect or potential competitors? How do their markets and services differ from yours?

6. Are there intermediaries in your market that you must sell to?

7. What threats or opportunities do you see that might require you to change your service mix, the markets you sell to, or the way you are seen by the market?

8. What is the single most powerful attribute of your firm?

9. How would you like to change the way you are seen?

Rate the positions you have identified from 1 to 10, with 10 being best, on the basis of the following criteria:

I. Market Considerations
   a. *Believability:* Will clients find this position easy to believe? That is, are they likely to believe that this position describes your firm?
   b. *Market Appeal:* Will clients give preference in hiring to a firm fitting this description?
   c. *Differentiation:* Does it differentiate you from competitors?
   d. *Simplicity:* Is it easy to understand?

II. Internal Considerations
   a. *Cost:* How much will it cost to implement?
   b. *Divisiveness:* How much might it divide your firm?
   c. *Acceptability:* How acceptable will it be to the rest of the firm?

sentences, and when they ask you what your firm does, seldom want to hear more. This kind of short, rehearsed statement is sometimes referred to as the "elevator description" because you should be able to describe a firm clearly in an elevator ride, if someone asks you. Similarly, if you have trouble describing what your firm does briefly and clearly at social gatherings, your firm is probably not clearly positioned, and this assignment will be difficult for you.

After writing out a short description of your firm, consider what the statement tells you about the effectiveness of your targeting and positioning. The more the description differentiates you from similar firms, the better it is. Compare these sets of descriptions.

Set One

a. We are the largest general-service law firm in the state of Michigan. We have contract, tax, securities, litigation, environmental, and other departments to be able to provide full-service support to corporations doing business in the state.

b. We are architects who work largely on correctional facilities, that is, prisons and related buildings. It's a field that requires a high degree of specialized knowledge about materials, security systems, layout, cost management, and other areas, which is one of the ways we bring value to our clients.

c. We are benefits consultants who help large corporations design creative benefits programs that help them recruit, retain, and motivate the best people in their fields. Like other actuaries, we can help clients meet regulatory requirements, but unlike others, we focus on using benefits creatively to achieve corporate goals through people.

Set Two

d. We are a management consulting firm that helps clients develop creative solutions to business problems. We have offices in ten countries and work for many large, international corporations.

e. We are consulting engineers and have environmental, asbestos abatement, and soils engineering departments. We work for a lot of public-sector clients in a three-state area, as well as for hospitals and corporations.

f. We are a full-service public accounting firm with thirty employees in two offices.

Each of the first three descriptions provides a clear idea of what the firms do, who they serve, and what makes them different from competitors. Critically, each offers a unifying concept: one-stop shopping for corporate legal services in Michigan, correctional facility architecture, and creative benefits programs to achieve business objectives through people. The second three all lack a unifying concept. They are also weak for other reasons.

The description of the management consulting firm in (d) is so vague as to be meaningless. We learn it is a large firm serving large clients, but get no idea of what it does.

Anyone who knows consulting engineering would find the mix of services described in (e) odd. Nor is there a unifying market. The listener would be hard-pressed to have a reason to recommend this firm over others and is likely to remember but one of the services it provides, at best. The message is confusing.

The description of the accounting firm in (f) fails on the criterion of believability. PricewaterhouseCoopers and Deloitte & Touche may be full-service firms, but the listener is unlikely to believe that so small a firm can meet that standard. Instead, it sounds like a firm with big pretensions. The message fails to capture anything really distinctive about the firm.

A good description is brief and clear about services and markets, and it offers a unifying concept that differentiates your firm from others.

What you write in response to this question represents your effort to capture your current target and market position. By buying a few lunches, you can confirm whether your clients actually see you this way.

2. *Whom do you sell to now?*

Building off the positioning statement you have just created, describe whom you now sell to by service, industry, function, geography, size of company, demographic characteristics of individual buyers, and any other categories of importance to your practice. Consider what the list you create tells you about how you would answer the question, "Whom do you target as clients?" Is there a unifying concept here? If not, try looking at how your revenues break down by market. Looking only at those markets that provide a significant portion of your revenues, does a unifying concept emerge?

Some professionals go so far as to describe the personal attributes that create an attractive prospect. For example, in addition to looking for clients fitting the right business profile, one of the rainmakers surveyed looks for people with a thirst for knowledge. He feels that a person without a thirst for knowledge will treat his services like a commodity and, therefore, won't be an attractive client. These kinds of criteria help your professionals interpret what they hear from prospective clients.

3. *What kinds of clients are most profitable for you? Are there markets or kinds of clients you are serving that are unprofitable or marginally profitable for you? If so, what are they?*

Answering these questions can help clarify where you need to focus your attention and help surface a unifying concept. If you have not done a formal profitability analysis by client and by client type, you should. As noted in the example cited earlier, it can bring out information you need to know about where you make your money.

4. *How does your description of your firm compare to the way competitors describe themselves?*

Review any of your competitors' promotional materials and Web sites. Reflect upon how you have heard them describe themselves at association meetings. Ask a few of their alumni how they describe themselves. Then consider how what they do and how they describe themselves compare to your firm.

Exhibit 6.2 provides a set of tables to help you analyze the information you collect. Once again, you need to look for ways that you are different from competitors. Do you offer a broader line of services or a narrower one? Are you more focused by industry or by size of company? Do you sell to a particular kind of person, or do you have particular strength in a geographic area? Look for possible unifying concepts. They don't have to be perfect, but they must capture something special about your firm that you believe is important to your clients.

Exhibit 6.2

Competitive Positioning Form

Firm Name	Market Strength by Attribute				
Your Firm					

Attributes include such factors as range of services, geographic scope, cost of service, and other factors of importance to the market. Try to capture the reputation of your firm and each competitor for each attribute in a few words.

Exhibit 6.2 (continued)

Competitive Positioning Form

Firm Name	Market Strength by Attribute		Market Position
Your Firm			

After reviewing the relative strengths of your firm and competitors, try to capture the market position of each in a few words.

5. *Who are your indirect or potential competitors? How do their markets and services differ from yours?*

The competitive landscape can change rapidly as indirect competitors find a way to capture market share from you or as potential competitors become real ones. American Express's acquisition of many small accounting firms has rapidly altered competition in the accounting industry. Other financial service firms may follow its example. These events are transforming the market for accounting services for individuals and small companies. Structural changes are probably occurring in your business, too. You need to keep such things in mind when you target and position your firm.

6. *Are there intermediaries in your market that you must sell to?*

Many professionals must sell to intermediaries before they sell to the ultimate client. If this situation applies in your profession, you must either target and position yourself with these intermediaries or find a way to disintermediate them. Both approaches can work.

Traditionally, architects and large engineering firms have served as prime consultants in the pursuit of major projects and assembled teams of specialists to support them. Many successful engineers have found ways to position themselves effectively with these intermediaries. By doing this, Judy Nitsch, founder of Judith Nitsch Engineering, Inc., has worked her civil engineering and land surveying firm onto *Inc.* magazine's list of the 500 fastest growing businesses in the United States. The major firms competing for public-sector projects are often required by law to use small, minority, or women-owned business subconsultants. Nitsch's firm is registered in Massachusetts as a Women-Owned Business Enterprise (WBE). As Nitsch says, "My largest market is public-sector projects, and on these our immediate clients are large architectural and engineering firms. Our goal is to be the WBE of choice for these people, and they are the ones I target." How she has done this is described in Chapter 9. For the present, note that it is clear whom she targets and how she wants these people to see her. That focus extends to her future markets as well. She says, "My firm's goal is to be the prime. The work we do now introduces us to the agency, allows me the opportunity to see how the large firms manage these projects, and teaches my employees the agencies' procedures."

Eugene Anderson of the law firm Anderson Kill & Olick, P.C., notes that for certain kinds of real estate transactions, the real estate broker is the intermediary for the lawyer:

> The real estate manager at the corporation contacts the broker first, when he is looking for space, and the broker becomes the buying influence who recommends you. You have to have a reputation with the brokers that the clients will be satisfied and, at the same time, you won't be an impediment to the deal, because the broker doesn't get paid until the transaction is complete.

Anderson attributes a part of his success as a rainmaker to becoming sensitive to the needs of intermediaries.

It is also possible to disintermediate intermediaries so that you can sell directly to the ultimate client. Several engineering firms, such as PWI Engineering of Philadelphia, successfully positioned themselves as prime contractors of major clients, without the need to work through architects on most projects.

Changes in buyer behavior can rapidly change the roles of intermediaries. As noted previously, architects have historically been prime contractors on building design projects in the United States. Today, they are increasingly forced to work as subcontractors to construction firms because clients are asking for design/build proposals. Under this contracting approach, a construction firm submits a single bid for a delivered project, which includes design. This has been a standard approach in other countries for a long time. Architects have found that selling to a construction firm differs from selling directly to a client in several respects.

Consider the intermediaries in your market. Do you want to position yourselves with them or to go around them, directly to the ultimate client?

7. *What threats or opportunities do you see that might require you to change your service mix, the markets you sell to, or the way you are seen by the market?*

Changes in the environment you operate in can threaten your current practice or create opportunities to grow it. As an example, demand for actuarial services exploded in the United States during the 1970s and early 1980s because of provisions in the Employee Retirement and Income Security Act (ERISA). In the 1980s, the Tax Equity and Fiscal Responsibility Act and the Tax Reform Act of 1986 partially reversed this trend. These changes in the legislative environment led to major changes in demand for actuarial services and in the way actuaries do business. Some firms have adapted far more successfully than others.

Should tort reform go into effect, the consequences for trial lawyers could be huge. Though to date there has been little significant change in the way litigation is handled, in part due to the successful lobbying efforts of trial lawyers, savvy firms are hedging their bets by developing alternative dispute resolution and other services that would thrive, should litigation become more difficult. Adding new services usually changes the way a firm needs to be seen by its market.

Though you don't want to get too far in front of the market, the position you pick should help you compete more effectively in the future. A good rule of thumb is to follow the money. If you can figure out where money will be spent in your area of expertise, you can position yourself to get it. The traffic engineering firm Vanasse Hangen Brustlin has grown from 6 people in 1979 to almost 500 today by figuring out where there would be funds backing a demand for their services and then staffing to meet those demands. Jimmy D'Angelo, a rainmaker at the firm, notes, "It's easy to be a rainmaker, if you find out where it's raining."

8. *What is the single most powerful attribute of your firm?*

As you seek to refine your targeting and positioning, you will not want to look too far away from your core strength. If you do, the market is likely to reject any new position you try to establish. Professionals who have neglected this risk have often paid a steep price.

For example, in the early 1990s, management of PHH Fantus, then the best known location consultants in the country, decided to reposition the firm as general management consultants. Founded in 1919 as the Fantus Factory Locating Service, the firm had a long and distinguished history as specialists, reinforced by extensive geographic information resources and an experienced staff. To reposition the firm, new professionals with general management consulting expertise were hired, and huge expenses were run up touting the firm's new position. Almost no clients were signed for the new services. The market simply rejected as unbelievable the firm's repositioning. The president who had pushed the repositioning was fired, and the firm was sold to Deloitte & Touche LLP, where it is experiencing a strong revival in its old specialty.

Firms that build on their strengths can capture an edge in the market. The engineering firm Smith Seckman Reid has done that. It has always done a lot of health-care work, originally for for-profit hospitals. In 1983, when work for this market was drying up, it targeted not-for-profit hospitals. By 1986, its success with health-care providers was strong enough that two of its engineers, Hugh Nash and Kenneth Diehl, decided to make it the best health-care engineering firm in the country. They have pursued this position relentlessly. Though some might argue whether or not they have achieved their goal, few would question that they are a contender.

In light of your answers to questions one through seven, what do you feel is the single most powerful attribute of your firm?

9. *How would you like to change how you are seen?*

Based on your answers to the preceding questions, you may decide that you want to change the way your firm is seen by its clients. Within limits, you can do this by changing how your professionals talk and write about the firm, what they do, and how you present your firm to the media. Of course, changes in how you want to be perceived may require changes in the services you offer or the markets you serve. Reflecting on your answers to the preceding questions, list as many visions of the firm as you can think of that would differentiate you from competitors. This should be a brainstorming exercise, completed without any attempt to evaluate the relative attractiveness of the alternatives.

Once the list is complete, rate the alternatives on the basis of the following criteria:

I. Market Considerations
Consider all of your major kinds of clients and intermediaries when rating alternative positioning concepts on these issues.

a. *Believability:* Will clients find this position easy to believe? Does it fit with the attributes for which the firm is best known?

b. *Market Appeal:* Will clients give preference in hiring to a firm fitting this description?

c. *Differentiation:* Does it differentiate you from major competitors?

d. *Simplicity:* Is it easy to understand? Is it the clear, unifying concept that you need?

II. *Internal Considerations:*

a. *Cost:* What major costs does the position imply, such as acquiring a specialist firm or recruiting specialists in new areas?

b. *Divisiveness:* Will the new position require you to de-emphasize or even eliminate a practice? What would you have to do to minimize the pain for the people affected? Given the ownership structure of your firm, how possible is this?

c. *Acceptability:* Would the position be acceptable to the majority of the members of the firm? Does it meet their standards of professionalism?

As you review the alternative positions, remember that the market ultimately decides what position you occupy, not you. You can influence market perceptions, but only so far. A major shift in position is a long-term venture. Trying to do it too quickly can weaken a strong position that you hold now for no market gain.

It is wise to test two or three positioning statements with clients. They may react more positively to some than to others or suggest small changes that will help you hone them. When you have done that, you can pick the one that you feel presents the firm most advantageously.

Targeting and positioning will help your firm only if you act on them. Once you have clarified your target market and identified the position you want to occupy relative to competitors, you should:

- Make sure that all the professionals and the support staff understand how you want the firm positioned and how they can help you do it. Providing a sample, two-sentence description of the firm reflecting the new positioning helps.

- Update all written documents to reflect the new positioning. This includes brochures; proposal, letter, and presentation boilerplate; and anything else that describes who you are and what you do.

- Begin to modify the firm to fit more tightly with the new position. This includes recruiting necessary talent to complement your current staff, modifying the services you deliver and how you deliver them, and writing articles and giving speeches that support the new position. It can even include such things as changing how your offices look.

These steps are necessary to ensure that the market and the people who work for the firm take the new positioning seriously.

Individual Targeting and Positioning

Within the context of the firm's target market and position, each of your professionals who is on track to become a rainmaker also needs to target and position himself. Each needs to be seen as an expert in specific areas for specific kinds of clients. This will help him or her develop a selling proposition that differentiates him or her from others in the firm. But becoming an expert is only a means to a larger end and only a first step. Once professionals are seen as experts, they need to become generalists all over again because true rainmaking results from understanding a client's business issues and bringing whatever services to bear that are needed to resolve them. This double-switch requires some explanation.

A partner with a major law firm describes this process. First, he describes the hard work needed to become a specialist:

> I am known as a securities and mergers and acquisitions lawyer, and I have built my practice based on those relationships. The first thing is to do good work. There is no substitute for busting your tail and learning about what it is you're supposed to be doing. I have spent a lot of time lying on my back reading dusty tomes to learn about things I needed to know.

Then he describes how he became a generalist:

> The relationships I have from this work have grown into what is really general counsel work. Clients look to me to help them with a broad set of problems because I have earned their confidence as a problem solver. Now I need to be on top of tax, estate, real estate, litigation, and other areas of the law. I have made the transition attitudinally from being a lawyer to being a businessperson.

From Generalist to Specialist

The importance of specialization is illustrated by the case of an architectural firm that sought to develop specific second-tier people as marketers, but found that it succeeded only with specialists, including one who had not been identified for development. The need to succeed at sales was so great that senior personnel almost always bumped the generalists from sales calls and presentations because the seniors were perceived to have a higher probability of winning. Specialists seldom got bumped because they had knowledge and credentials that the seniors didn't. The specialists also brought opportunities to the company. They were consulted by third parties who recognized their expertise, and these conversations sometimes turned into leads. When a third party had a more general question, he or she almost always went to a partner rather than to one of the younger generalists.

Some professionals resist specialization or want to specialize in areas already saturated with talent at their firms. They cite two principal reasons for this feeling.

First, many say they fear becoming overspecialized and thereby reducing their marketability, should they need to find another job. This concern is particularly common among people who work for a firm or practice that they perceive as already being in a niche market. The fear is usually disproportionate to the risk. By the time a professional is ready to go on a track to become a rainmaker, he or she usually has well-established generalist credentials. Becoming a specialist does not necessarily imply doing only specialist work; often the professional can continue to do some work outside the specialty. Over time, many professionals have developed more than one specialty. Specialists are also more likely than generalists to get market recognition through speaking engagements, and this is helpful when looking for work.

Though seldom voiced, I suspect another reason for the fear of overspecialization comes from the role model that some firm specialists provide. Senior specialists are sometimes brilliant, quirky people who thrive on being experts in a narrow field. They are not seen as movers in the firm, surviving because of their much needed expertise. The young professional cannot see that many of the more dynamic partners in the firm also specialized. Because they possessed broad problem-solving abilities, they became generalists again later when their clients asked them to deal with broader issues or when they were put in charge of a practice or an office. Specialization was, nevertheless, a critical step in their careers.

Professionals also say that they want to remain generalists because they enjoy the diversity of the work they do. In a world in which advancement increasingly requires specialization, these people may have to pay a high price for their pleasure.

These facts need to be explained.

Specialization occurs serendipitously to many professionals. Shortly after founding their own architectural firm, the partners of Butler Rogers Baskett were working on an interiors project for an advertising agency. A friend of Jonathan Butler asked him to take over a project for a law firm in the same building. The friend worked for the law firm and was unhappy with the current architect. A second law firm engagement came in a similar fashion. These two projects became the foundation for a specialization in law firm interiors design. Today, the firm is the premier designer of law firm offices. Joe Flom has acknowledged that his specialization in hostile takeovers and takeover defenses resulted from a similar string of luck.

Although luck will always play a part in the emergence of specialties, firm management can help the process along by helping young professionals identify opportunities for specialization and helping them build knowledge and experience in the area.

Things You Can Do

1. *Assign a professional to enough work in a specific area to build the professional's knowledge and confidence.*

   Encouraging people to develop a unique specialty begins early in some firms. Chi Systems, a management consulting firm that specializes in the health-care industry, has been particularly successful at this. Its chairman and CEO, Karl Bartscht, notes, "We don't have many people doing the same thing. One will have an emphasis on mergers and acquisitions, one on physician/hospital relations, and so on. We encourage people to develop an expertise." This, in part, is done by giving them the chance to work on engagements that build a specific expertise.

2. *Give a professional the responsibility for learning about, and then helping others in the firm understand, an issue.*

   As a young attorney, Lloyd Leva Plaine, of Sutherland, Asbill & Brennan, was asked to give a speech to the firm's partners about the (then) new Tax Act of 1976. She asked a partner what he thought would be the best way to learn the material, and he suggested out-lining it. This assignment became the basis of her current expertise in tax law. Asking young professionals to develop a methodology or approach to a specific problem can serve the same purpose.

3. Encourage the person to speak and publish.

We deal with these subjects more fully in the next chapter.

Once professionals have developed an expertise, they can identify and target the people who need it. Each professional should be encouraged to start a personal contact list, as a subset of a larger firm contact list, of people interested in the specialty. These can be past and prospective clients, people who have attended speeches, or others who have expressed an interest. This list will become the foundation for a contacting program to be discussed in a later chapter.

From Specialist to Generalist

Once they become specialists, some professionals also resist becoming generalists again. This transition can be more difficult. Becoming a specialist requires hours of tedious work. Once a professional attains recognition in an area, much of his or her professional identity and stature in a firm are likely to derive from it. Stepping away from it requires both a change in attitude and the development of new knowledge.

In an earlier quote, a partner at a large law firm noted that he had made an attitudinal transition from being a lawyer to being a businessperson and had to acquire extra knowledge to do so. One hears this in various forms again and again from the rainmakers:

- I am really a businessman who happens to be an architect.

- He was hands-on with all his clients and knew what was going on and could talk about their business issues with them. [an accountant]

- Building the knowledge base and personal confidence on a broader range of material than my own particular specialty was a challenge for me. People don't want to show their ignorance and are uncomfortable talking in areas outside their expertise. Building that broader knowledge base on business issues is key [to becoming a rainmaker]. . . . You have to make up your mind to find out enough about [a business issue] to talk about it intelligently. [an actuary]

Clients often push these professionals they develop confidence in to broaden their knowledge by asking for advice in areas outside their narrow expertise. Firms can also start the change by giving a professional responsibilities to run an office or perform other duties, such as selling, that force him or her to think more broadly. Relatively few firms have any formal way for helping professionals make this transition.

Things You Can Do

1. *Help all professionals understand how the work they are doing affects a client's broader business and personal concerns.*

   This should be a part of the briefing that begins every project. The message should be reinforced at every meeting at which the engagement is discussed in any detail. Partners should ask professionals working on a project how the specific decisions and recommendations they are making will affect the client. If they don't understand how the work they are doing fits with the larger business and personal issues that their clients face, they will not become rainmakers. Of course, such discussions take time, but the time is an investment.

2. *Provide or subsidize training in areas that will help create a deeper understanding of a client's business issues.*

   Many professionals need education on business issues. Nonaccountants are likely to identify this with training in accounting. ("I tell younger lawyers that if you want to be a corporate lawyer, don't tell anyone you don't understand about accounting. Take the time to get out and learn it. Know how to read a balance sheet and an income sheet. You are just a hack if you don't understand these things.") Although an understanding of some accounting basics is essential to understanding business, nonaccountants should note that accountants complain as much as other professionals that their young professionals don't understand their client's basic business issues.

   Professionals need to learn how the fundamental drivers of a particular business affect the way the management of a client organization thinks about problems. These drivers have a profound effect on organizational economics, finances, and relationships with customers as well as on the underlying structure and interpersonal dynamics of the organization itself. This is more than accounting. Additionally, this broader understanding requires an ability to assess human wants and fears and a knowledge of how to address them in a manner appropriate to a professional advisor. Short of a miniature MBA program, no publicly available courses provide this training, as far as I know. A few firms have done an excellent job of building their own programs.

3. *Assign aspiring rainmakers responsibility for becoming expert in an industry and specific companies.*

Becoming knowledgeable about what is happening in an industry or at a company will help professionals gain broad business knowledge. They should be required to track an industry or specific companies in the press, attend a trade association meeting, and make calls on people who can provide information. Professionals will not take this kind of assignment seriously unless management monitors and comments on their progress.

4. *Invite clients and other people knowledgeable about business to speak to your staff from time to time about the issues they are facing as businesspeople.*

For many professionals, nothing has greater impact than the words of a client.

As professionals reposition from specialist to generalist businesspeople, they will communicate that to clients in the questions they ask about the clients' problems and the interest they show in broad business issues. Let us now look at how professionals can position themselves to broader audiences through thought-leadership activities, like speaking and publishing.

7

Creating Value
with Ideas*

I n the absence of machinery and raw materials, ideas and knowledge form the basic capital of professional firms. Professionals
draw on them to create value for their clients and so generate fees
that keep the firm running. Firms rich in intellectual capital grow and
prosper; those poor in it are less likely to. A little over half of the rainmakers in the survey include writing books or articles and speaking
frequently as elements in their rainmaking systems. Their words show
that they see the promotion of ideas as an important part of their business development efforts.

- He developed the idea and the goal of becoming the top executive compensation consultant in the nation. He was smart
  enough to figure out how to do that and set out to get it. He was
  a gifted writer and speaker and very adept at turning a phrase.
  He had almost a comedian's ability to be humorous and pithy at
  the same time. Using those skills, he built his personal promi-
  nence. He wrote a key book on executive compensation and
  worked skillfully at getting his name in *Fortune, Forbes, The Wall
  Street Journal* and the rest of the business press, so that reporters

* This chapter is based on an article that originally appeared in *Journal of Management
Consulting* and was co-authored by Annette Felzani Dwyer, then director of the Thought
Leadership Program in financial services at KPMG Peat Marwick LLP and now Principal
of AMFDwyer Consulting. Ms. Dwyer focuses on governance, strategy, operations, and
implementation management for small to medium-sized companies, not-for-profits, and
faith-based organizations.

would call him if a subject came up that dealt with executive compensation. He would always have a quotable quote. He would keep the names of any journalists he spoke to and would follow up with them from time to time and try to plant ideas for stories. [Bud Crystal, management consultant, Towers Perrin]

- I wanted to build our reputation in the area of energy conservation, where I thought there would be a lot of work. I knew something about the subject and hired a PR firm to get our name out as energy conservation experts. I felt we needed good PR because, as with athletes, the firm that gets the most publicity is seen as the best. I wrote articles and spoke on the subject. I made a point of meeting people at magazines, who are always starved for something to publish and will work with you, if you have something to say. This was part of the identity I wanted to create for the firm as one with innovative solutions. It helped get the word out, and word does get around. [Norman Kurtz, engineer, Flack + Kurtz. Kurtz used fundamentally the same tactics to promote other ideas, too.]

- I began early in my career to write articles, thereby credentialing myself. In 1974, when Interstate Stores went bankrupt, they came to us, in part, because I had published articles on bankruptcy and retailing. Interstate Stores later became Toys Я Us. This project made it easier for the firm to sell similar services to other bankrupt companies and helped establish our bankruptcy practice. I continue to publish. [Ed Weinstein, accountant, Deloitte & Touche LLP]

- Publishing articles and having the reprints impresses clients. A lawyer with thirty reprints will get hired for a case, when one who hasn't got any will come up empty-handed. I would also speak, in the beginning, at any organization that would have me. [Eugene Anderson, lawyer, Anderson Kill & Olick]

- I grew this company primarily through marketing: by writing books and articles, and by giving seminars. The articles and books are especially necessary when you start a firm. They create your credibility. [Kirk Tyson, management consultant, Kirk Tyson International Ltd.]

- We have worked hard at staying visible in the world of lawyers, who comprise an important part of the market. We speak at legal gatherings and at design gatherings with a law firm focus. We write for legal publications and write about legal issues for other publications. We send reprints of our articles to clients and prospective clients. [Jim Rogers and Charles Baskett, architects, Butler Rogers Baskett]

Professionals in the survey have devoted many hours during their careers to speaking and publishing. They do it because they believe that the publicity that comes from well-promoted, good ideas brings in business. In other words, it creates wealth. Yet, we seldom stop to think about how that exactly happens. Perhaps this is because balance sheets constructed under traditional accounting rules don't adequately capture the value of intellectual capital. The accounting industry and several large corporations recognize this problem and are struggling with it, and a small number of large consulting firms seriously plan how they create and manage intellectual capital.[1] Most professional firms, however, approach the subject haphazardly.

This is shortsighted because ideas give us access to the best clients. Most senior executives have a small brain trust of thoughtful people whom they turn to for counsel. Members often include accountants, lawyers, and consultants. Functional specialists within organizations also have outsiders whom they look to to keep them abreast of things they need to know about. They often turn to these same people when they have problems. So, for example, many general counsels have brain trusts of lawyers, human resources managers have brain trusts of consultants and actuaries, and facilities managers have brain trusts of architects and engineers.

Professionals compete intensely for the opportunity to participate in these brain trusts because doing so lets them talk with executives about the executives' most urgent business problems. Professionals may have services that apply to only one of every five or ten of the problems they discuss, but when they do, they are in an excellent position to make a sale. As a result, brain-trust membership can be the source of interesting and profitable engagements.

So, a reputation for having ideas that work gives us an entry pass to brain trusts. The ideas themselves allow us to offer fresh perspectives on old problems. A professional who has earned a close relationship with an executive by consistently contributing sound, new ideas has created a substantial barrier to any competitor targeting the same account.

Well-publicized ideas also help us obtain new clients by creating "demand pull" for our services. Some prospective clients will seek out the proponent of a provocative idea. Others will gladly agree to a meeting to learn more about it. The greater the demand pull for a firm's services, the easier will be its sales efforts. Ideas provide the substance around which name recognition programs can be built. They lie at the core of a firm's branding efforts.

As if all this were not enough, firms closely associated with the creation of an idea can often charge a premium on engagements to which it is applied. Clients recognize that a work force's productivity is a function of the amount of capital invested to support it. This is as true of a professional staff as it is of an assembly line team. The more of the right kind of knowledge and ideas that professionals have access to, the higher their billing rates are likely to be.

As with most capital, intellectual capital grows most surely for those who make steady investment. Like all investments, steady investment in intellectual capital has a compounding effect. Peter Drucker's stature as a thought leader, to cite the preeminent example among management consultants, results from a steady flow of good ideas over many years. These include the concepts of "decentralization" and "knowledge workers," among others. He has made a steady investment in the generation of ideas over a lifetime.[2]

But making this kind of steady investment isn't easy. Like all investment decisions, this one is heavily influenced by the competition for resources needed for day-to-day delivery of services. Like all investments, this one is easily postponed in the face of that competition. Like all investors, professionals who fail to invest in intellectual capital today pay a price in the future.

Here we will look at the things you can do to increase the consistency of investment in the development and promotion of ideas. Some firms leave this work entirely to the individual professionals. Others centralize parts of it. We will look at both of these possibilities.

Knowing What You Know

The first step in the development and promotion of ideas is often a careful documentation of what it is you know that has value. Leading with your thoughts implies that you know what your thoughts are. One might think that professionals, the archetypical knowledge workers, would know this, but most don't. To really know requires conscious effort, usually in the form of a disciplined process. That process can be writing an article or book or preparing a speech or seminar. The need to develop a clear understanding of their own thoughts is one of the reasons thought leaders do these things. Writing a brochure or documenting a methodology are other processes used to clarify thinking. Joseph Pine, the author of *Mass Customization*,[3] has said:

> I put everything I knew about mass customization into the book ... and then some. By that I mean that writing it helped stretch my own understanding. I found that there were issues that I had to cover that I hadn't thought about sufficiently and that forced me to research them, talk with people and think about them in ways I hadn't before.

In everyday discussions about our areas of expertise, we often feel that our thinking is sharper than it really is because we slip past weak spots in our logic or knowledge. A good process ensures clear thinking by forcing us to articulate our thoughts to a targeted audience logically and persuasively. It exposes our thoughts to scrutiny and so makes weak points apparent. That is, it points out what we *don't* know, so that we can think through these areas and research them. Processes that ensure rigorous thinking are the foundation of a thought-leadership program.

Thinking requires discipline. While preparing a speech, I once interviewed CEOs of large companies to ask what they would like to hear about. One said that the speeches he got the most out of took one idea and really explored it well. This is what thought leaders do. Simplifying the complex and going to the nub of an issue, talents attributed to thought leaders, often boil down to taking the component ideas of an argument and exploring each carefully, one at a time. Most people, including most of our clients, are too busy to do that kind of thinking themselves.

George Bernard Shaw once wrote, "Few people think more than two or three times a year; I have made an international reputation for myself by thinking once or twice a week." This assessment is perhaps caustic, but most clients don't think much about the issues that professionals dedicate their work lives to. They don't have time. They lack the breadth of experience required to extract broadly applicable insights from the process or the technical depth to plumb an idea for its full significance. Yet, it is from that kind of thinking that breakthroughs come. Professionals are well-positioned to have the needed breadth and depth. James O. McKinsey, among others, was particularly accomplished at this kind of in-depth probing. His book, *Budgetary Control,* for example, was the first to explore in detail the implications of using budgeting as a management tool.[4]

Management can help this process along. Lloyd Leva Plaine, an attorney with Sutherland, Asbill & Brennan, described how she received such help from the firm early in her career:

> I started practice in 1975. A year later there was a change in the tax laws with the Tax Act of 1976, which radically changed tax practices. I was asked to give a speech to the partners about it, something I obviously wanted to do well. I asked a partner what he thought would be the best way to learn about it. He suggested that I outline it, which I did. Once I had finished, I saw I had something in the work I had done that might interest others. Using the outline and presentation to the partners as a base, I started writing articles and giving speeches.

Plaine has since gone on to write many articles and a book and to give many speeches. These efforts have been the source of much of her new business.

Deciding What to Think About

Managing the thought-leadership process requires deciding which ideas to put through this time-consuming process. This is similar to the problem that research and development laboratories face when deciding what research projects to invest in. You will need a steady flow of new ideas, but you cannot afford to invest in all that the members of the firm come up with. This means you must have a screening process.

Sometimes the individual professional decides this, as Plaine did:

> I tried to pick out areas where expertise would help others. I worked on subjects that were complicated enough that others might not invest the time needed to get to know about them. Further, I picked subjects of importance to my target market, people who have a certain amount of property. I tried to pick areas that people would link to my name, when they thought about them.

If firm management chooses to make the decision about what ideas to develop, its initial direction must come from the firm's strategy. Firms that wish to be identified as leading-edge innovators must produce leading-edge ideas. Firms with a strong implementation orientation can often do well by adapting or extrapolating on an idea originally put forward by others. Raymond Manganelli and Mark Klein, for example, successfully created and marketed the *rapid* reengineering concept in this way.[5] Firms with strong market niches can sometimes do quite well by interpreting ideas generated by others for their narrow audiences.

When management selects ideas for development, there is a tendency to look for blockbusters. This tendency has resulted in the management consulting industry being accused, with some justification, of pushing the latest consulting fad, be it reengineering, quality, just-in-time manufacturing, core competencies, or any one of a number of big ideas that have produced many engagements for their proponents and followers. Certainly, most consultants would like to be seen as the originator of one of these blockbuster concepts, but that is not the only way to be seen as a thought leader.

Some of the most enduring thought leaders, like Peter Drucker, are less associated with one big idea than with a long series of high-quality, smaller ideas. Da vid Maister, an advocate for the use of articles, speeches, seminars, and proprietary research to market professional services, has emerged as a thought leader in the professions by following his own advice. He is not associated with a single big idea, but with many valuable, if smaller, ones. This is reflected in his book, a collection of many of his articles, each of which elaborates on a different idea.[6]

The selection of an idea for development also requires a sense of timing. There is often a window of opportunity for an idea. Promoting it too early or too late will result in reduced impact. Leaders know that they cannot get too far ahead of their constituents if they want to be followed. History is full of brilliant people who did not emerge as thought leaders during their lives because they were ahead of their time — Gregor Mendel, the father of genetics, being one we all know from high school biology classes. That W. Edwards Deming and Joseph Juran, two founders of the quality movement, found little audience for their ideas in the United States until the Japanese began to grab market share with superior quality products shows that this is also true in the professions. As late as 1980, a consultant and former auto executive, James Harbour, advised GM executives of many of the competitive problems they were about to have with the Japanese, but they were unwilling to hear him.[7]

Professionals who want to be recognized as thought leaders today must deliver a message their clients are ready for, rather than a more radical, but unacceptable, one. (A few clients are ready for radical ideas and seek them out. A few trend-setting firms and patient thought leaders deliberately seek out such clients. Many pursue a more conservative clientele and adapt their ideas accordingly.) It is not by chance that the big consulting concepts over the past fifty years helped clients address issues of immediate importance to the business community of their time. For example, in the 1960s, the growth of national, high-volume markets made it possible for corporations to use the experience curve to capture cost advantages; in the 1970s, portfolio management helped recently created conglomerates improve the allocation of financial resources; in the 1980s, the quality movement helped corporations regain competitiveness against foreign imports; and in the early 1990s, reengineering helped corporations use modern computing technology to slash overhead in the face of intensified global competition and worldwide recession.[8]

In other professions, thought leaders also take advantage of market readiness for an idea. The late John F. Hennessy Sr., one of the founders of the engineering firm Syska & Hennessy, was particularly adept at identifying an idea ripe for development. This story related by Duncan Finlayson, who worked with Hennessy, exemplifies that talent:

> Jack had the ability to come up with ideas that captured people's imaginations. Often they anticipated needs that affected a great many organizations. Once, in the 1970s, there was a fire in a high-rise in New York. He had lunch with the mayor shortly after that, and the mayor told him that he worried that there were many other buildings in the city where the same thing could happen. The mayor was looking for a way to address the problem. Hennessy suggested that they find an unused high-rise and burn it down so that they could study what happened and then develop standards for high-rises and ways to deal with fires in them. Other people were brought in, including a developer, the fire department, and a university. They found an old building and burned it, using special cameras in fire-resistant boxes to film what happened and special instrumentation to record heat levels and other things.
>
> Out of that came landmark legislation on high-rises. It established fire safety codes, the concept of compartmentalization, requirements for sprinkler systems and fire coatings and stairwell pressurization and safe havens. All this was new. Hennessy got a lot of work as a result of his leadership in this project because we were now the experts and every building had to meet the new codes. He had a knack for getting paid for things that were good for everyone.

Each idea has a life cycle, and monitoring the movement of a firm's existing ideas through the cycle provides another tool for the management of the thought-leadership process. A good idea promoted well can generate business long after efforts to enhance it and publicize it end. This is one of the great benefits of thought-leadership efforts, but it is also a seductive trap. Old ideas eventually lose their market appeal. When this happens, the number of engagements that apply them decline, and the margins on these engagements fall. With a little reflection, most of us can think of firms or practices that rode jaded ideas too long and saw business deteriorate as a result. Firms or practices that do this are disinvesting in their intellectual capital the way a landlord sometimes disinvests in physical capital by failing to spend on building maintenance and improvements. This approach can produce high short-term returns, but ultimately results in the destruction of the asset.

New ideas, then, must be developed to replace or reinvigorate old ones before this happens. The ability to do this repeatedly, to generate a continuous flow of marketable ideas, separates firms that are true thought leaders from everyone else.

Because timing is so critical to thought leadership and because firms need a steady flow of new ideas, they must learn what issues clients want to deal with now. That information, of course, can come only from listening closely to clients. Any thought-leadership program must have a system for capturing this critical intelligence from the hundreds or thousands of conversations that a firm's members have with clients during the course of selling and delivering engagements. It is particularly important to work with those clients who push you to expand your own thinking, who stimulate the creation of new ideas.

Idea selection can be left to the individual professionals, but can also be done by management. PWI Engineering has grown from a 12-person to a 100-person firm in 10 years in part because one of its owners, Tom Bathgate, feels that it is a part of his job to identify issues that the firm's clients want to know about:

> I spend 20 to 30 percent of my time in an informal exchange of information with clients, which I don't expect them to pay for. I have built a network of people who want to stay on top of issues, and I try to be a clearinghouse, finding out about things for them. When an issue comes up that would be of importance to many of our clients, we research it thoroughly and share it.

Once you get an idea, you have to decide what to do with it. It is hard to weigh the merits of ideas because they are so amorphous and may not initially emerge from a professional's mind in a clear and usable form. Creative people come up with many ideas. A few are brilliant, many are good, and some stink.

The process a firm uses for screening ideas, then, must not shut off the flow of new ideas by discouraging professionals with too many rejections on the basis of unrealistically high standards. Initial screens can include fit with the firm's strategy, cost of development, timing, downside and upside risk, and market receptivity for the idea. Ideas that meet these screens should then be subject to more critical evaluation and selection.

At firms serious about developing reputations as thought leaders, ideas that pass these screens should be assigned a development priority and budget. Management may suggest the professional write an article on the subject as time permits or, a greater investment, a full-scale research effort. Projects to develop ideas felt to warrant large investment require careful budgeting and project management. Only those firms willing to invest time and money in good ideas are likely to see a significant return.

Of course, we cannot know exactly what ideas will capture the market's fancy even if we listen closely to our clients and apply a rigorous screening process. The business sections of bookstores are filled with books that appear briefly and leave little mark when they have gone. Thought leaders often test their ideas in the marketplace to see if they will catch on. Joe Flom, of Skadden Arps, the greatest rainmaker in the history of the legal profession, is famous for this. Others in the firm refer to his "flavor of the month," the idea he is testing in the market in conversations with clients at any given time. Many leading business concepts first appear as articles. The authors quickly elaborate on them in books when they see a promising response. So, for example, the concept of reengineering was first put forward in an article by Michael Hammer,[9] before he and James Champy wrote *Reengineering the Corporation*.[10]

Actions to Support Ideas

Of course, if you want to lead with your ideas, those ideas must be accessible to your market. This means the ideas must be presented in forums where many people hear them and in ways that make them easy to consume. A learned friend once told me that popular business books often read "like *Readers' Digest* versions of more substantive books." There is some truth in this assertion. Successful thought leaders realize that few clients will wade through an academic treatise. They make their ideas accessible and save detailed technical explanations of their research for those few expert audiences who care.

The power of popularization is well-documented in the quality movement. Several consultants vied for the position as the leading spokesperson on quality. Phil Crosby captured an early lead for that position by publishing the accessible *Quality Is Free* in 1979.[11] But Deming was featured as the ultimate authority on quality in the 1980 NBC television white paper, *If Japan Can ...Why Can't We?* The delivery of his ideas in this most popular of all media had tremendous impact. Among those who saw it and called Deming was Donald Petersen, Chairman of Ford Motor.[12]

Joseph Juran, who had passed on the opportunity to be featured on this program (a questionable business decision), captured a reputation as a thought leader by producing how-to videos on quality. Corporations bought $30 million worth of these videos and showed them to thousands of senior and middle managers. At the time, this was a highly innovative approach to promoting an idea.

Thought leaders write articles, white papers, and books. They give speeches and seminars. Increasingly, they produce videos and are now developing compact disks and Web homepages that advance their ideas. They promote their ideas in words that everyone can understand and in forums accessible to large audiences.

An idea can be fascinating and an argument compelling, but to deliver benefits to a client and profits to a professional firm, it must somehow be linked to a change mechanism. In management consulting, this usually means a methodology supported by an organization that can deliver a complex engagement. In law, it is language and procedures that either create or avoid legal consequences. In engineering, it can be a methodology or a technology. Each discipline has its own ways to deliver change. Even these will do little good unless the thought leader has a system for bringing willing followers into the fold. Many politicians with brilliant ideas have failed because they did not have the organization to make use of the energies of the converts they created. So it is with the professions. Thought leaders who do not have the organization in place to: (1) develop engagements with clients who hear their message and seek their help, (2) develop a methodology, technology, or other change mechanism, (3) train employees in the application of this mechanism, and (4) deliver a complex engagement with quality service, risk losing their leadership position to a better organized competitor.

When Tom Peters and Bob Waterman published *In Search of Excellence*, they captured the imagination of a generation of businesspeople.[13] They introduced many appealing concepts, including getting close to the customer, quality, management by walking around, and sticking to one's knitting. But ways to deliver results on these concepts were largely developed by others, who captured huge economic benefits from doing so.

It is through the details of selling and delivering engagements that your investment in ideas will be turned into cash.

Large firms, small firms, and sole practitioners all live off the ideas and knowledge they command. Just as many investors fail to maximize their wealth through inattention to their financial investments, so many professionals fail to maximize theirs through inattention to their intellectual capital. The time to take control of this key asset is now.

Things You Can Do

1. *Reward your people for ideas.*

   A firm that consistently produces better ideas than competitors will grow more rapidly and make more profits. But those who produce ideas often go unrewarded. Some of the leading management consulting firms reward their employees with such things as extra vacation time for coming up with good ideas. The expense is well worth the cost when the alternative may be losing ideas that can be captured this way and later turned into cash.

2. *Assign a professional to report on an area of special interest to firm management, members of a practice, or clients in a presentation or briefing document.*

   If you make this assignment seem an honor and performing it well seem important, you will develop an expert who probably has something special to say to the market. You will, of course, have to make sure that the professional has enough time to do it. It will be a legitimate use of nonbillable time if the professional succeeds in educating other members of the firm or clients about something that clients need to know.

3. *Encourage professionals to write and speak about areas in which they have expertise.*

   This expertise can result from work done as a part of the preceding recommendation, from client work, or from some kind of special research. Encouragement can include cash rewards, public accolades for those who succeed, support from a professional writer, or provision of training on writing and speaking. For example, a training class on article writing at one technology consulting firm has helped firm members publish in *Harvard Business Review, CIO Magazine, InformationWeek, Total Quality Review, Law and Order, HR Magazine* and many other journals. Some firms support professionals with ghost writers and writing and speaking coaches.

At some firms, publishing and speaking are weighed when considering professionals for promotion. In some, they are included in annual performance goals. These forms of encouragement, of course, will mean little unless the implicit provision or withholding of rewards is adhered to.

4. *Package ideas for distribution by the firm's professionals.*

Some firms package ideas in a way that makes it easy for professionals to distribute them to clients. Hewitt Associates, a compensation and benefits consulting firm, provides its professionals with documents that give them something of value to leave behind with a client after a meeting. PWI Engineering, a firm with 100 employees and therefore not large in comparison to many others, produces technical bulletins that its engineers can distribute to their clients. Most large firms provide their professionals with some material of this kind. Few do it consistently. Many midsize and small firms provide far less support of this kind than they could.

8

Finding a Lead Generation Approach That Works

"Our people are too reactive. They're good at selling when a client comes to them with a problem, but they don't go out and find opportunities," a senior partner at a management consulting firm told me shortly after I began my current practice. Since then I have heard similar words from many people in many professions.

Before you can sell, you must have a lead. A lead is an opportunity to sit face to face with a prospective client to talk about a problem that the client recognizes he or she has and that you can help solve. Many firms suffer because they don't have enough leads to grow their practices. Often this is because they take a reactive approach to lead generation, waiting for former clients to call or send a request for proposal. Leads obtained this way differ in both quantity and quality from proactively generated ones. As architect A. Eugene Kohn says, "Proactive marketing creates work where there is none. It allows you to get work without competing for it. Those are often the best opportunities."

Real rainmakers generate leads. Getting young professionals to do the same is hard. Because lead generation lies at the heart of a rainmaking system, both this and the next chapter are devoted to the subject.

Lead generation can usually be broken into two parts: obtaining introductions to people you want to do business with and developing a relationship with them so that they consider hiring you when they have a need. This chapter deals with the first of these problems. Chapter 9 deals with the second.

Obtaining introductions to the people you want to do business with can be disheartening work. It requires call discipline, many hours worked for no immediate return, getting past gatekeepers, and resilience in the face of rejection. It can be a comedown from the ego-enhancing experience of working with clients. Clients almost always return phone calls; prospects often don't. Clients listen to what you say because they are paying for your opinions. Prospects often aren't sure they want to hear your voice at all. Clients pay you; prospects don't. No wonder lead generation is so easily postponed in favor of client work. Still, rainmakers must make time for this crucial work. In my experience, true rainmakers spend far more time generating leads than in actually selling. It is here that their optimism, systems, and large networks pay off.

Guidance on lead generation can be hard to come by. It is an area in which aspiring rainmakers can get little help from literature on selling products. The Product Model of selling presumes a dedicated sales force that spends almost all its time calling and meeting with prospective customers to sell product manufactured by someone else. This assumption fits most professional firms not at all. At virtually every law firm and most accounting and management consulting firms, leads are generated and sales made by the professional staff. This is because most clients want to buy from those who, in their perception, will deliver the service they need. In the words of Warren J. Wittreich, they want to deal with a professional who sells, not with a professional salesperson.[1] Professionals must balance client development with managing and performing engagements. This is sometimes called the Seller-Doer Model or the Sell-Manage-Do Model.

At best, the assumption of a dedicated sales force has a partial fit at some firms. Many architectural and engineering firms do have full-time business developers responsible for generating leads. A few consulting firms and some accounting firms also have dedicated lead generators and salespeople. But the fit remains partial because, unlike people selling products, final sales at the overwhelming majority of firms are still made by professionals, not by salespeople. Lead generation processes that start with a full-time business developer must be constructed in a way that makes transition of the sale to a professional smooth and natural.

Whether professionals or dedicated business developers generate leads, you must have a system for generating them. As noted in Chapter 1, there has been a lot of debate about the best way to do this. There are advocates for cold calling, networking, giving speeches, writing articles, holding seminars, direct mail, and other approaches. These advocates are of two kinds. First, there are those who describe many different ways without recommending one over another. Two authors who have written for consultants, Howard L. Shenson[2] and Herman Holtz,[3] exemplify this approach. Though their books are helpful in other ways, they do not help a practitioner decide how to allocate scarce lead generation time and dollars. Regarding this choice, Holtz states, "...the guiding principle is still: whatever works is right."[4] This is more accurately a nonprinciple that leaves it to the reader to learn by trial and error.

Other authors recommend a specific approach or clearly rank approaches by preference. These include Maister[5] and Schiffman,[6] among others. They have a one-size-fits-all mentality and recommend that whether you are an audit, tax, or transaction-support accountant; a trial, tax, or real estate lawyer; a strategy, benefits, or turnaround consultant, the methods you should use to get leads remain the same. All these books, and particularly Maister's, have made a contribution to the professions, but their recommendation of a single or single set of lead generation approaches for all firms simply does not fit with the facts.

Over the past twenty-five years, I have seen firms succeed with a huge range of lead generation techniques, including all those listed here. A practice at one large technology consulting firm I know brought in many leads from advertisements, an approach generally not felt to be effective for lead generation in the professions. (Its services were productlike in that they could be readily understood by the client, were very much the same for all clients, and were needed by many. The buyers could be clearly identified and targeted in specific periodicals, and the firm had a unique position in the market that could not be imitated and that it could tout in its ads.) I have also seen firms waste huge amounts of money on approaches that didn't work for them, though they had worked at other firms. It would be convenient if there were an approach that worked for everyone, but the professions are too diverse for this to happen.

Management seeking to create rainmakers must guide its professionals toward lead generation approaches that do work. Some firms have an approach that works in place. If yours does, you can skip the rest of this chapter. If not, you must help your aspiring rainmakers develop one. To do this, I recommend the following methods.

Developing Lead Generation Approaches

1. *Look at what has worked in the past.*

Sometimes a firm doesn't need to do anything new; it just needs to do more of what it has done in the past. Several firms have greatly increased the number of leads they have generated by analyzing the way their successful rainmakers have worked and turning it into a firmwide system. Doing this, some have turned lead generation into what can be called a "core competency" in current management argot. Something that has worked in the past has probably been honed and adapted over the years to the situation the firm faces when it goes to market. Young professionals will benefit from the knowledge about the approach that is resident in the firm. These things are not true of any new approach you try.

Simply doing more of what you have done in the past won't work for all firms. Circumstances sometimes change, making an approach less successful than it had been. One consulting firm, for example, had been built around a series of seminars that attracted high-level managers from large corporations. If cultivated during and after the seminars, these managers became an excellent source of business. But it didn't last. Over the years, the firm found that increasingly lower-level managers attended. The people the firm wanted to do business with were no longer coming to the seminars. At first, it reacted by holding more seminars overseas where high-level managers continued to come, but eventually it had to find another approach to supplement the seminars.

Furthermore, an approach may not be transferable to young professionals. Rainmakers may choose to carry their secrets with them into retirement or be incapable of sharing. In Chapter 1, we saw that many rainmakers are poor mentors. Some rainmakers' approaches are based on personal attributes that others can't imitate. Some law firms, for example, have hired former government officials who have built practices based on the prestige of their former positions and contacts made while doing government work. Their successors in the firm often don't have these attributes.

2. *Identify the characteristics of your practice that affect how you should go to market.*

At some time or other, most firms have tried new approaches and found that they have wasted money and time. To reduce the risk of this happening, you must adapt any new approach you try to the special characteristics of your firm, its services, and its markets. Some approaches cannot be adapted at all. As a first step, clearly articulate the marketing problem you face. You should be able to describe it in a few sentences that capture its most important characteristics. Parameters that often define a professional firm's marketing problem include:

- *Frequency and Confidentiality of Need:* The problems faced when selling services that are needed constantly, periodically, and infrequently are quite different. People who sell services that are needed infrequently, for example, are likely to seek leads through intermediaries who are in a position to be aware of the client's need and make a referral. This tendency is increased when the need is confidential as well as infrequent. The buying procedures for periodic needs tend to be well established with readily identified buyers who must be cultivated. Many of these buyers hold staff, as opposed to line, positions, and people in staff positions tend to be insecure and, therefore, conservative in their buying decisions. Firms that sell services needed constantly by the client often develop close personal relationships that create loyalty.

- *Urgency and Size of the Need:* Urgent problems with potentially large impact, such as the need to fend off a hostile takeover effort, will receive high-level attention. Buyers will be less concerned about price and formal evaluation processes than about retaining the services of the best advisor fast. Positioning and reputation become extremely important in such markets.

- *Visibility of the Service and Demonstrability of Its Impact:* If the service you deliver is highly visible in the marketplace and its impact is clear, you can rely more on referrals based on the quality of your service than if your service is relatively invisible or if its impact is unclear. So, for example, a lawyer who wins a big case or otherwise represents a client well against adversaries is likely to attract other clients on that basis. He or she is seen in action by potential clients and the results are clear, so word gets around fast. This kind of success also generates opportunities to speak and publish articles, which, in turn, sometimes generate leads. The database of rainmakers has many lawyers who have built their practices this way.

An actuarial firm that provides a steady flow of information to a client, mostly by phone and mail, does not enjoy this advantage. Only one or two people at the client company may be aware of the service. Its impact may also be hard to demonstrate or to differentiate from a competitor's service.

- *Range of Services and Size of Firm:* Firms offering a broad range of services have many more points of access to a prospective client than do niche firms. A logistics consulting practice that is a part of a big, multiservice firm faces a different marketing problem from that faced by a small, independent firm specializing in the same area. Similarly, very big firms have relationships with many of the clients they want to service. For them, doing more work with their existing clients may be more important than adding new ones. A small, young firm may face the opposite situation. Because big firms tend to have a broader range of services than small ones, these two problems are closely interrelated.

- *Cost of the Service:* The more costly a service, the more people are likely to be involved in the hiring decision, all other things being equal. This has important lead generation implications because you will need to reach as many of the people involved in the decision as possible.

These and other factors interact in complex ways to create a special marketing situation for each firm. Your task is to describe that situation in a few sentences. Three fairly typical situations follow as examples:

- *The Needle-in-a-Haystack Problem:* When a client's need for a firm's services is likely to be infrequent and highly confidential, the professional may have difficulty finding the client (and vice versa) at that moment when the client has a need. This is true, in varying degrees, of location consulting, bankruptcy law, and some transaction-support accounting services. Markets for such services have several common characteristics.

Clients who don't have a need today are reluctant to spend time learning about the professional's services. No one, for example, wants to learn about a bankruptcy lawyer's services when things are going well. This makes it difficult to capture mindshare. Because of the infrequency of the need, many clients are likely to be first-time buyers who have not dealt with the business situation in question before. When a person does have a need, he or she will be reluctant to openly seek out a professional who can help, fearing the consequences of a breach in confidentiality. So, companies planning to relocate their headquarters are usually extremely reluctant to have this fact known. Management fears tipping off competitors and headhunters to a move before plans are complete, disrupting their own work forces, incurring political pressure to stay at their current location, or seeing real estate prices in chosen communities escalate.

Occupying no share of the client's mind and unaware of his or her need, the professional is likely to be overlooked at the critical moment when the client is ready to buy. Clients often know they are naive about the business issue in question and so will talk to a few trusted advisors. Professionals operating in Needle-in-the-Haystack markets often seek to develop referral relationships with these advisors. Advisors, however, can become competitors because they, themselves, are in a position to sell the needed service to the client even if they are not experts in the area. The clients are too naive and too concerned about confidentiality to realize that they are not dealing with a true expert.

- *The Many-Points-of-Light Problem:* Some professionals sell services that many others also offer and that fulfill a need created by a specific kind of event, say, a real estate transaction. If these events occur periodically, say, every other year or so, a professional will have difficulty building client loyalty when many competitors are also seeking to obtain the client's attention between events. Architects who design standard suburban office space, interior designers who design general office interiors, many real estate attorneys, and other professionals face this problem in varying degrees. In this environment, professionals must differentiate themselves from the many other points of light also seeking to impress the client. These markets also have some common characteristics.

Knowing that they will need the service in question repeatedly, many clients establish formal buying procedures for it. Generally, there is a clearly identified buyer, who is also a specialist. This might be a company's general counsel, its facilities manager, its human resources manager, or someone else. These buyers, who can heavily influence the decision to hire a professional even if they are not the decision makers, must be cultivated by the competing professionals. In some cases, they come to expect wining and dining as a form of perk.

There is much competition among firms for early warning about the events that drive the need for services, so as to gain early access to the buyers to learn the details of the engagement and their needs. Once the event becomes public knowledge, buyers are often so overwhelmed by calls from people soliciting their business that they stop returning phone calls to protect their time.

These markets tend to be highly networked. Usually, several different kinds of firms can benefit by learning about an event early. So, environmental engineers and environmental attorneys both want to know about a corporate environmental problem. They benefit from a mutual exchange of information and introductions.

- *The One-Dog-Client Problem:* Clients need some services constantly. In such cases, the knowledge of a client that a professional develops and relationships nurtured over months of close contact create a formidable barrier to competitors seeking a client's business. This is true of accounting audit services, many standard legal services, and increasingly, information technology consulting.

  A firm or practice seeking new clients in this environment must overcome a prospective client's loyalty to the professional currently providing the service. This may be done by offering a service that the professional currently serving the client does not provide and seeking to expand the relationship from there. Law firms often employ a variation on this theme by seeking opportunities to work for a client where current counsel is conflicted.

Any long-term relationship ebbs and flows, and competitors seek to exploit times when the client seems dissatisfied with its current professional's service. Often this dissatisfaction is related to price. To keep price down for such standard services, clients increasingly ask for periodic competitive bids. Many will then show the lowest bid to their current provider and ask him or her to match or at least come close to it. The combination of price pressure and high switching costs for the client create an incentive for firms to bid work below cost for the first year of a relationship with the expectation of increasing fees in future years, once the client is locked in.

Your firm or practice may fit one of these categories. Even if it does, you should carefully modify the description to more exactly capture your situation. If none of the descriptions fit, you will need to come up with your own. Exhibit 8.1 provides a form that will help you write one.

Exhibit 8.1
Defining Your Marketing Problem

1. *Frequency:* How frequently is a client likely to need your services? Does the same person within a company need them, or do different people in different parts of the organization need them at different times?

2. *Urgency:* When need for your services arises, how urgent is it likely to be? How far in advance do clients typically foresee the need for the service? How big an impact can your services make on the client company's performance?

3. *Visibility:* How visible is your service? What people within the client company, other than the buyer, are likely to be aware of what has been done and the fact that you did it? If you do a good job for one client, how likely are others to be aware that you did? When you work for one client, do others get to see you in action?

4. *Reach:* How big is your firm, and how broad is the range of its services? How do these compare to your major competitors?

5. *Cost:* How expensive are your services, and what does their cost imply about approval levels and pressure to obtain competitive bids?

6. *Other Factors:* What other factors are critical in defining the marketing problem you face (level of competition, geographic concentration of market, firm reputation, and so on)?

Reviewing your answers to these six questions, describe the marketing problem you face in a short paragraph.

---

3. *Evaluate lead generation approaches in the context of your marketing problem.*

Once you have prepared your description, you can test any lead generation approaches against it to see if you can make them fit.

Ignoring the characteristics of your firm's marketing problem when trying a lead generation approach is likely to be costly. Under pressure from its parent, one firm I worked for developed a cold-calling technique based on an approach used successfully at other firms. A sophisticated telemarketer was hired to obtain meetings with high-level executives at large corporations for the firm's senior professionals. Unfortunately, the technique was not well suited to the Needle-in-a-Haystack situation the firm faced. The professionals found that continuing a conversation with the prospective clients was difficult once the client had said, "Yes, but we don't need that service now," as the majority of them did. Maintaining a relationship after the call was difficult because the clients didn't see value in frequent conversations given the infrequency of their need for the service. They soon began to say, "We'll call you when we need you." Making regular calls in the hope of finding a few companies ready to buy proved inordinately expensive relative to other lead generation approaches. After great expense and much wasted time, the program was abandoned. Few firms with Needle-in-a-Haystack problems have been able to make cold calling work. Rather, most have succeeded by obtaining referrals through networks of people who have warning of clients' needs and by attracting interest from prospective clients through publicity about their successful projects.

Exhibit 8.2 lists a variety of lead generation techniques and describes situations in which they are often effective. If your situation is dissimilar from that described for any technique, you should ask yourself these questions:

- Why do I believe this approach will work for my firm or practice?

- If it doesn't seem to fit naturally with the marketing situation I face, what do I have to do to change the situation or adapt the approach to make the approach work?

Exhibit 8.2

Lead Generation Techniques

1. *Cold Calling*
   - Flexibility:
     Low. Does not work well for some firms, such as those whose clients have an infrequent need for their services.

   - Strengths:
     Gets you face to face with a client to talk about issues you may be able to help with.

   - Weaknesses:
     Incurs high cost per contact, especially with geographically dispersed market.

     Requires high level of selling skill.

     Usually needs high possible conversion rate or high value per project to justify high cost per contact.

   - Works best with:
     Firms whose services are needed by most clients most of the time.

2. *Seminars*
   - Flexibility:
     Moderate. Logistical requirements are substantial.

- Strengths:

    Prequalify prospects because they attend based on interest in issue.

    Provide opportunity to get face to face.

- Weaknesses:

    Require long list of prospects to ensure audience of sufficient size.

    Require ample staff support to manage logistics.

- Works best with:

    Frequent and expected needs, which create an incentive to stay on top of trends and approaches.

    Infrequent needs being faced by many firms simultaneously, such as changes in laws or technology.

3. *Publicity*
   - Flexibility:

       High. Can be made to work at some level for most firms.

   - Strengths:

       Reaches broad audience with low cost per contact.

   - Weaknesses:

       Lessens your control over lead generation; client must call you after receiving message.

   - Works best with:
       Services with high news value.

4. *Relationship Marketing* (staying in contact with current and former clients)
   - Flexibility:

       High. Works well for most firms.

   - Strengths:

       Incurs low cost per contact.

       Results in relatively high conversion rate.

   - Weaknesses:

       Does not broaden base of business.

- Works best with:

    Frequently needed services.

    Broad range of services so that there is always something to offer.

5. *Direct Mail*
   - Flexibility:

        High. Can be adapted to most firms' situations.

   - Strengths:

        Incurs low cost per contact.

   - Weaknesses:

        Provides low control over lead generation; you expect client to call you.

        Requires high level of selling skills if you follow up with phone calls.

   - Works best:

        In combination with other approaches.

6. *Public Speaking*
   - Flexibility:

        Moderate.

   - Strengths:

        Prequalifies prospects because they attend based on interest in issue.

        Provides opportunity to get face to face.

   - Weaknesses:

        Requires professionals with strong speaking abilities.

   - Works best with:

        Services for which there are many potential audiences.

7. *Trade Association Activity*
   - Flexibility:

        Moderate. Depends on number and strength of associations in your area of practice.

- Strengths:
  Gets you face to face with prospective clients in a situation where it is easy to introduce yourself.

- Weaknesses:
  Is a competitive environment; most of your competitors will be there, too.

  Will be less effective if relevant association has no active local chapters.

- Works best with:
  Services for markets with highly active associations.

8. *Networking*
   - Flexibility:
     High. Can be made to work in most situations.

   - Strengths:
     Creates a quasi-sales force of contacts.

     Helps capture market information unavailable from most other sources.

     Gains access to prospective clients through referrals; warms up cold calls.

   - Weaknesses:
     Does not provide as direct access to clients as cold calling, speeches, or seminars.

   - Works best with:
     Markets that are geographically concentrated.

     Highly networked markets.

---

4. *Determine how the firm will have to change to accommodate a new lead generation approach.*

   The more complicated and sophisticated the lead generation process that you install, the more the firm will have to change to accommodate it. You may be able to run an occasional seminar or attend a trade show without changing much else about your firm, but if you want to install a substantial new approach, you must remember that it must fit into an entire sales system to work. The professions are awash in lead generation processes unrelated to a larger sales system. These processes are largely a waste.

So, for example, a firm that plans a series of seminars to generate leads must do the following in addition to running seminars:

- Modify its targeting process to generate names and addresses for the mailing list required to find attendees.

- Ensure that the professionals involved in the seminar have time to prepare and rehearse.

- Assign professionals to develop relationships with the attendees over the course of the seminar.

- Record pertinent information on the attendees gathered during the seminar. This includes information gleaned about the companies they work for, their business needs, and their personal needs and interests.

- Follow up with attendees shortly after the completion of the seminar with something of additional value.

- Develop long-term relationships with the participants through periodic contact by mail, by phone, and as appropriate, in person.

If you are not willing to do these things, you probably shouldn't run the seminar program in the first place.

5. *Recognize that your professionals will select different approaches based on their personal interests and abilities.*

Firms that have a firmwide system for developing leads tend to place a strong emphasis on recruiting people who will succeed at developing business that way. One firm, for example, has a day's worth of psychological tests that it administers to people it is considering for client relationship career tracks. If they don't meet a certain profile, they aren't hired. As one person who had worked with the firm noted, "We all tended to be very much alike."

Most firms employ a far more mixed group of people; one consultant said drolly of her firm, "We have one of each kind, here." If this is the case, one approach to developing leads is unlikely to work for all. Different people will have to select approaches that will work for them. Attorney Dixie L. Laswell says:

> To the extent possible, you should be doing things you like to do. If you don't like giving speeches, you shouldn't do it. If you prefer to run, you can get to know people at the club where you work out. I tell my women friends that when they're at that Little League game, it's easy as pie to strike up a conversation with the person cheering next to you. He probably works outside the house and may need legal services. As a woman, you have to integrate your professional with your personal life to get everything done that you need to get done.

As we have seen, many men feel the same way.

I have described the lead generation processes most commonly used by professionals in my first book, *Rain Making: The Professional's Guide to Attracting New Clients,*[7] and will not go into them here. After identifying two or three approaches that seem promising, firm management should not spend much time in figuring out which is the best. The hard part is getting professionals to apply any of them with sufficient consistency and discipline to generate a stream of introductions. Too often, they will devote weeks to debating strategy and planning approaches, and then take no action. One often suspects that deciding on strategy becomes a way to avoid the hard slogging of lead generation. It reminds me of the situation that Lincoln faced during the Civil War:

> The root of his problem, he began to realize, was that neither the generals nor the people recognized that they were at war and that it would take hard, tough fighting to win. "They have got the idea into their heads that we are going to get out of this fix, somehow, by strategy!" he exclaimed. "That's the word — strategy! General McClellan thinks he is going to whip the rebels by strategy; and the army has got the same notion."[8]

Ultimately, to get business, professionals have to act, and act with relentless determination, even when this action doesn't seem natural at first. Few understand the sheer amount of action that is required to get new clients and to push themselves up a client development curve that will look something like the one shown in Exhibit 2.3. An example of this relentlessness in applying a technique to get introductions to prospective clients is provided by the late Carol Berlin Manzoni, a partner at the Chicago-based law firm of Ross & Hardies. Early in her career, she began to give speeches. "What speeches really get you is more speeches," she comments wryly. Still, she stuck with it tenaciously:

> I spent a significant amount of time giving speeches to groups of people I hoped would know and remember me. I spoke at chambers of commerce, hospital associations, and many other groups. Once one is on the circuit and has topics of interest, you get requests to speak. I would also ask clients if they were members of an association that would like to have me speak. There were years when I was doing twenty-five speeches a year, and it was very, very fruitful.

Leads came, but not after the first speech, and not after the second.

Things You Can Do

1. *Provide a centralized process that will help professionals in your firm meet the people they want to do business with.*

    The firm can help aspiring rainmakers get introductions to people they want to meet by using dedicated marketing staff to arrange for speeches, set up a seminar series, run direct mail campaigns, or do a variety of other tasks. When this kind of effort is begun, the professionals who will be involved need to know what the firm will do for them and at what point they are expected to pick up responsibility for assisting in the effort and developing relationships from the introductions that result. If they aren't involved early, the chances that they will do their part diminish.

2. *Ask professionals to develop personal marketing plans that include actions they will take to generate leads.*

    Firm management may have to help the young professional think through the implications of actions committed to in such a plan. So, for example, if the professional plans to get involved in an association as a means of meeting people, he or she will need help thinking through exactly what needs to be done to get results, including attending meetings, participating in committee work, obtaining business cards at each meeting, and following up with letters and phone calls after each meeting. The professional should then be asked to schedule these activities as a part of the development of a plan.

Often such plans will include too few activities that will get the professional face to face with prospective clients. If you receive such a plan, you need to point out this oversight and have it corrected. For example, a young professional is likely to include creation of a brochure for a specific service as a major plan element. Brochures are greatly overrated by young professionals. Most can be done without completely, and time devoted to creating them simply delays efforts that will get the professional face to face with a client, where something useful might actually happen. Article writing and mailings are worthwhile activities, but they will never replace getting face to face.

Plans will be worthless unless you monitor and manage their implementation.

Once a professional has met a prospective client, he or she must develop a relationship that will increase the chances of getting business when the client has a need. This subject is so important that the next chapter is devoted to it.

9

Building Relationships That Produce Business

A t one point in my career, I was transferred from Chicago to New Jersey to turn around the Eastern regional office of the firm I worked for. The office was losing twenty-five cents on every dollar it took in, and there had been two previous attempts to fix it. I was told that this time we would either fix it or close it. I had a one-way ticket, a wife, a kid, and a mortgage.

The situation was, in some ways, much simpler than the turnarounds many professionals have faced. One competitor was shellacking us in the marketplace. Debriefings with clients after losses showed that the competitor tended to know people at the companies we were both selling to before an opportunity arose. In contrast, we hadn't known anyone at these companies. This translated into better knowledge about the client during the sale than we had and, in some cases, early warning about the need for the service we both provided. No wonder we were losing business.

In short, our competitor was better networked than we were. As we have seen, most rainmakers have large networks of contacts. These networks can be of three kinds:

- *Classic networks* comprised of noncompeting professionals and businesspeople who refer business. The many networks that exist among lawyers, accountants, and bankers provide one example. Those between architects, consulting engineers, real estate brokers, and builders provide another.

- *Cross markets* comprised of people offering different services within the same firm. The referrals made between the audit, tax, and consulting arms of some accounting/consulting firms result from cross markets, as do the referrals between different practices within a law firm.

- *Relationship markets* comprised of professionals and their clients. In this case, the professional provides the client with a variety of help, such as knowledge of industry trends, information on changing laws, and leads for a job search. The client helps the professional get business. Many professionals compete for the role of trusted advisor to senior executives of major corporations as a means of developing relationship markets.

These three kinds of networks help the rainmakers in several ways. Because of them, the rainmakers sometimes get opportunities that competitors don't; strong relationships can result in sole-sourcing. Sometimes rainmakers' networks give them early warning of a need. Sometimes rainmakers are able to break into a hiring process that is already well underway and that they have learned about late because they have a relationship with the right person at the client organization. They can get access to more people than competitors can during a sale. This helps them get better information on which to base their sales effort and can also predispose the buyer to hire them.

Most rainmakers support themselves and their firms through the relationships they build. Though every human being knows something about building relationships, rainmakers do it with professional discipline. This discipline distinguishes them much as the discipline with which a Steffi Graf approaches tennis or a Tiger Woods approaches golf distinguishes them from the rest of us. Aspiring rainmakers must develop discipline, as much as an aspiring athlete must. Management must support the development of discipline, and the first step to doing so is to understand how networking works.

I learned the rules of networking the hard way when I came east to head up the troubled office. As soon as I learned that our competitor was better networked than we were, I set out to develop a network of my own by flying off to the annual conference of a trade association where I could meet many prospective clients. I spent three of the most miserable days of my life working from early in the morning, through the conference sessions, through dinner, and on into the night at hospitality suites introducing myself to strangers. The whole time I felt like a shoe salesman at a haberdasher's convention. Everyone was extremely courteous, but I felt out of place.

At the end of the three days, I was exhausted, no closer to solving my problem, and anxious to get home. I grabbed my bag and went down to the curb in front of the hotel where I ran into a friend who suggested we share a cab to the airport. During the ride, I was about to comment on what a waste of time the conference had been, when my friend said, "What a great meeting! It was the best I've ever attended. I must have gotten five leads!" I realized then that I was doing something wrong, and on the plane home I wrote out a list of people who I considered to be good networkers. Back in the office, I called these people and asked them what networking was all about. They told me.

Since then, I have learned that they were describing rules already identified in an area of game theory and that these rules apply to all three kinds of networks, though the application varies somewhat from one kind of network to another. The area of game theory relevant to networking is called the Prisoner's Dilemma, about which much has been written. An accessible description of research on this problem can be found in Robert Axelrod's *The Evolution of Cooperation*.[1] It is based on the premise of two criminals arrested in the act of committing a minor crime. The police, rightly, suspect them of having committed a much more serious offense together, but do not have enough evidence to get a conviction on this offense unless one of the prisoners turns state's evidence against the other.

Each prisoner has a choice, as shown in Exhibit 9.1. He can cooperate (C) with the other prisoner by remaining silent about the serious crime or defect (D) by turning state's evidence. With two prisoners, there are four possibilities. The prisoners can cooperate with each other (C,C), by remaining silent about the serious crime, in which case they both go to jail for a year for the minor one. The first prisoner can turn state's evidence against the second even though the second cooperates with him by remaining silent (D,C), in which case the first goes free, whereas the second prisoner spends five years in jail for the serious crime. The second prisoner may defect and go free, while the first cooperates and serves five years (C,D). Finally, both may defect by trying to turn state's evidence against each other (D,D), in which case there is a glut of confessions, causing them to lose market value, and both serve three years. The police keep the prisoners in separate cells so that they cannot communicate with each other prior to making their choices.

Exhibit 9.1

The Prisoner's Dilemma

		Prisoner Two	
		Cooperate	Defect
Prisoner One	Cooperate	C,C 1,1	C,D 5,0
	Defect	D,C 0,5	D,D 3,3

This problem can easily be converted into the Networker's Dilemma, as shown in Exhibit 9.2. In this case, each of the two networkers has the choice of either giving time to help the other get business (Cooperate) or using that time to do something beneficial for herself (Don't Cooperate). For the logic of the Prisoner's Dilemma to apply, the cost of giving time, here shown to be $200, representing the opportunity cost of time not spent helping oneself, must be lower than the value of the time received, here shown as $1,000. As you can see, the problem has the same win/win–win/lose–lose/lose/win–lose/lose structure that typifies the Prisoner's Dilemma. As in all such cases, there is the risk that the participants will end up in the lose/lose quadrant in an effort to gain advantage over each other.

Game theorists have conducted studies of the Prisoner's Dilemma and determined that those who spend the least amount of time in jail after many rounds of play with the same people, that is, the winners, employ something called the Tit-for-Tat Strategy. Reworded for our purposes here, the rules of this strategy are:

- *Be a giver.* Realizing that it is in your best interests to establish a cooperative relationship, try to establish one in the first round of play by cooperating with all other players.

- *React to the other player.* In the second round and each succeeding round of play, you are faced with two possible situations. Some players cooperated with you in the preceding round. In this case,

Exhibit 9.2

The Networker's Dilemma

<u>Where</u>
Cost of giving time = $200
Value of time received = $1000

		Networker Two	
		Cooperate	Don't Cooperate
Networker One	Cooperate	C,C $800,$800	C,D -$200,$1000
	Don't Cooperate	D,C $1000,-$200	D,D $0,$0

the choice is easy. Simply continue to cooperate with them. But others defected in the preceding round. If you cooperate with them in this one, you may encourage them to defect again. It is important to show them that you are not a sucker and will not be taken advantage of, so you defect in this round. Thus, you react to the other player's preceding move by responding in kind in this one. Cooperation leads to cooperation. Defection to defection.

- *Be forgiving.* By the rules of the Tit-for-Tat Strategy, you consider only what happened in the immediately preceding round. Once someone demonstrates a willingness to cooperate by giving you a green card, you reciprocate in the next by doing the same. It doesn't pay to hold grudges.

My survey shows that rainmakers employ something close to the Tit-for-Tat Strategy even though most of them are unaware that they do. Listen to the way Kirk Tyson, a management consultant and founder of Kirk Tyson International Ltd., describes his method of developing business:

> We market to people who attend one of our seminars. My personal network is about 4,000 — a lot of people have attended our seminars. After a seminar, I call the people I met there. I try to start each call with the mindset that my mission is to facilitate the person's success and his company's success. [Be a giver] I will always relate to them on a personal

level first. I then progress to their situation in the industry, and because I am a voracious reader, I often am more up to date than they are, and they thank me for informing them. [Be a giver] If things aren't going well for them, the conversation often comes back to their personal concerns, and I help them as best I can. When appropriate, the conversation progresses to a discussion of their needs for research.

I remain close to 400 to 500 of these people by calling them more frequently than I do the others. These are the ones who progress to research and consulting clients and become repeat clients. [React to the other player]

This is what accountant Ira Yohalem, of Yohalem Gillman & Company, says:

I have a huge network of resources and rely on them for many things. If I don't know something a client wants to know, I know someone who is the expert. I am constantly asked for advice for that reason and that puts me in the position to refer business. I'm very careful about the business I give out. The person has to be good at what he does. If he passes that test, I refer some business [Be a giver] and try him for two years, and then, if nothing comes, if he isn't at least trying to help me, too, I will let the relationship cool. [React to the other player]

Or this partner at a big accounting firm:

I generate business by having a very large group of contacts that I stay close to. I have about 300 people on my mailing list, broken down into four categories: bankers, attorneys, clients, and other accountants. I know every one of these people, and, with a large part, [my wife and I] have a close relationship. You pay attention to those who are responsive to you. There are only so many days to have lunch or dinner. [React to the other player]

Creating Structure

The rainmakers in the survey don't play exactly by the rules of the Tit-for-Tat Strategy because the rules work for a simple game and the rainmakers live in a complex reality. The simple game, for example, has a formal structure consisting of rounds of play, exchanges of messages about one's choice to cooperate or defect, and so on. But in the complex reality, there is no structure except that which the rainmaker chooses to create. As I have explained elsewhere, the systems that rainmakers use to develop business are a way to impose structure on a complex activity. Within most rainmaking systems, processes help the rainmakers make sure they get close to those they meet attending association meetings, doing client work, or making cold calls. The processes also make sure that contact is sustained over time. Here are a few examples of some of the processes that rainmakers use to structure and discipline their relationship building. Note, especially, how relentlessly they are performed. In all cases, they represent but one part of each rainmaker's system:

- I needed a way to bring the people I met into closer contact. I'm not into golf or tennis and not a sports enthusiast. Nor do I belong to a club. So I had to find a way to compensate. People love to eat and I love to cook, so I invited them to my home. Once every six weeks or so for fifteen years, I have invited six or seven couples and prepared a banquet Chinese dinner. I now have a reputation as "The Chinese Cook." This activity has enabled me to establish closer relationships than the usual relationships you have in business. People remember where they ate dinner on Saturday; it is something different about me. This could not have been done without the support of my wife. [Jack Kaye, partner, Deloitte & Touche LLP]

- He used cold calls. He would identify the people he wanted to meet and send them a letter. He might send 100 letters and get 2 responses. Then he would go to the city where he had a meeting set up, say Columbus, and start calling from his hotel room on Monday morning to get other meetings. He would say that he was in town and would like to stop by. He would see them again and again for years, maybe for no more than twenty minutes. [a management consultant who founded a successful firm]

- He used the financial community. He said, "I have bought lunch for every important banker in Chicago and New York at one time or another, and nearly every one at one time or another has given me some work. . . . except one." This man was an executive in a New York bank. He said, "I have been courting him for several years and I have never gotten a nickel's worth of business from him and I can't figure out why he is the exception." About six months later, he came to the office one day. He used to walk up and down and drop in on people. He said, "I have completed the circle. Remember the guy from that New York bank? Well, I found out that he's the one who got us the XYZ Company study. I never knew how it happened. I never knew and I always worried about this guy. Now I know."[2]

- An audit partner brought us an opportunity to sell business to a division of a large cosmetics company. We won the business, and during the sale, [the rainmaker] got to know the controller. Once the project began, he took the controller to lunch or dinner, not often, but maybe every six months. I managed the project, and whenever I would bring him an issue related to it, he would say, "Let's call Jim (the controller) and see what he thinks about it." He would do this just to have a reason to call. We did five projects with the division, and he did this again and again. After we were done, [the rainmaker] would look for any excuse to stay in touch. When we did work for another unit of [the same company], I would come in with an issue and he would say, "Let's call Jim and see what he thinks about it." It was an automatic reaction. He does this with many people. After twenty-five years in business, he knows a lot of people. [a consulting partner at a big firm]

- I am a member of several associations where I have the opportunity to work with prospective clients. Over the years, I have learned a lot about working with volunteers and making things happen. I chair committees and was the first woman and youngest person ever to be elected president of the Boston Society of Civil Engineers. I will be the President of the New England Chapter of the American Consulting Engineers Council in 1998. People learn who I am and what I do. It's important to be competent when volunteering for association activities, because the people assume that if you are competent there, you will do good work and be as responsive on a project when you are being paid. I always try to have association committee meetings in our offices to show we are credible and substantial. People who come say, "I didn't know you had so many people," and "You've got better computers than we have." That makes an impression, and it helps some of them become clients. The relationships I have developed doing association work have been the source of a lot of business. [Judy Nitsch, Judith Nitsch Engineering, Inc.]

- Every week we get together to talk about potential new business. We each tell about potential projects we have heard about. From these meetings, he makes up a task list of twenty names or more of people he needs to call, maybe five people per project. He works through that list. He calls these people to get a meeting or more information. Sometimes he has his secretary call for him to arrange a meeting. He also does a lot of shotgun calling to people he knows. The people he calls tell him what's going on and who he needs to see. Sometimes they make additional calls for him to get the information he needs. Then we go to see those people, 99 percent of the time with some kind of entree. [a consulting engineer]

- He gets a lot of referrals from New York [law] firms. He goes there every spring to see the Metropolitan Opera. He always schedules a long list of clients and other lawyers to see while he is there. It is exhausting just to read. If he doesn't know someone well, he will send a letter to reintroduce himself and then call. Last time, he made five visits a day for several days. [a lawyer from a western city]

- He has built five groups that have turned into associations over his career. He sees groups that need representation and issues that are best addressed by a group. These groups, of course, provide him with a forum for getting in front of people and a way to build relationships. He views this as a civic contribution, though he probably wouldn't describe it that way. [a Washington attorney]

These methods provide a sampling of the ways professionals develop close relationships and stay in regular contact over the years, once they meet a potentially valuable contact. All place the burden on the professional to initiate and maintain contact; rainmakers take responsibility for developing relationships. Other professionals often mean to, but don't. This is particularly true of relationships with clients. Nonrainmakers often believe that rainmakers are such trusted advisors of their clients that the clients call them regularly to discuss problems. Calls usually go the other way.

It has been shown that frequent contact increases the level of cooperation between most people.[3] By employing methods that assure frequent contacts, rainmakers are making a critical investment in increased cooperation. Often these increases are worked at deliberately. Joe Kosakowski, of the consulting firm M. F. Smith & Associates, says, "I always try to improve a relationship and view all relationships on a scale of one to ten. When someone treats me like a four, I try to treat them like a five. If they treat me like a six, I treat them like a seven. If they treat me like a nine, I treat them like a ten." This is an example of how rainmakers draw up the level of cooperation. It will work only if you discipline yourself to meet with people repeatedly.

Defining Cooperation

In the Prisoner's Dilemma, cooperation is defined only as not turning state's evidence. In the complex reality in which we live, there are many kinds of cooperation. You can introduce people to prospective clients, inform them about trends or events in an industry, or even in their own companies, that they need to know about; help them find a new job; coach them on a sale; give them the name of someone who can help solve a problem; make them look good to their bosses; congratulate them when something good happens; or give a supportive word when they are down. Rainmakers must learn what will be helpful to each contact they know so that they can always recognize an opportunity to help. This requires time getting to know people whom you want to develop a relationship with and is another reason rainmakers need calling and meeting discipline.

Though much of the giving that rainmakers do must be customized to specific contacts, even in this area one can create a system that makes giving more consistent. Many rainmakers read the business press and other documents not just for themselves, but also for their many contacts, in effect, becoming a clipping service for others. Bob Dubner, a partner at Coopers & Lybrand Consulting, describes this process and captures the compulsiveness that many rainmakers feel about keeping abreast of current information for the benefit of their contacts:

> I maintain my network with phone contacts because I enjoy the interpersonal touch. I also read a lot and send clients articles of interest. If I see information that is of immediate interest, I give them a call. It's harder and harder to keep up with this. The information is coming so fast you feel you are drowning in it. As I have gotten older, I have to read more and more and expose myself to more thoughts to stay ahead of the curve. I must read a couple of hours a day, even on vacations. I find I make good use of planes and trains to keep up. My reading and efforts to help keep clients informed by sending them things isn't just a technique to get business; I do these things because I value my business relationships and find them and the subject matter interesting.

Deciding Whom to Network With

The Prisoner's Dilemma game also differs from the complex reality in the selection of players. In the simple game, you are assigned a small number of people to play with. In the complex reality in which we live, there are many more people whom we can network with than we have time for. The Affinity Principle described in Chapter 2 makes the importance of spending time with the right people clear. Chapter 6 provides guidance on making the selection.

The large number of people you can develop relationships with in the complex reality in which we live makes possible many different degrees of relationship that are not possible in the Prisoner's Dilemma. Large networks tend to split into two groups: primary networks, comprised of people with whom the rainmaker has a close relationship based on mutual cooperation, and secondary networks, comprised of people with whom the rainmaker has weaker ties.

Primary networks usually consist of between twenty and fifty people. Dixie L. Laswell, an environmental lawyer, says, "I probably have thirty to fifty people in my core network, but it grows like Topsy from there." The rainmaker often has an informal name for this group, and the rainmaker's spouse often seems to be the source of the name. One accountant distinguishes between his friends and his semifriends. Another accountant's wife refers to his primary network as his Mafia. Attorney Gene Killian says:

> As my network has gotten bigger, it has really shrunk. You know who the quality contacts are — people who give good service, are ethical, and who want a two-way street on the giving. You spend more time with them. I have about twenty of these people. My wife calls them my Breakfast Club.

The name tends to reinforce the close affinity of these groups and the established nature of the mutual cooperation. It can become an informal society. Members have to *pass* a core network test, as shown in Exhibit 9.3. They must be:

- *Physically in the market.* If they are not, they won't be able to pass opportunities to the rainmaker. Other professionals you network with must be out working with clients and meeting new people. Clients who belong to the group must also be well-positioned to provide business or be likely to be in that position in the future. As one management consultant interviewed during the survey says, "If you know someone in a company who is really good,

Exhibit 9.3

The Core Network Member Test

Are the contacts:

- **P**hysically in the market?
- **A**lert to opportunities for others?
- **S**avvy about handing off and coaching on a sale?
- **S**killed at what they do?

---

don't look at that person as just a company contact; look at him or her as someone who is really important to you. I have several of these people who I have known for years. One has been in four different companies. He tends to go to troubled companies, and there is always a flurry of activity for us when he gets there."

- *A*lert to opportunities for others. Unless contacts are likely to be aware of an opportunity for you when they hear it, they cannot help you. Rainmakers recognize opportunities to help others, and so do the people they network with most closely.

- *S*avvy about handing off and coaching on a sale. Recognizing an opportunity for someone else is not enough. A primary network contact must be skilled at getting you in, either because he or she has the authority to hire or because he or she has influence with someone who does and is savvy about how to introduce you.

- *S*killed at what they do. Rainmakers know that it doesn't pay to network with hacks. You will have to recommend people you network with to others, and your own reputation is at stake every time you do.

Rainmakers know that secondary networks remain extremely important even after they have established strong primary networks. This is for two reasons. First, the members of a rainmaker's primary network soon get to know each other and develop their own relationships. When that happens, the rainmaker can no longer provide much value by passing on information given to him or her by another. By continuously developing the secondary network, the rainmaker brings back a flow of introductions and information that maintains his or her value to the primary network. To those who study networks this is known as the Theory of Weak Ties.[4]

Further, a lot of opportunities come from secondary networks even though fewer opportunities come from each person than come from the primaries. Many such opportunities won't come if you don't stay in touch. Dennis Hill, an information technology consultant who spent a part of his career as the Chief Information Officer of a large company, once told me that during that period in his career, he learned that the next piece of business a client has is likely to be given to the next consultant to make a visit. The client has a need that he must address quickly and is often less concerned about a formal selection process or remembering a friend than about getting the problem solved now. If you aren't in front of him, you have a good chance of being passed over. Many of the rainmakers in the survey reinforced this point:

- I recently had lunch with a banker, and he referred me to an account that will have recurring revenues in excess of $400,000 a year. I guarantee you that if I hadn't had lunch with him that day, I wouldn't have gotten the referral. He would have given it to the next accountant he had lunch with. This is different from someone you're close to. He wasn't saving it for me as some people would do. You have to stay visible with all of your referral sources. I have lunches with bankers, lawyers, and other referral sources at least three times a week. [Jack Kaye, partner, Deloitte & Touche LLP]

- I just got a piece of business last year from a friend who was a senior accountant for whom I had worked thirty-seven years ago. He knew he could trust me, that I was professional and would take care of his client, and that I was interested in getting the business. We had seen each other only over the years, so he remembered me. [Edward Weinstein, partner, Deloitte & Touche LLP]

- The more exposure you get, the more opportunities you get to touch something. On an airplane back from Singapore, I struck up a conversation with a woman sitting next to me. Her daughter was studying to become an architect, and I offered to have her come work with us to gain experience. A year later, the woman called me to design a building in Manila. We never would have had that opportunity, if I hadn't met her. Being out there meeting people is helpful. [A. Eugene Kohn, Kohn Pedersen Fox Associates PC]

- You never know where business will come from. My last two referrals came from two accountants I had worked with thirty-five years ago at another firm. I had never been referred a piece of business by either of them before, but I kept in touch with them over the years. [Richard A. Eisner, Richard A. Eisner & Company]

"You never know where business will come from" is a phrase I heard over and over again from many rainmakers while conducting the survey. Usually, it was said to reinforce the need to develop and maintain secondary networks.

Attorney Peter Sarasohn aptly described the value of developing both primary and secondary networks at client companies:

> I have a billiard ball metaphor that explains why these relationships with second-tier people are important. Picture the leadership team at a company formed in a tight pyramid with the chairman at the top, like the balls in a game of pool set up for a break shot. At some time over the next five years, a cue ball in the form of a merger or bankruptcy or change at the top or just a falling out is going to strike that group with such velocity that it will break apart. If you have developed relationships with all the people in the pyramid, when the group splits apart, you have the chance of obtaining many new clients as the people move to other companies.

Leonard Gubar, a partner at Reid & Priest, uses a different metaphor for growing a practice this way. He compares it to the growth of trees, with new branches forming as old contacts move to new companies. Turnaround consultant Jay Alix calls the network of contacts he has developed "the daisy chain."[5] All the rainmakers who build strong networks work from one contact, from one relationship to others in this way. One excellent story of how this was done was told by consulting engineer Robin Greenleaf:

> A client with whom we had a really strong relationship was planning a new biotechnology building. The request for proposal was sent to twelve architectural firms. We asked permission to contact all of them and ended up on all twelve teams and built relationships with all of them. This got us many new projects — one for the biotech building with the firm that won and, eventually, others with firms that lost that project but put us on teams for others.

Uncertain Returns

This brings us to another aspect of the complex reality that differs from the Prisoner's Dilemma: the uncertainty of returns. In the game, cooperation always produces value; that is, the other prisoner spends less time in jail than he would have if you had defected. In the complex reality, we often make an effort to help others, but they receive no economic value from our effort and vice versa. We may, for example, introduce a contact to a prospective client with an immediate need for his or her services, yet the client may hire someone else. The effort was made to cooperate, but no benefit was received. More patience is required in the complex reality than in the simple game. In this environment, it is important to get pleasure out of helping others and the exchange of networking because, at times, that is all that sustains you:

> I like people and like to help people. I'm not uncomfortable doing things for people and not having anything come back to me. Though, as a mature businessperson, I recognize that a percent does come back, that's not my motivation. [Bob Gaida, partner, BDO Seidman LLP]

Most of the rainmakers expressed similar sentiments.

The structure of the game builds in other kinds of uncertainty as well. In the game, exchanges are always simultaneous. In the real world, there are always delays, and often long delays, between giving help and receiving help in return. What's more, the opportunity to exchange is always equal in the game. In each round of play, both prisoners have the opportunity to help each other equally by not turning state's evidence. In the real world, the ability to help is seldom evenly balanced. Sometimes there is great imbalance.

These two aspects of reality make it difficult to determine whether someone is really engaged in an exchange, is seeking to return the help you give, or has simply accepted your help without intending to make a return. Rainmakers must make judgments about whether a two-way relationship is developing within the context of uncertain returns. They use several indicators. First, they ask themselves if the contact has asked sufficient questions about them and their services to be able to identify an opportunity when he or she comes across one. Contacts who don't ask this kind of question probably aren't serious.

Second, they ask themselves if the person has shown a sense of obligation or urgency to return help given. Is he or she surfacing a few opportunities for the rainmaker? Even if these opportunities aren't the kind the rainmaker wants, the attempt shows that the contact wants to return the favor. Does he or she call? Much is said about a relationship by the degree of urgency and obligation we show in our efforts to respond to others. This is especially true of relationships with clients. A partner at Akin, Gump, Strauss, Hauer & Feld makes the point with this story:

> I have a client who is a great marketer, and he once told me that I am a great marketer. It interested me that he should say so, and I asked him why. He said, "Because you return phone calls. Even if you are in Paris or Timbuktu, I know you will return my call. Even if I say it isn't important, you return my call." I said, *"That's because you are important, even if the issue isn't."* (Italics added.)

Third, does the person respond to a direct request for help? This is a basic test:

> I go to a client and say, "You must be unhappy with the work I'm doing." They ask me why I would say that, and I say, "You haven't recommended me, and that's the sign that someone is unhappy." They will say, "I didn't realize you wanted me to," and ask what they can do. I ask for ten names and we review them together, and then I suggest we focus on two and we explore the best two further and so get qualified leads. Usually the client introduces me personally, saying, "This is my guru," so I come with a great testimonial. You can do this with anyone you make happy. You should hit them at the time they're happy with what you have done.

Be explicit about the kind of help you want, and make sure that it is something the contact can do:

> I will help a banker or attorney, and they will offer to try to help me at some time in the future. I say that what I'd really like is to have them take me to an event, social or business, where I can meet the kind of people I want to know, and they are usually happy to do it. [Bob Gaida, partner, BDO Seidman LLP]

The unevenness in ability to give creates problems for those who can give far more often than they are likely to receive. This is true of accountants, who know so much about their audit clients' businesses and have such close relationships that they are in a much better position to make referrals than are most other professionals. It has also traditionally been true of architects relative to engineers because architects have traditionally been prime contractors who invite engineers to participate on their teams. Accountants and architects, then, have been in the enviable position of being able to pass work around. The best rainmakers do this without giving the appearance of looking for one-for-one swaps of help.

Other professionals, like actuaries and engineers, have traditionally found it harder to provide leads to others. Often they solve this problem by offering other kinds of help. In Chapter 7, I described how Norman Kurtz, one of the founders of the consulting engineering firm Flack + Kurtz, positioned his firm as innovators by staying abreast of the latest technologies in his field and educating architects about them. Educating architects became a networking tactic:

> The idea was to bring innovative ideas to a profession that was often seen as tired. I would call architects and tell them about technologies that they might not know about and that would help them with their designs. I wanted us to be seen as innovators. When I got a favorable reaction from someone, I pushed it.

These are the things that rainmakers do to build and maintain a network that is the source of most of their leads. Getting professionals to do them is hard. There are several things you can do to help.

Things You Can Do

1. Get them to start early in their careers.

As Norman Kurtz says, "It's not hard if you start early. In your twenties, thirties, and forties, you have to develop a lot of relationships with the people you work with. Some will make it big and some won't, but by the time you are older, some can give you work." At one firm, young professionals are asked to collect four business cards a month. At the end of a year, they will have about fifty, of which five will be useful. In five years, about the time the professionals become managers, they will have twenty-five to thirty contacts and be on the road to building a network.

The Investment Principle described in Chapter 2 shows why consistent investment in the development of a network from as early as possible in one's career is so important. Even a low target of five calls a week to contacts is a good way to build discipline.

2. Review their contacts with them.

Once a year, ask young professionals to bring their list of contacts to you, and discuss each person on the list, one at a time. Make suggestions about whom to keep up with and how to keep up with them. When the contact list gets so long that this becomes difficult to do, you probably don't have to do it any more.

3. Show them how to leverage time.

The most common reason that professionals give for not developing business is lack of time. In Chapter 2, I described the Time Allocation Principle and showed the ways that rainmakers make time for business development by combining it with other activities. Professionals need help figuring out how to leverage their time in this way. Often, they simply need ideas on how to do it until the thought patterns become natural to them. For example, a senior manager is traveling to another city to visit a client. Suggest that she walk the halls for half an hour while she is there, just to touch base with people she knows at the company, but is not scheduled to see on this visit. A junior partner is preparing an internal training seminar. Suggest that he briefly interview five clients by phone to learn what they would like to see the young professionals in the firm learn. Teams are making recruiting trips to campuses. Suggest that they visit briefly with a few professors to see if there might be an opportunity to refer business to the professors and for the professors to refer business to the firm. Someone has a problem on a project. Suggest that she call the client to get an opinion. Suggest that a partner hand-deliver a bill to a client. Suggest that everyone have at least one lunch a week with a client or other business contact. Push them to act.

4. Teach them to look for dissatisfaction.

Whenever someone is dissatisfied, you have an opportunity to help them. Aspiring rainmakers should be coached to listen for dissatisfaction when their clients and other valued contacts speak, and to seek ways to help by providing information, advice, or an introduction.

10

Questioning and Synthesizing Methods

When a professional says, "I sold the XYZ project," it can mean anything from, "I took an order over the phone from an old client," to "I spent the last three years pursuing this contract and finally landed it." In this book, "selling" means what you do when you are talking with a prospective client about a problem that he or she acknowledges having and that you can help solve for a fee. Often these discussions occur face to face, but much selling is also done by phone. Some selling may also be done in carefully constructed letters. This chapter and the two that follow deal with three aspects of selling.

More has been written about selling than any other subject in this book. Much of the literature is oriented toward the sale of products, but several books describe selling methods applicable to the professions.[1] The survey of rainmakers generally supports the approaches in these books, and I have no wish to repeat at length what has been described well elsewhere. Rather, I will cover the basics of selling briefly for the sake of continuity and spend more time on those aspects of the process of particular importance to professionals and to the question of rainmakers.

Today, most professionals realize that selling skills are crucial to the well-being of their firms and to a successful career. But not all. Some professionals do not see themselves as doing much selling because prospective clients are, to a large degree, presold before discussions about a problem begin. Prospective clients often visit a litigator only on referral from another attorney, who has prequalified their need. Such clients seldom shop around. Other professionals count on clients to come to them on the basis of long-standing relationships, rather than on selling skill. But ignoring selling skills is risky, as the experience of one large, old firm that grew explosively after putting in a sophisticated sales system shows. A principal in the firm told me, "We are blowing away the competition, even where there were long-established relationships between clients and our competitors, because our selling approach brings value to the meetings." In an increasingly competitive world, professionals need strong selling skills, if only to protect themselves from aggressive rivals.

There are three approaches to selling. People who employ a *hard sales* approach push a product at customers by stressing its attributes and by using a variety of closing tactics to pressure them to buy. Car salespeople usually use this approach and are despised for it. I doubt any professional has succeeded this way, and it is relevant here only because it has given such bad connotations to the word *selling* that some professionals want to avoid the whole topic.

Most professionals employ some form of *needs-based selling.* Using questions, the seller explores the buyer's situation until the buyer's needs become clear. The seller then shows how his or her services can address those needs. The more sophisticated versions of needs-based selling, such as Rackham's SPIN Selling,[2] also use questions to build the buyer's commitment to taking action before discussing a service. Most rainmakers use the needs-based approach. Probably all of them do so much of the time:

- McKinsey didn't pontificate. He was much more conversational. One of the standard techniques which he outlined to us in staff meetings was that you ask questions, you don't start by giving answers. He often used an illustration about selling textbooks, emphasizing that first you learn what the teacher is concerned with and then explain how your book could help serve that purpose. He said, in the first place you can appear a lot smarter if you ask questions than if you simply give answers, but more than that — if you really try to help the other person — until you understand what the nature of the problem is, you had better not begin to guess how to go about it. He really was a super salesman. . . .[3]

- He was the best salesman I've ever seen in my life. The key was he was a good listener. He would never think of talking, himself, as long as he could keep the prospective client talking. . . . He allowed the person to tell what his problems were and, once need was established, would convince him to let [our firm] help. [a management consultant; the speaker was a former IBM executive and a rainmaker in his own right, and had seen a lot of good salespeople in his time]

- When you meet with someone who is considering hiring your firm, you first have to understand their needs. You have to ask them about the case and the situation underlying it. You also have to ask them about their business approach. Do they want to fight to the end because they think they're right? Do they have a litigation budget that they don't want to exceed? [Merton E. Marks, lawyer, Lewis & Roca]

- He listens well and always understands the business issues of the prospective client and is good at figuring out what is bothering the prospect personally, too. He doesn't talk that much, but hears what is being said and has an appropriate, helpful response. [Bob Hillier, architect, The Hillier Group]

- You have to listen carefully to what people say. One client gave me the business because I hit every point he had mentioned in my proposal. He said the others had hit most of them, but that I was the only one who hit every one. You have to listen well. [Ralph Anderson Jr., accountant, Richard A. Eisner & Company]

- He has the ability to sum up. He has an uncanny knack to bring all the pieces back together to the original purpose in an eloquent way. [Marvin Mass, engineer, Cosentini Associates]

The needs-based approach is appropriate in many situations. It is low key, because the professional makes no effort to make a sale unless the client states a need, and effective, because it allows the professional and the client to develop a clear understanding of the need before talking about solutions. It is the best approach when a prospective client comes to you with a problem or when you meet with a client informally, say, over lunch, without a specific agenda other than to catch up.

The less talking a professional does in such situations the better. When selling to a group, there may not even be much need to ask questions, as this description of a technique used by a management consultant shows:

> [A big metalworking company] had a lot of productivity issues and asked us to come in. [The rainmaker] was unimpressive during this kind of meeting, but took meticulous notes. But at the end of the meeting, he was always the one who could summarize key points. At this particular meeting, the executives rambled on for forty-five minutes in front of the chairman, and [the rainmaker] hardly said anything. At the end, he read back the issues and a package, one, two, three, four, five. It became pretty clear what was needed and who would do it.[4]

No one is born with needs-based selling skill. Though some of the rainmakers in the survey developed this skill early in their lives, before they became professionals, many did not. Their technical training and early work experience did not prepare them for the need to sell. Alberto Galgano, the founder of an Italian management consulting firm, described how painful learning on the job can be:

> How I started to bring in business is a sad story. I received no training in business development at the technical university in Milan that I attended. Nor did I learn much about it during my early years, working as a manager in private corporations. This made bringing in business very hard for the first five or six years that I had my firm. We made many mistakes, which we overcame with enthusiasm and a will to succeed. At first, I talked too much and had to learn that I needed to spend more time listening. I learned that first you have to get the client to speak. You have to learn about his needs, first. Second, you must understand the language he uses when he talks about his problems and use that same language when you talk about your services. Then you can help him understand that you can help him solve his problem. We have spent years perfecting the approach we use now.

The current success of Galgano and his firm shows how well he has learned. Having had to learn the hard way himself, he now advocates training in selling skills.

As powerful as needs-based selling is, it isn't appropriate in all situations, and some professionals have worn out their welcome with prospective clients by misapplying it. It often won't work well when a professional requests a meeting with a busy executive and then uses the meeting to fish for opportunities. If the client doesn't have a problem that the professional can deal with now, there can be two bad outcomes. First, the client may feel that his time has been wasted: Yes, you, the professional, got value from the time spent — information on my company and a chance to fish. But what about me, the client? If you take my time, don't I have a right to expect a reasonable return on it? This kind of thinking is particularly true of senior executives at large corporations, who view their own time as a precious resource.

Second, a professional who works in an area that involves human suffering, and uses needs-based selling in a meeting he or she has requested, risks appearing ghoulish. That's the way you might feel about a heart surgeon, if he visited you at his own request and asked a lot of questions about your health. No respectable professional wants to give the appearance of reveling in other people's discomfort or, worse, of encouraging it to get business, as did a California divorce lawyer who reportedly hired models to flirt with men at bars and then hand out his card.[5]

Value-based selling will work in some situations where needs-based selling won't. When using this approach, a professional brings an idea or information of value to a prospective client and then structures a discussion around it. The professional does *not* give a presentation; rather, after a brief introduction of the subject's possible importance to the client, the professional uses a structured format to draw out the client's own thinking and concerns, adding value both by the structure of his or her questioning and by occasional commentary. Value-based selling is much like needs-based selling, but requires a carefully planned introduction, a format, and focused questioning that educates a client on a specific subject while giving the professional a chance to explore for needs.

Many rainmakers have used this approach:

- He would bump into an idea and then work it with his clients. Once he read an article on breakeven analysis and decided he would do one for each one of his firm's top fifty clients. He did and then visited them to talk about the implications of what he had found. He used to talk about how much business he got from this. He was great at selling [new services] to an existing client. [an accountant]

Value-based selling depends upon having a provocative issue to discuss, and so links closely to the thought-leadership process described in Chapter 7. The results of surveys, benchmarking studies, forecasts, and other research, as well as good ideas, form the basis for a meeting:

- He always has something to say when he goes to meet people. These ideas come from his business vision. Ten years ago, for example, he was talking to all the banking clients about turning trust accounts into mutual fund accounts. That is old news now, but he was way ahead of the curve then. Most of them didn't know anything about it. We were well ahead of everyone on this. [an accountant]

Seminars can be seen as a modified version of value-based selling. Firms that run them do so in the hope of engaging in a sales discussion with participants.

After a meeting, many rainmakers will follow up with a letter that gives a brief description of the problem and summarizes what the participants agreed to do. Roland Berger, president of Roland Berger & Partner GmbH, says, "I always confirm a meeting and follow up on a meeting with a letter. The letter will refer to the points we discussed or ones we might discuss next time. But I always send a letter."

Clients are busy and preoccupied. The letter a professional writes following a meeting helps clients recall what occurred and what was agreed to. This makes it easier for clients to explain what took place to others and reminds them of any actions they said they would take. In short, it helps clients do their jobs better. It also provides the professional with a chance to get his or her name in front of the client again, to show his or her understanding of the problem in question, and to look practical and professional. It increases the chance that the client will take the next step toward solving his or her problem, which, quite probably, increases the professional's chances of getting hired. Every professional should write such letters.

Gathering information on a client's needs in sales meetings is critical to winning. Sometimes the sale is made at the same time. But for many professionals, sales are increasingly won or lost in a beauty contest in which final contenders for the engagement make formal presentations to the client. This subject is covered in more detail in Appendix D.

Things You Can Do

1. Train your professionals in sales techniques.

The questioning, listening, and presenting skills required to sell can be learned. Excellent books and programs are available that have been used successfully by others. To protest, as the senior members of some firms do, that these abilities can't be taught shows about as much awareness of the world we must compete in as a belief in the flat earth theory shows about a person's awareness of geography. You greatly hamper your firm's ability to compete by ignoring these tools. When selecting a trainer, be sure to select one with experience in the professions.

2. *Give your professionals an opportunity to practice.*

Training doesn't work if it isn't reinforced on the job. To train people and then not give them the chance to practice what they have learned is a waste of time and money. If you expect professionals to sell only when they bring in a lead themselves, you must give them training in how to bring in leads and an opportunity to do so, or sales training will be wasted.

3. *If you expect your aspiring rainmakers to initiate sales meetings with clients, as opposed to reacting to clients' requests for meetings, help them prepare discussion frameworks suitable for value-based selling or prepare those frameworks for them.*

Unlike needs-based selling, little has been written about value-based selling. Providing such tools and education for their use is a legitimate task for a centralized marketing function and one way to leverage centralized resources over a large number of people. As one actuary said to me, "I need packaged ideas that I can deliver to my clients. Just give me the ideas, and I will get them out."

These frameworks need not be complicated or long. They are not presentations. Instead, they should be structured in a way that helps the professionals draw information from a client with questions.

11

Anecdotal Selling

"**I**'ve had some bad experiences with architects. How can I be sure you're going to bring this project in on budget?" asked the prospective client. Everyone in the room knew that the engagement hung on the answer to this question. I looked at Bob Hillier, the founder of the firm and one of the best rainmakers I know. He responded with the following story:

> When I had only been in business a short time, I won a project to help renovate a classroom building at a local university. Our design substantially exceeded the client's budget, but I thought it was so beautiful that I could talk them into spending the money. When I met with the facilities manager, he looked at my design and immediately asked what it would cost. I told him, and he handed me back my drawings and told me the engagement was over. I said I would redo the work to fit his budget, but he said no, he couldn't work with someone who didn't listen to him. I've never forgotten that lesson.

With that story, so much more effective than promises or statistics, he won the engagement.

The degree to which stories are used to make points is one of the distinguishing characteristics of selling professional services. It is noted in early literature on the subject. In a article entitled "How to Buy/Sell Professional Services," Warren J. Wittreich stated that "of all the extrinsic considerations, the persuasion by success story makes the most sense."[1] He is right, though the stories aren't always about successes as we have just seen.

Why Professionals Use Anecdotes

Most professionals tell stories to persuade clients to hire them, but not all do it well. To develop rainmakers, firm management will want to make sure that their professionals learn anecdotal selling skills by making it clear why anecdotes are so critical to making a sale and how they are constructed. After that, practice will build fluency.

Anecdotes help persuade in many ways. Most critically, they help make a highly conceptual service seem tangible. Professional services cannot be seen or touched or tested prior to purchase the way a product can. They don't have specifications that can be measured. Usually, they are one-of-a-kind purchases because no two client situations are exactly alike, and services need to be adapted to each client's situation. Once a client buys a professional service, the cost of changing vendors is high, often prohibitively so in midengagement. In these circumstances the professional must help the client visualize the benefits he or she will receive. Anecdotes are the best way to do it.

Look at how this story, told by Phil Michel, a consultant who helps relocate data centers, makes tangible the value of experience to a prospective client considering doing the work in-house:

> We work for a lot of large companies that have a lot of smart people. What we bring is experience in data center consolidation. Most people get involved in these issues only once every ten years or so, but we do every day.
>
> For example, we recently completed a consolidation analysis for a large insurance company. Management planned to consolidate the small data center run by its non-insurance subsidiary into its main center. The analysis showed a three-year payback.
>
> The head of the subsidiary brought us in to evaluate the consolidation because the data provided by the center was so critical to his operations. We went through a step-by-step review of what it would cost to consolidate and run the center. Because of our experience, we were aware of many costs that hadn't been taken into account in the original analysis and showed that the consolidation would cost four times the original estimate and had an actual payback of over six years. The consolidation was scrapped. We weren't any

> smarter than the people who did the original analyses; we
> just had more experience.

This story is more convincing than a simple listing of the many data center consolidations the firm has worked on. It is probably more convincing than statistics comparing consolidation success rates of the consultant against firms doing the work alone, were such data available. The persuasiveness of stories has actually been documented by researchers. Stories do tend to be more believable than statistics, even among quantitatively trained individuals.[2] Even though educated people have been warned against the limitations of anecdotal evidence, most find it seductively convincing.

Anecdotes are particularly powerful for demonstrating the value of process benefits, those benefits that derive from the way the professional does his or her work, as opposed to being an outcome of the work. They include developing consensus or commitment to action, building awareness of a problem, prioritization of efforts, and the like. Here is an anecdote told by Bob Grasing, a partner at Robert E. Nolan Company, a consulting firm specializing in performance improvement for financial institutions:

> We often have to work in organizations where the inter-
> personal dynamics are a major issue in getting the work
> done. Helping people build working relationships is a part
> of our job.
>
> I recently called on a big property and casualty com-
> pany we are working for that had this problem, and the vice
> president who had engaged us said that he can only judge
> by what he sees and what he sees is people eating lunch
> together who never did before, because they had always
> been adversaries. He commented that that will be the long-
> lasting benefit of our work.

Anecdotes can be used to confirm your understanding of the client's situation and can do so in a way more powerful than simply parroting back what the client has just told you because it shows you have dealt with similar issues before.

Anecdotes are also used as indirect probes when a direct question might prove offensive or risky. Here is a story an office operations consultant uses to test whether a client needs to document its processes more carefully. It makes admitting such a need easier because it shows that even large, sophisticated companies have this problem:

Most companies have informal systems that employees have developed by themselves over the years that may not be in the company's best interests. Not long ago, we were helping the vice president for administrative services at a *Fortune* 500 corporation reengineer invoice payment processes, because the company was suffering from a slow payments problem. The first meeting was interrupted by a distraught administrator who announced that Xerox had just called to say that it would pull all of its 350 copiers from the 5,000-person headquarters at the end of the month if its bill wasn't paid. With less than two weeks to the end of the month, this required immediate attention.

We went with the vice president to the accounts payable clerk and asked her how she paid her bills. "I have twenty-six piles organized by vendor name, A through Z, that I stack bills in as they arrive," she said. "On the first of the month I pay the A bills. . . ."

Anecdotes can even be a polite way of telling a client that you think he or she is wrong. In this form, they can be used to help you redefine an engagement's scope. I once competed with a low-cost competitor for an engagement to find a new location for a plant that made small machine tools. The president of the company needed to lower his labor costs to meet foreign competition and felt that relocating was the way to do it. Rather than compete on price, I decided to suggest that he broaden the engagement to determine which of three possible approaches or combination of approaches — relocating, redesigning his product, or redesigning his manufacturing process — would allow him to reduce his price sufficiently to compete. I introduced this approach with the following story:

Are you sure that moving this plant will get your costs down far enough to underprice your competition? A couple of years ago, Plumbing Fixtures Corporation [name changed] built a $60 million plant in Louisiana to cut its costs so that it could meet price competition from Brazilian competitors. They cut their costs and prices 20 percent, and the Brazilians responded by cutting theirs by 30 percent. The price umbrella that Plumbing Fixtures had created was so large that the Brazilians could cut their prices that much and still make a profit. Plumbing Fixtures went out of business.

This story changed his thinking about the fundamental nature of his problem and led to a sale. The project I sold the client solved the problem he really faced rather than the one he had imagined he faced.

Anecdotes can perform another service that is difficult to accomplish in other ways; they show you have the characteristics of the kind of person the prospective client wants to work with. Because you are what the client is buying, it is important for him to know that you are smart, insightful, trustworthy, experienced, practical, tactful, and many other things that it would be immodest for you to claim directly. When you are sitting face to face with a client, anecdotes are one of the few ways to demonstrate these qualities. So, for example, professionals are sometimes hired because they can stand up to the boss when no one else dares to. Here is a story that one consultant tells when he suspects that this may be the reason a prospective client is considering hiring him:

> Sometimes we get brought in to do things that it would simply be impossible for someone inside to do. For example, we were hired by the president of a large Western utility to help him cut costs, though it turned out that wasn't the real reason we were needed. The real problem was that things just didn't happen in this company even when they had been agreed to. We would get a group together, develop a consensus on actions, and assign responsibilities, but nothing would happen. It didn't take long to realize that the problem was the seventy-eight-year-old chairman. Though he was semiretired, everyone was afraid to act, expecting him to step in, give them hell, and reverse the decision. I had to meet with him and tell him he was screwing things up and to back off. After that we could get things to happen.

The anecdote with which I began this chapter exemplifies a special kind of these self-revelation stories. It is called the sadder-but-wiser anecdote and can be extremely powerful. It usually starts out with words like "early in my career" and ends with a sentence like "ever since then. . . ." The power of this kind of story lies in the common belief that lessons learned the hard way are learned best. They also help build chemistry by showing the professional is willing to reveal his or her own past mistakes. Here is one I heard attorney Peter Sarasohn tell to an accountant he was hoping to get referrals from:

> When I was a young lawyer, I was trying a case in front of a judge with a reputation for being hard-nosed. I found myself getting so wrapped up in my client's case at one point that I stopped and apologized. The judge got mad at me right there in front of my client. "How dare you apologize," he said. "If you don't feel emotional about your client's case, why should I?" Ever since then I have never felt embarrassed about being emotionally committed to my clients' cases.

This story is far more persuasive than a statement like, "I will really fight for any client you refer to me."

Anecdotes can also help you build chemistry with a client because they are entertaining and more memorable than statistics. They may even be funny, and a prospective client who laughs is half sold. You don't have to be a raconteur to tell an amusing anecdote; you just have to have an eye for the quirky experiences of life. Here is an anecdote told often by a former colleague in the location consulting field:

> When we evaluate a town for a client, we talk to all the major employers to learn about their pay scales, labor relations, and recruiting experiences. You hear some pretty odd things. At one tired, old apparel company in a small town in East Tennessee, I was collecting this information from the president and the personnel officer. "How many holidays do you give?" I asked. "Six," responded the president. "No, no, B. J. It's seven," interjected the personnel officer. "Don't you remember? You gave them your birthday last year."

This story almost always got a chuckle and made working with us look like fun.

For a firm to benefit from the power of anecdotes, it needs two things. First, it needs professionals skilled at using them. Many aren't. Second, it needs a base of institutional lore so that its professionals have access to good anecdotes to meet a variety of client concerns. Most professionals learn this lore at the knee of the gray-haired rainmakers they see in action. This informal approach works well in many firms, but not in all. I will deal with each of these issues in turn.

What Makes a Good Anecdote?

To tell a good anecdote, a professional must first make it relevant to the prospective client. In the words of Warren Wittreich, "the most crucial thing that should be accomplished is to provide the buyer with some basis for identifying himself with the situation being described, i.e., provide him with a point of contact with what is being talked about and what he has in mind."[3]

Often this requires making a brief positioning statement before you tell the anecdote. "Developing a consensus is clearly half the battle in cases like this." "I can see that deadline weighs heavily on you; most work of this type is deadline sensitive." Statements like these let the listeners know that the story you are about to tell will be linked to a specific concern they have raised.

Then you must select an anecdote about an organization or person with whom the listener will feel some affinity. At its simplest level, this means that bankers like stories about banks. They are unlikely to be impressed by a story about a professional's successful efforts to help a state government's employment agency solve a collections problem.

Once you select an anecdote, you must describe the organizations and people in it in a way that emphasizes their similarity to the listeners and their organization. So, when telling a story to a banker in Chicago about a much smaller bank you have worked for in Cleveland, it becomes "another midwestern bank." A bank of similar size to the listener's but located in California becomes "another middle-market bank." An insurance company becomes "another financial institution." A Chicago-based oil company becomes "another major issuer of credit cards located here in Chicago." This kind of description comes naturally to old hands, but not to younger professionals learning how to sell.

The anecdote must have the four basic components of a good story: plot, character, action, and outcome.[4] Plot is built around the fundamental threat or opportunity that the character in the story faces. This might be dealing with a competitor who is rapidly taking market share, or an opportunity to use a new building to improve the communications among company researchers who will then develop better products, or any other issue that a client faces. It is imperative that there be only one plot per anecdote, even if the engagement being described had several and even if each of them has a valuable message for the client. Anecdotes are so brief that they cannot sustain multiple plots the way a novel can. More than one plot will result in a long, rambling, and confusing story that will not help you. This is a common problem among professionals inexperienced at telling good stories. You can always tell a second anecdote later using the same engagement as a base to make a different point. But each anecdote must have only one plot.

You need a character in the story to give the prospective client someone to identify with. A character also makes the story more interesting — people being more interesting than abstract concepts like a corporation. Perhaps the single most common weakness of anecdotes is the absence of a character. Action also increases interest by creating images that the listener can visualize. Note, for example, how the description of the facilities manager handing back the architect's drawings in the anecdote with which this chapter began creates a strong and memorable image. It helps you feel the architect's embarrassment.

A good story must have a clear outcome. Too often the teller leaves this for the listener to infer, a dangerous mistake. The listener may draw the wrong conclusion or simply end up confused. So, for example, the first anecdote in this chapter ends with the crucial outcome, "I have never forgotten that lesson," without which the teller might simply sound as if he were complaining. The only time that an outcome is not needed is when you are using an anecdote simply to confirm your understanding of a client's situation. The outcome in such cases can be expressly stated as "I understand what you have told me," words that are sometimes best left unsaid.

Finally, a good anecdote must be brief. If it gets too long, it ceases to be an anecdote. Most can be told in five or six sentences, excluding positioning statements. Longer anecdotes quickly become confusing and dull.

Exhibit 11.1 presents an anecdote told to me by a lawyer. Major components are described beneath the anecdote. In reviewing this exhibit and the other examples of anecdotes shown here, please be cautioned that they create a false impression of unvarying form — that there is only one correct version of an anecdote. This is what happens when oral traditions are described in writing.[5] In reality, an anecdote is seldom told twice with exactly the same words. Rather, it is modified to increase its relevance to a particular listener. It is lengthened or shortened depending upon the listener's level of interest. It is altered to make a slightly different point. It is only with practice that a professional builds the fluency with an anecdote needed to change it to meet the needs of different situations.

Exhibit 11.1
The Structure of an Anecdote

Here is an anecdote told by an attorney seeking to caution clients that they may not have the best approach for turning over their estate to their children. It tactfully shows that they may be wrong, educates them, and shows the value of the lawyer's experience, and so helps make the sale.

Anecdote

Not long ago I had a meeting similar to several others I've had in the past. An elderly couple had put their life into their business, and the children had come to work there. When the couple wanted to retire, they wanted to sell it to the children. All the parents wanted was money for their retirement. The business was valued and stock issued, and the parents were given a share of the stock, which provided the income they needed for their retirement. They moved to Boca Raton, enjoyed their retirement, and grew older. Then the business took a hard turn, and the children ended up having to close and liquidate it. There was nothing left for the parents because they hadn't protected themselves against this eventuality. It didn't help that the closure wasn't really the children's fault.

Components

- *Plot:* An elderly couple needs to transfer their business in a way that gives them funds for retirement and provides their children employment.
- *Character:* An elderly couple that the listener, also an elderly person, can identify with.
- *Action:* Moving to Florida. Liquidating the business.
- *Outcome:* The elderly couple left without money.

Structure

Note that the story is short, just eight sentences excluding the positioning sentence at the beginning. It makes one point and avoids tangents into such subjects as the tax reasons for transferring the business in the way it was done.

Building Institutional Lore

Most firms have anecdotes that form an institutional lore that their professionals can draw on when selling. As noted, younger members of the firm learn this lore from the older ones simply by being with them during sales meetings. To this lore, they add anecdotes from their own engagements, some of which eventually make their way into the firm lore.

This approach by itself will not work in very large firms, where a professional is likely to learn only a small fraction of the lore that might be useful. It also does not work in new organizations that have not had time to develop a common lore. Organizations facing this problem include consulting arms established by companies that have not traditionally been in the consulting business. In such cases, a more aggressive approach is needed to develop and institutionalize good anecdotes.

Because anecdotes cannot be cast in a permanent form, but must be adapted to the needs of a specific situation, you must present the basic information about engagements in a way that makes extracting an anecdote easy. One format for doing this is shown in Exhibit 11.2.

Exhibit 11.2

Sample Project Description

Project descriptions must be constructed in such a way that your professionals can extract anecdotes from them, complete with plot, character, action, and outcome.

Project #301
(Discount Stores Corporation)

Client:	An off-price women's apparel retailer with more than 300 stores in the Midwest and Great Plains with sales in excess of $1.5 billion.
Issue:	Operating in independent fiefdoms, line managers viewed IS personnel as peripheral to their concerns. IS personnel were not involved early in the planning process, were treated like order takers, and were not given support once a project had begun. The CIO

wanted an IS strategy to integrate IS into the mainstream of corporate planning.

Needs: *Awareness Building:* Merchandising and other functions needed to see IS as crucial to their concerns.

Information Access: Management needed information faster to improve buying and other decisions.

Speed: Lack of support was creating unacceptable delays in application development.

Project Outline: XYZ Consulting was hired to develop an IS strategy to increase the company's return on its IS investment. After basic information on needs, competitors' strategies, and available technology had been collected, focused committees of managers worked with XYZ consultants to prioritize goals and tasks. The process was designed to build commitment to the final strategy.

Results: The IS strategy has been accepted by senior management and is currently being implemented with XYZ's help. All projects have been assigned both IS managers and business sponsors. Applications development is proceeding on schedule for the first time in years. Point-of-sale reports are now being delivered three weeks faster than previously. The use of contract applications developers has been reduced by 20 percent.

Things You Can Do

1. Teach young professionals the institutional lore of your firm.

Young professionals need to learn the anecdotes about past engagements that they will use when they are selling. They will learn best by accompanying senior partners on sales calls. Informal firm gatherings are another good place to learn. When another member of the firm tells a good anecdote, point it out to young professionals and ask this person to repeat it.

2. *Have your professionals record the major aspects of engagements in formal project descriptions.*

Establish a standard format, like the one shown in Exhibit 11.2, and insist that it be filled out. Many large firms require that this be done as a part of every project close-out. Someone with strong marketing instincts needs to review these documents from time to time to make sure that the major points are captured. Review the database you create this way with aspiring rainmakers, showing how these descriptions can be converted into anecdotes. The database will, of course, also serve as a source of project descriptions to send with letters and proposals to demonstrate the firm's experience.

12

Finessing a Sale

Marvin Bower, the man who built McKinsey & Company after the death of James O. McKinsey, and a man who has left a lasting mark on the consulting profession, once said, "There is no such thing as business ethics. There's only one kind — you have to adhere to the highest standards."[1] This admirable sentiment is not much help in practice where we must make many small decisions about ethics every day and must decide, often instantaneously, what meets the highest standards and what doesn't. Nowhere in business is this more true than in client development work, where we make many claims and commitments subject to ethical interpretations.

Take, for example, this description of the way Mr. Bower's mentor often handled a meeting with a prospective client:

> McKinsey told us that he often attended a meeting of the executive committee or the board of directors, and that his general tactic was to keep his mouth shut and listen to what went on. He found that usually everybody there had problems and wanted a chance to tell about them and how bad they were, and maybe get some sympathy and help.
>
> And so when the sales manager was telling about his problems, nobody else was really listening much. The next man was getting his story ready mentally, and the finance man, when his turn came, also talked about his problems. When the meeting looked like it was about to close, McKinsey would speak up and say, "Gentlemen, it seems to me we have been talking about seven problems this

afternoon. Now, problem number one is . . . , and problem number two . . . ," and he would name the seven problems. . . . He said he didn't restrict himself to the problems they had mentioned. It was easy to add any he wanted to because nobody would remember what anybody had said. . . .[2]

Clearly, there is a small but deliberate deception here, yet one that, I believe, most people would find unobjectionable. Why does this deception "adhere to the highest standards" (assuming for the moment that it does), when others clearly don't?

Because of the implied trust in the professional–client relationship, the thought of deceiving a client is particularly abhorrent. Most professionals believe that they are honest and serve their clients' best interests. Yet many do deceive their clients before they are hired. Clients know this, but hire the professionals anyway. This may sound cynical, but it is not meant to be. The practice derives as much from the nature of human communications as it does from a desire to win engagements. If we are to train professionals to develop new clients, it is best to address this issue head on.

Professionals learn to stretch the truth early. When new to their firms, they are encouraged not to volunteer that fact to prospective clients. They are told to answer evasively when asked, "How long have you been with the firm?" I remember one seasoned professional advising a newly hired consultant, "Say that this is your first year."

Later they learn to cite former clients by the well-known parent company's name, regardless of how obscure the division was that they actually worked for. They learn to list big-name clients for whom they completed a one-day consultation alongside those for whom they worked for over a year as if there were no distinction between them. Sitting in a client's office in Detroit, they state boldly, "We completed a reengineering project for the XYZ Company," though the work was done by the firm's Singapore office years ago, before the term *reengineering* had been invented.

A young professional who questions such claims will usually be told that it is not really lying and that it is common practice. The tone with which this message is delivered shows the speaker's discomfort with the subject and often communicates that further questioning of the issue might be career limiting. Professionals soon come to believe that if they don't stretch the facts, they will be at a disadvantage against competitors that almost certainly do. And those who avoid distortion by meticulously explaining possible misunderstandings of the facts they present about their credentials probably do lose sales. Their careers suffer.

Deception through the careful use and abuse of facts is the art of finessing, and it is here to stay. Much practiced, it is little talked about. Because it is so little talked about, many questions about how it is accomplished, its ethicality, and its practicality go unanswered for those who are learning to sell. For me, these questions are:

- How is it done so that, to the degree that it is ethical, I can teach it to professionals who want to become effective client developers, and, to the degree that it is unethical, teach them to avoid it?

- On what basis can we make ethical and practical decisions about when to finesse and when not to?

- What are the alternatives to finessing, and how well will they work?

I will attempt to answer these questions.

Types of Finesse

There are several common types of finesse.

The Rubber Ruler: Professionals often choose that reference point or measure that will make them look best, even if by some other reference point or measure they would look less attractive. The professional who has been on the job for two months and says, "This is my first year," makes herself look good by choosing years as her unit of measurement instead of months, weeks, or days. Similarly, the head of a firm who tells a prospect from a bank that "Twenty percent of our business over the past year came from banks" is employing the same technique if 20 percent of the firm's engagements came from banks but only 5 percent of the revenues.

The Lowest Common Denominator: In this case, the professional uses general facts instead of specific ones because they make him look better. So, for example, a professional selling to a manufacturer of high-precision aircraft parts may refer to a previous client as "another metalworking company" instead of stating explicitly that the company made common household screws. "Another metalworking company" suggests a common denominator between the prospect and the past client, whereas "a wood screw manufacturer" makes the difference clear.

The Withheld Fact: A professional will sometimes withhold some facts while stating others because doing so makes her look better. "Have you ever done any work in our industry?" a prospect asks, and the accountant responds that two years ago she helped the XYZ Company design a new credit approval system for its sales force. She chooses not to burden the prospect with the fact that the system was never implemented.

I have seen a version of this finesse that is common in the architectural and engineering industries where employment levels fluctuate greatly depending upon work in house. A consulting engineer giving a prospective client an office tour showed us down a corridor where, by peeking over dividers, we could see engineers busily at work on CAD machines. Halfway down the hall, the engineer waved a hand in the direction we had been going, and said, "From here on out the workstations are very much the same." He led us back to his office to discuss the client's project, neglecting to say that the workstations we had not seen were all unoccupied and leaving the impression that the firm was bigger and busier than it really was.

The Two-Faced Fact: A professional can use words that have two meanings, on the chance that the prospect will take the one that is most favorable even though it is not true. He can state, for example, that "in two of three projects of this type, our clients were able to reduce their costs more than 50 percent." He wants the client to believe that such savings have accrued in two-thirds of the many projects the firm has done, when actually the firm has done only three.

This is a very common kind of finesse when presenting credentials. In a recent *Fortune* article, an ex-consultant criticized the industry for this kind of deception:

> When consultants are pitching business, the "we" in "We promise to make you well" is always an interesting thing. Just because "we" have fixed a company like yours in the past doesn't mean "I," the guy who's pitching your business, was actually a part of it. Six of the people who did that kind of work before may be dead, and the other three have probably left the firm. My old firm is selling my experience even though I am not there, and they are selling it over and over again![3]

The Artificial Link: Sometimes by carefully juxtaposing two unlinked statements a false impression is created. The professional may describe one of her past engagements for the XYZ Company and follow it up immediately with a brief description of another project for ABC Company that her firm didn't work on. She makes no claim that she worked on the second project because she didn't, but the client is likely to infer that she did because of the close sequencing of the descriptions. An example of such a finesse is provided in Exhibit 12.1 on page 181.

The Lie: Sometimes outright lies are employed. A professional may say his firm has more employees than it actually has to make it look more substantial. Another professional, pressed to cut her fee, does so, saying that she has reduced the engagement's scope to arrive at the lower number. In fact, the service she intends to give is almost identical to that offered at the higher fee. She has lied because she does not want to appear to have overpriced the project on the first quote nor to seem so desperate for the work that she will take a lower margin to get it.

Michael Kelly describes how a lawyer who wanted to broaden his practice beyond his civil rights specialty used this finesse:

> The civil rights lawyer is typecast, even by other lawyers who might refer business. It is like the movie star who has made her name in TV sitcoms who tries to get dramatic roles. It is a struggle telling people you are available. Nowadays when Staughton is asked what he is doing, he tends to respond by saying what he would *like* to be doing: "I've started trying malpractice cases."[4] [italics in original]

What Is Right?

All professionals have employed at least some of these techniques during their careers. Most will raise an eyebrow at specific examples, feeling that they go beyond what is ethical. But what is right? Where does one draw the line? These are not easy questions to answer. The most thoughtful work on the ethics of misrepresentation defines lying as "any intentionally deceptive message which is stated,"[5] a definition that would cover most finessing. Yet even the most adamant anti-finesser must choose what facts to present to a prospect. That choice will create distortions no matter how careful the professional is. Few would deny that a person has the right to present himself in the best fair light. But what is fair?

The answer depends, in part, on the model one chooses for business. In a landmark article on the subject, Albert Carr compared business to a poker game in which bluffing is expected and considered ethical within broad limits.[6] He makes a strong case for this view. Although clients may complain about professionals' posturing, few are above it themselves, either with their own customers or with professionals. A consumer products company that in its ads portrays every user as young or glamorous distorts deliberately, to cite but one mild example. Another classic work, *How to Lie with Statistics,* describes methods that we all recognize that companies use to distort information.[7] In most cases, they do not consider themselves, nor are they considered by the public, to be unethical for such behavior.

Clients deal much the same way with their professionals when it is to their benefit to do so. Most, for example, would not hesitate to tell professionals that they should eliminate the markup they charge on expenses because the firms they are competing with bill expenses at cost, while withholding the fact that the professional fees that these competitors are seeking are much higher. Few would consider such a ploy unethical.

Anyone who plays poker and holds himself to ethical standards more constraining than those of others at the table will lose money. Similarly, if your clients and competitors all engage in finessing and you don't, you will be at a serious disadvantage. By this analogy, finessing is not only ethical, but necessary.

Still, the poker analogy implies that there are ethical standards, unlike, say, an ultimate fighting match analogy. For example, in poker it is considered unethical to collude with another player against a third. But what are the limits when trying to persuade a client to hire you?

Deciding When to Finesse

Here, there is no clear guidance. In a complex business world with many shades of gray between truth and falsehood, and between ethical and unethical behavior, few rules are so clear that they can replace good judgment. It may even be that the rules of ethical behavior vary with those of the industry that you sell to. Yet by claiming to be part of a profession, we imply that in some ways we meet standards higher than those of other businesses. What are they? I will not attempt to lay out rules for others but can cite some questions that have helped me arrive at a position I can accept.

Does it pass the stink test? I have borrowed this question from Laura L. Nash, a specialist in business ethics. Independently and earlier than I did, she suggested using a list of questions to help resolve questions of business ethics.[8] When I discovered her list after creating my own, I realized that this question was missing from mine and feel it is important to include it explicitly. If you feel that a finesse is wrong, don't use it. The deception used by McKinsey, described at the beginning of this chapter, passes this test, at least for me. Its principal value is in avoiding an explanation, which could be perceived as self-aggrandizing, that the clients have missed several key aspects of their problem. It does not mislead the clients about the credentials or capabilities of the consultant.

If the client sees through the finesse, will he feel that he has been treated unethically? I must first make clear that I am not asking this as a practical question — I will deal with the practical aspects of finessing later — but as an ethical one because I am trying to determine the rules by which the client is playing. If he would not feel that he had been treated unethically, I have surmounted one ethical hurdle.

So, for example, most clients would probably feel that a junior professional had treated them ethically if she said, "This is my first year" when she had been with the firm for two months. Clients have all had to write resumes and know how credential stretching is done. They know their question about tenure to a junior person is potentially embarrassing and will not be surprised by a less than precise reply. If, on the other hand, a client were to privately ask the engagement leader about the tenure of a junior professional, he might well expect a more direct answer and feel abused were the engagement leader to equivocate. Here the personal embarrassment to the professional is removed.

The approach used by McKinsey, described at the beginning of this chapter, seems ethical to me because it so clearly passes this test.

Of course, you cannot know for certain what a prospective client's ethical standards are, but by asking yourself how he or she would feel about a particular finesse, you force yourself to make judgments that should not be ignored. This is particularly true for professionals who work with diverse organizations; for example, the standards of a stock brokerage firm may differ from those of a charity. This is not to say that a professional should adopt the prospective client's definition of ethical behavior, no matter what it is. Rather, it means that if you can meet his ethical standards, you then only have to worry about your own.

Would other parties described in your claim disagree with it? This question most often applies when you discuss a past project. A description that a past client would accept as a fair representation passes a crucial test. So a claim that "after our engagement, their profits went up 30 percent" implies a causal relationship that almost certainly oversimplifies reality. If the client would acknowledge that your work contributed strongly to the profit turnaround, it seems a fair statement.

The description of McKinsey's finesse meets this test, too. Though the people who he was supposedly summarizing were present, no one argued that he was giving an unfair representation of what he had heard. This was so even though he added things that hadn't been said.

What issue is under discussion? Ethically, far more freedom to bluff exists when negotiating the terms of an engagement than in any other area. Here the poker analogy most obviously holds. Here the client is most likely to finesse you and most likely to expect to be finessed. Bluffing on why a fee is as high as it is, or why you have lowered it, or why the work will take as long as you say it will are indistinguishable from the bluffing that goes on in business-to-business transactions of all types.

An example of finessing in this context is provided by Charles Luckman, who sat on both sides of the table in the purchase of professional services during a long and distinguished career. For example, as a head of Lever Brothers' U.S. subsidiary, he hired Louis Skidmore and Nathaniel Owings to design the company's New York headquarters. Later, as the founder of what became one of the nation's largest architectural firms, he sold major master planning and design projects. He reports using *The Two-Faced Fact* without any embarrassment when describing the sale of a master planning project for what later became Edwards Air Force Base:

> "Mr. Luckman, what would be the fee for this master planning assignment?" the senior colonel asked. I looked at [my partner] and he looked blankly back at me. Neither of us had ever heard of ARDC (Air Research and Development Command, the client organization and the forerunner of NASA); we knew nothing about jet aircraft, nor had we ever done any master planning.
>
> While I didn't have the slightest idea how much work would be involved, I did know it was terribly important to get that job. Taking a stab in the dark, I said, "Two thousand dollars." When I saw the shocked expressions on their faces, I could tell I had blown the ballgame, and hastily added, "Per sheet of drawings, of course."

When they asked us how many sheets were involved, we were right back in the soup. This time I decided to live a little dangerously: "Forty sheets of drawings," I told them.

They smiled. "That makes it eighty thousand. Fine, that seems to be in our range. Get to work and we'll be back in thirty days to see what you have."[9]

Negotiations about terms and conditions is the area in which *caveat emptor* applies most clearly and is the only area in which outright lies, such as the example cited under *The Lie,* may be considered an acceptable practice in either selling or buying a professional service.

Even here, there are limits to what is acceptable. Although there is great freedom in arguing why a term or condition is as it is, the implications of the term or condition, that is, exactly what it means, should be clear to all parties. For example, I believe that most professionals would feel it is unethical to promise completion of a project in thirty days if they know it actually will take much longer.

Finessing about qualifications and deliverables requires far more judgment. The ethical distinctions between exaggerations, misrepresentations, and lies become important, and it is an area where I can see little agreement in practice within the professions. So, for example, though the majority of professionals probably believe that outright lying about credentials is unethical — a belief I share — my observations suggest that lies and misrepresentations that amount to the same thing are common, at least about minor aspects of credentials and in some tight situations. This is, in part, because the professional has little time during the give and take of a complex sale to decide what to do.

How critical is the issue to the client? The more critical an issue is to a client, the more careful a professional must be about finessing. Take these two different ways that a client might ask the same question of the partner selling an engagement:

1. What will your role be in the engagement?

2. We've had difficulty in the past with professionals whom we see during the sale and then never see again once we have hired the firm. What exactly will your role be in the engagement?

For ethical as well as practical reasons, the second question requires the professional to answer more accurately than the first.

Once again, the McKinsey practice passes the test. The prospective clients almost certainly didn't care if he gave a precise recitation of the problems as originally stated, as long as his description accurately captured their situation and would lead to a solution.

Is the finesse necessary? This sounds like a practical consideration, but I ask it for ethical reasons. The more a person finesses, the easier it becomes and the less that person is likely to bother with ethical distinctions.[10] Finessing can be addictive. I have known several professionals who without compunction lied and misrepresented in ways that by my standards were shameless. These people were willing to take grave risks by finessing in situations that didn't seem to call for it on practical grounds. Part of such willingness seems to be based on the pleasure derived from getting away with it. In the case I know best, the individual, a powerful rainmaker, clearly took pleasure in his daring and would dismiss as naive any suggestions that he moderate his behavior. You do not want to become inured as he was. You do not want to get hooked on pleasure of this kind.

Determining what are acceptable ethics when selling a professional service remains a troublesome subject that deserves more attention than it has received. Exhibit 12.1 outlines two examples of situations where reasonable arguments can be made for or against finessing.

Does It Help You Win?

The practicality of finessing is far easier to discuss. Most of the debates about finessing that I have heard quickly moved to discussions of practicality. I believe this happens for two reasons. First, at least one debater wants to move away from ethics for fear of appearing either prudish or unprincipled. Second, if a finesse is inappropriate on practical grounds, the ethicality of it becomes irrelevant, saving a lot of debate likely to be unresolvable because it centers on values.

The practical argument against finessing runs roughly as follows: Professionals have a reputation for posturing and bluffing that affects how clients perceive both the professions and each of us individually. (Two humorous books are devoted entirely to this subject,[11] and a third also deals with it extensively,[12] showing how common and comical the image of the posturing professional is.) Because clients expect professionals to bluff, they are suspicious of what we say and are likely to see through most bluffs. If we are caught, it may cost us the sale. Even if it doesn't, it can result in an adversarial tone in the relationship with our clients that reduces trust. Since long-term relationships are based on trust and most professionals want long-term relationships with their clients, stretching facts is likely to be counterproductive.

Furthermore, candor is often a satisfactory alternative to finessing; most clients admire it, and it does not hurt you as often as some professionals seem to think it does. Yes, it can be risky, but so is bluffing.

Against this position, I have heard a pro-finesser argue that sometimes finessing is necessary to win. Because clients expect it, and, indeed, behave the same way in their own business dealings, they are unlikely to hold finessing against you, as long as you stay within reasonable bounds. Just as people can bluff each other in a poker game and have trusting relationships after the game is over, so can professionals and clients have trusting relationships once the sale has been made.

It follows from this logic that the amount of bluffing a person does depends on how strong his or her position is when making a sale. In making a sale to a prospective client from an industry and with a problem that the professional has dealt with often, the professional is likely to bluff less than when having to stretch his or her knowledge and experience to new areas. This may explain why I have had several gray-haired professionals tell me that finessing isn't really necessary, but never a young one. Indeed, the founders of many well-established firms probably finessed a good deal more when they were starting up than they do now. An interior designer in my survey told this story:

> When I went out on my own, my first large project was a 300,000-square-foot interiors job for [a major financial institution]. I saw brochures from [several large competitors] on the facilities manager's desk when I visited him. He never asked how many people I had in my firm, and when he said he wanted to come see me, I said I wanted to make it easy for him, so I went to see him. That way he didn't see my office which had only me in it, though it had a good address. I won the job without him asking me how big my firm was. It was an eight-week project, and I did it in five with the help of some friends I brought in to help me out. Later, when [I was working another project for the same company and] had six or seven people, the facilities manager came to see me. When he saw the office, he said, "If I'd known you were so small, I never would have given you that job."

This is a highly ethical and successful man who got started with some fast footwork that he almost certainly wouldn't use today. I suspect that if the client learned the truth now, he would laugh.

The practical positions for and against finessing are not as far apart as they might seem. A professional taking either position would be likely to argue that you should not finesse any more than you have to and not in ways that would embarrass you if the client were to ask follow-up questions. I suspect that this is where the norm in the professions lies though there is wide variation in practice.

There are alternatives. Those who finesse least may do so because they have learned that the more your prospective client talks and the less you do, the greater your chances of making a sale. The less you feel compelled to talk about your firm, the less you will feel the need to stretch facts. Silence is the best alternative to finessing because it, too, helps you win.

Human beings do bluff; a life of total candor would be lonely and intolerable. One who tried it would end up like Anthony Trollope's Josiah Crawley, bitter and contentious. In the fast give-and-take of a sales meeting, there is seldom time to deliberate on whether to finesse or how far to go. If we talk about the subject when there is time for reflection, we will probably make better decisions about finessing when under pressure.

Things You Can Do

The subject of finessing should not be ducked. I have seen young professionals who have made such a meticulous effort not to mislead a client that they either bored the clients with more detail than they wanted or undercut the firm's reputation with unnecessary caveats. I also have seen young professionals who risked compromising their firms' reputation for fair dealing. People in both categories need help.

It is not possible to draw up a set of rules that covers the vast diversity of situations that professionals face when selling and in which they must decide instantaneously what they will say about the firm and its credentials. But limits can be set on such common issues as how a professional's experience at a former employer will be represented or how recently hired people will describe their tenure with the firm.

Beyond that, when a young professional raises the issue of finessing by expressing concern, joking, or perhaps, bragging, you should not let the opportunity to discuss it slip by, as I believe, many senior professionals do. That they do may be because they themselves need to think through how they deal with the issue.

Exhibit 12.1
What Do You Think?

The professionals in these cases are faced with decisions about finessing that they must make instantaneously. Do you believe their decisions were right? Were they practical?

Case 1: The chief information officer at a large bank invites an information systems consultant to meet with him to discuss a merger of his bank with another of about the same size. The CIO serves under the new vice chairman on a committee that is planning the merger of the two banks' information services departments. He is looking for a consultant to work with the committee. It is potentially a large and profitable engagement, which the consultant needs because his firm has just completed a similar project for another bank and has a number of consultants who are unassigned.

After a positive two-hour discussion, the CIO shows the consultant to the door, saying that he has to get on to another meeting. As they shake hands, he says:

> By the way, as we discussed, the merged IS department will be much smaller than the two separate departments that exist now. A lot of people's jobs are at stake. As we go through the process of deciding who will work best in what job, I want you to remember that you work for me.

The consultant is not sure whether the CIO is trying to protect his own job or those of people who work for him, but he is certain that he is being asked to compromise his objectivity. The CIO does not let go of his hand and looks him steadily in the eye, apparently seeking confirmation.

The consultant feels that to say yes would be unethical. But to state simply that he cannot compromise his objectivity will probably cost him the engagement and result in the layoff of several members of his practice. Instead of taking either course, he returns the CIO's gaze and says:

> Of course, we are obliged as professionals to recommend what is best for the bank, and I'm sure that's what you want us to do. And I want to say how deeply I appreciate your thinking about us for this engagement. It's exactly the type

of work we want to do, and if we get it, I know it will be because of the interest you showed in us.

While driving home, the consultant reflects on what he said. He has finessed using the artificial link and realizes that the CIO could draw several messages from this juxtaposition of two unrelated thoughts, including "I'm your man," or "I must maintain my professional objectivity, but I'm a reasonable person and I'll do what I reasonably can," or "I'm deliberately finessing you, and if you're smart you will listen only to the first half of this statement." He is not sure if he was ethically right in using the finesse. What do you think? Was it a good approach from a practical standpoint? Please keep these issues distinct.

Case 2: On the basis of good work she had done for Very Quarry Tile, a quality consultant is asked to meet with the chairman of another company in the same industry. Most of the conversation centers on this prospect's needs, and the consultant makes several allusions to her work for Very Quarry Tile, the only company in the industry she has worked for in her ten years in quality consulting. At one point, the prospect asks her if quality circles are a good idea. She answers:

> That depends on the situation. Very Quarry Tile didn't use them because there was already a very open flow of information between management and workers. At Superior Bathroom Tiles, they were essential to breaking down a hierarchical environment in which the workers were never heard. Each case has to be looked at separately.

The consultant has never worked for Superior Bathroom Tiles and learned about its quality circles in a trade journal article. She does not feel it is necessary to spell this out even though the prospect might infer that she had worked for the company. Soon thereafter the chairman says that he thinks her broad experience in the tile industry could be of great help to his company and asks her for a proposal.

On her way back to the office, she has second thoughts. Was her failure to mention that she had not worked for Superior Bathroom Tiles ethical? From his statement, it seems probable that the prospective client assumes she did. Should she have clarified her (lack of) relationship to Superior Bathroom Tiles after the prospect commented on her extensive experience?

Responses by Professionals
Fred L. Fox
Geonics
Tucson, Arizona

Mr. Fox's firm specializes in ethics and ethical issues. Here are his comments on the two cases:

Case 1: The client has deliberately put the consultant on the spot in this case by asking him "to remember that you work for me," but the client's choice of words leaves the consultant an ethical out. The consultant can simply say yes. Implications be damned, the consultant would be replying in total honesty without committing himself to doing anything inappropriate later. It would be a terminally ignorant consultant who would *not* remember that the job came from the man who hired him; this is simply affirmed by saying yes.

By finessing, the consultant has erred for no good reason. There was no need to say anything, and by saying what he did, he implied that he was agreeing to play a game. As is often the case when responding to difficult questions, a long response may have gotten him into a tight corner that he could have very simply avoided.

To answer your questions, the consultant was *wrong*. He said too much, and the finesse is obvious. From a practical standpoint, that is undesirable. As his client, I would also question his ethics.

Case 2: The consultant is in charge here, and she's done nothing unethical in getting there. She merely described why some company used quality circles after describing why the company she actually worked for did not. Had she gone into some detail about the other company's use of quality circles without having been party to it, she would have implied that she worked on the project. As it was, she did not; she merely reported knowledge.

The chairman asked for a proposal on the basis of a successful presentation. The proposal should contain the consultancy's credentials, so the chairman has ample opportunity to reconsider. Also, this gives the consultant the opportunity to spell out her credentials in detail should policy demand it.

To answer your question, she is *right*. She did not need to clarify anything.

* * * * * *

Richard O. Neville, CMC
Neville Associates Inc.
Fort Myers, Florida

Your comments on finessing reminded me of my own early days in consulting. My firm hired bright but inexperienced MBAs, and we were regularly confronted with the question, "How long have you been with Harbridge House?" Until I read your article, I hadn't thought of our answers as finesses, but in retrospect they were.

With this preface, let me offer my thoughts on the two cases.

Case 1: I think the consultant handled it about right. As he drove home, he might also have realized that his "client" will not be the CIO alone, but the committee planning the integration of IS departments. Undoubtedly, the other bank will be represented on the committee, and for the consultant to seem too loyal to one member of the merger over the other would not only compromise his objectivity — it would likely result in the nonimplementation of his recommendations, however good they might be.

Thus I believe the finesse was practical; the alternatives were not to get the job at all and face layoffs, or to get the job and deliver a service of little or no value to the client. It was also ethical in that it took place in a selling environment, where the client is as likely to finesse as the consultant, and he told no untruths.

Case 2: In this case, I believe the consultant could have given a better answer. With ten years' experience as a quality consultant, she can be presumed to have a wide knowledge of the effectiveness of quality circles. She has probably consulted for some companies that used them. It would have been far more effective, and less misleading, to cite examples from her own experience rather than from something she has read.

I don't think it was ethical (or practical) of her to leave the impression that she has wide experience in the tile industry. Since she was referred to this prospect "on the basis of good work . . ." for another tile company, her qualifications both in the industry and as a quality consultant are not at issue; there is no need to finesse or inflate her experience. From a practical standpoint, this misimpression could backfire if the client learns — and he will — that she has done only one job in the industry. If she submits a written proposal, she should clarify her experience.

* * * * * *

Donald W. Seymour, CHC
National Health Advisors, Ltd.
McLean, Virginia

Case 1: The consultant has acted both ethically and, in the larger scheme of things, practically. The CIO has placed the consultant in a difficult situation, essentially soliciting a black-or-white response to the question of loyalty. The consultant, from an ethical standpoint, has responded quite appropriately by making it clear that, as a professional consultant, his job is to provide a service to the organization (as opposed to the CIO). This consultant has been quite skillful in giving a direct answer but avoiding confrontation. From a practical standpoint, I think it was also a great response. True, it may cost the consultant the job. More optimistically, there is the potential that the consultant's skill in dealing with the CIO's question will help him secure the contract and establish a good working relationship.

Case 2: This consultant has both an ethical and practical problem. When she referenced Superior Bathroom Tiles, she needed a qualifier. For example, "it is my understanding that Superior Bathroom Tiles. . . ." Absent this qualifier, her new client has assumed that Superior Bathroom Tiles was one of her past clients. She now also has a practical problem. When it comes to light, as in all likelihood it will, that Superior Bathroom Tiles was not her client, she will have a credibility problem that will endanger her existing engagement and perhaps destroy her relationship with the new client. Obviously, should this occur, it will also damage her reputation and that of consultants in general.

13

After You Are Hired

Most of what happens after a client hires you is beyond the scope of this book. But not all. Providing good service is inextricably tied to business development because it is the foundation of your reputation.

> You have to remember that this is a service business. The client is the one I want to make happy. If he is happy, word will get out.
>
> To provide good service, you have to be sensitive to what a client is trying to accomplish instead of just responding to the question being asked. The client is probably not an expert in the law or a particular aspect of the law and may not see that what can't be done one way can be done another. You have to understand the business objective and help achieve it. There is no separation between business and law in this context.
>
> Good service is also the cumulative effect of many small acts. For example, clients need to know they can count on you to return phone calls within an hour or two or, at most, four. [Joe Flom, lawyer, Skadden, Arps, Slate Meagher and Flom]

By changing a few words, this statement could be made to apply to any profession.[1]

Selling and service, I believe, require the same kind of thinking. Both require sensitivity to clients as people. Both require an ability to understand the business issues that underlie the problem you are to solve. Both require a sense of urgency and obligation to satisfy the client. Brilliant people who are insensitive to these issues may produce good technical work, but they often fall short on both service and selling.

This suggests that developing professionals to provide good service also helps them develop as rainmakers. A few of the rainmakers in the survey acknowledged as much. The late Carol Berlin Manzoni, a partner with the law firm Ross & Hardies, and, at the time of this quote, Co-chair of the firm's management committee, recalls:

> The senior lawyer I first worked for had a high service ethic. You were expected to move mountains for your client, not just be an excellent lawyer. This lesson was important to my later business development work.

Others, less fortunate, had to learn from clients. One attorney described an important lesson about service that he learned this way:

> When I was a young lawyer, an accountant who was a client came to visit me. He drove [for over an hour] to see me in my office, and I kept him waiting for forty minutes because I had other pressing things to do. When I brought him into my office, several other people stopped by with questions and I answered them, and I also took several phone calls. After the last of these calls, the accountant, who was much older than me and really a very nice man, looked at me and said firmly, "You're going to talk with me now without interruption." He went over and closed the door to my office and then reamed me out for the next ten minutes. "How dare you treat me like this. I'm your client and I've come a long way to see you and you keep me waiting and then act as if anything that comes up is more important! Don't ever let this happen again." I told him he was right and that it would never happen again with him or any other client. And it hasn't. It's easy for a lawyer to become arrogant without realizing it.

Young professionals do need to learn about servicing clients.

Service should start as soon as an engagement is sold. Often, when a firm sells a major engagement, there is a sense of great relief. Over the months that it takes to make the sale, anxiety increases as the professionals get closer and closer to winning. In a formal competition, for example, pressure goes up noticeably once a firm is short-listed to make a presentation. After the presentation, pressure increases again as you wait to learn what the client has decided. The good news that you have won brings joy and, usually, a great reduction in anxiety. There is a tendency to turn to matters put aside during the frenzy of the pursuit.

Meanwhile, the client's anxiety level is moving in the opposite direction. During the months of searching for a professional, anxiety falls as the selection committee becomes confident that it is focusing on the right firms. The minute the committee makes a selection, however, that changes. Suddenly, the members realize that they are stuck with the firm they have chosen and that if anything goes wrong they will be blamed. Anxiety skyrockets. The bigger the engagement, the higher the anxiety.

Professionals must not let their own reduction in anxiety lull them into confidence that everything is well. Rather, there is often need to show the clients immediately that they made the right choice by taking rapid action on the engagement.

When work gets underway, both good service and effective selling dictate that a professional get to know any significant players at the client who will be affected by it. A young professional may see these people as mere sources of information needed to complete a project. Management needs to point out that their acceptance of the firm's work will depend, in part, on how well the professional understands that the engagement will affect their work and their lives.

The work that many professionals do results in some people being hurt, and no professional can afford to let some people's displeasure with the work interfere with what is best for the client. Accepting this point does not justify a cavalier attitude toward other people's troubles or alienating people unnecessarily. Problems of this kind are avoided if one takes a long-term view of relationships. Most rainmakers do. They will extend themselves to be accommodating within what their work allows:

- People may not be able to help you for ten to twelve years. Young people often don't see that; they're too short-sighted and feel the need for expediency and quick results. They don't spend time on people who can't help them right now. But the analyst who wants a little help now may be a vice president and a charger in eight years. [Michael J. Zimmer, lawyer, Reid & Priest]

- I always try to meet this standard: I am going to leave the person I am talking with happy that he spoke with me. Even when we are talking about a problem, I try to meet this standard. You want people to feel motivated to help you. [Bob Gaida, accountant, BDO Seidman]

- I always believed that you have to play with the hand you are dealt and work with those people assigned to a project. That means dealing with some people who aren't that qualified. A client will usually pay extra for you to put more people on a project if you work with the people who are there and don't disrupt the company. [Gene Delves, information technology consultant]

These long-term relationships can develop with anyone you come into contact with on an engagement:

> I zealously represent my clients and strive to get the best deal for them. At the same time, I also treat the other side and their lawyer ethically, professionally, and with respect. This is the right thing to do, and these people may be a source of business tomorrow. [Ken VanWinkle Jr., lawyer, Lewis & Roca]

These quotes, of course, bring us back to building relationships, which has been discussed at length in Chapter 9. To avoid repetition, I limit this chapter to those aspects of building relationships that are essential to conducting engagements.

Your main contact at a client company requires special attention. Rainmakers recognize that their job includes making this person look good. This is both a service and a marketing issue, a point brought home by a management consulting client who told me this story:

> We did a performance improvement study for [a major utility] many years ago. At the time our contact, a senior vice president, was vying for the top job in the company against two competitors. McKinsey was also working in another area for this same person. When our work was finished, we made a presentation to the board that was well received. Afterwards, our recommendations were implemented, and the project was a success. When it came time to present the findings of the McKinsey study, they prepared a presentation for the SVP to give and helped him rehearse his delivery. The SVP got to stand up in front of the board at a critical time in his career. The McKinsey recommendations were also accepted and successfully implemented. The SVP always gave us a good recommendation after that, but when he needed more work, he went to McKinsey.

Most opportunities to make a contact look good are less dramatic than the one in this example. You must keep the contact informed about what is happening on your engagement, warn him or her about any problems as quickly as possible, and deliver results so that they are easily understood. All these things need to be taught to young professionals, but in the rush of getting work out the door, sometimes aren't.

If professionals are thoroughly trained on providing good service, they will be in a position to develop the lasting relationships with clients who are the source of future work.

Of course, you must make sure that the client feels that you actually did do good work. Many firms now conduct a formal audit of client satisfaction at the end of an engagement. Many tie the compensation of the engagement team to the results of these audits. These kinds of audits are essential business practices today. An unhappy client can cause you terrible damage in the marketplace. One you don't know about is the worst.

Sometimes a client needs help appreciating what you have done. This may not be necessary if you have done something dramatic and obvious, like win a major court settlement, but many professionals deliver services that are less visible. Much of what an actuary does, for example, may not be apparent to important people at the client company. Accountants do many things for people at the companies they audit that can go largely unrecognized. A rainmaker makes sure that clients are aware of the services they are getting. Here is how one rainmaker does that:

> Each year I try to have an audit report meeting with the top people at a client company. The clients know what's in the audit already. Our real purpose is to begin by thanking the client for the chance to work for them and describe what we have done for each department and what was the result of it, so everyone knows what we did for everyone else.

Another approach is taken by Gary Pines of Towers Perrin:

> I try to deliver the first bill and any other important bills to the client in person. These informal meetings provide a good way to review what you are doing and how it is going at the client. It also provides a good time to find out about any problems that may be festering and about opportunities. It demonstrates how important the client is to you.

Large firms with large clients for whom they do many different things must often take a team approach to client relationship management. Keeping the team of people working with a client in communication with each other improves service and helps sell more work. The team members meet regularly, sometimes by phone, to discuss what is happening in different parts of the client company, bring each other up to date on their projects, sort out problems, and identify opportunities for each other. These teams are good training grounds for future rainmakers because young professionals have the opportunity to learn about the major business issues facing the client and hear experienced client developers talk about clients' needs and selling approaches.

Things You Can Do

1. *Establish a quick-start policy for all new engagements.*

   Require professionals to offer to meet with a client to kick off a new project within three days of authorization. Delaying startup beyond seven days should be permitted only at the client's request.

2. *At the beginning of every new engagement, remind your professionals that their goal is to make each person they work with on it a client for life.*

   When we meet someone that we expect to have to work with for many years, we naturally react to the introduction differently from the way we would if we expected the relationship to last only a few months. If you encourage your professionals to take a long-term view of relationships, they will be more likely to do the many little things that create lasting ties. They will be more attentive to personal information that clients give out, to avoiding and clearing up misunderstandings, and to helping clients advance their careers.

3. *At the beginning of each month, ask your professionals to commit to doing one thing that will advance a relationship with a client.*

   They can take a client to lunch, do a personal favor, send a birthday card, send a note complimenting someone's work, or anything else they can think of that will help advance a relationship. They should choose for themselves, then report in front of their peers thirty days later on what they have done, and finally make a commitment for the following month.

4. *Ask your professionals how they will help the principal contact on a project look good.*

   Ask them this at the beginning of each project and at regular stages throughout it.

14

Creating Rainmakers

In the preceding pages, I have tried to capture both the simplicity and complexity of what rainmakers do. What they do is simple. They extend themselves to keep their current clients happy and, at the same time, look for new ones. They build large networks of the right kinds of people. They stay at the front of these people's minds through frequent contact. They pursue many business opportunities to win a few.

Professionals are smart, analytical people who have no difficulty grasping these messages. But many smart people confuse understanding something with mastering it, and rainmaking is so complex that it is not easily mastered. Complexity derives from doing all these things with hundreds, even thousands, of people with limited time. As I have said, it is like playing the piano. Anyone who spends the time you have devoted to reading this book to learning about pianos would have a good understanding of how they work. That would not be enough to play one well. Your fingers just wouldn't do what you understand needs to be done. Your mind wouldn't race fast enough. Playing a piano well requires practice. Playing one professionally well requires compulsive practice. So it is with rainmaking.

Commitment. Discipline. Relentlessness. Willingness to experiment. Resilience. Those are the qualities needed to succeed. Fortunately, these are qualities that many professionals possess in ample quantities. We have good raw material to work with. The challenge is to get people to apply these qualities to rainmaking.

Systems help. We have seen how most rainmakers have developed systems that they work relentlessly. The systems help them master the complexity of juggling many things simultaneously. They help create a balance among the many individual activities required to make rain. They ease automation and delegation.

Many of the rainmakers are driven people. No doubt, much of that drive is innate, but I suspect some of it derives from their systems. You drive a car, a complex mechanical system, but take your foot off the gas for a moment, or worse, fall asleep at the wheel, and you will find that the car also drives you. It doesn't just stop the instant you stop driving. Create a system for managing a network of 200 people, add people to it until you have 1,000, and you will find your system driving you. It will push you to do more and more. Even if you are temporarily distracted from client development work, the momentum of the system will drive you on.

It is because systems are so important to creating rain that so much of this book has been devoted to their individual components. I hope the suggestions in the "Things You Can Do" sections of these last several chapters help you get the pieces of a system working. In this chapter, I want to step back and discuss things you can do to get a whole system working. I want to set aside the things the firm can provide to professionals — like packaged ideas for distribution to the market, support in setting up a seminar, or names of prequalified prospects — and focus on the coaching that goes on between you and the aspiring rainmakers.

Things You Can Do

1. Start them early.

The earlier people start to build client development into their weekly routines, the easier it will be for them to bring in business later. Many of the rainmakers in the survey began their business development efforts early in their careers, usually during their first year or two as professionals. This is a pattern you want your people to emulate. The firm should set expectations about the kind of effort it is looking for at each level in a person's career. It should then support these expectations with appropriate training for each level. Training should begin as soon as an employee is hired. During the initial firm training process, provide an hour's instruction on client development. That will help the new hires realize that they will have to bring in business later in their careers and that they can start building a foundation for later business development efforts immediately. The quantity of education on client development should increase as people advance in the organization.

When groups of young professionals gather, use the opportunity to describe how senior professionals began to develop business early in their careers. Role models help establish expectations. Firm lore helps build a marketing culture.

2. *Focus on long-term career and personal goals.*

When your professionals reach the point in their careers when they should begin bringing in business, the focus on the subject needs to increase. This is the time to establish substantial goals.

In my experience, young professionals are motivated more by long-term career and personal goals than by the need for immediate sales. If you can link their client development efforts to these goals, you increase your chances of creating rainmakers. Start your people off on rainmaking by having each develop a personal marketing plan. This plan should be built around career goals that will require from three to five years to achieve. Most of these goals will fall into one of four categories:

- *Reputation Goals:* These are goals to be a recognized leader in an area of practice important to the firm and to its clients.

  Examples
  a. I plan to become the best known consultant in the world in the field of retail logistics.
  b. I plan to become the best known tax, trust, and estate attorney in the Houston area.
  c. I plan to become the best known architect in school design in the state of North Carolina.

  This kind of goal often requires writing and speaking frequently and getting oneself quoted in the press. But by themselves, those things are not enough to attain the desired recognition. For that to occur, the professional must also know either most of the people at prospective client organizations who might hire his or her firm for work of the kind in question or major third-party influencers. He or she must also have done significant work in the area.

- *Client Relationship Goals:* These are goals to have your firm seen as the professionals of choice at specific client organizations and to be the trusted advisor of their leadership.

Examples

a. I plan to make my firm the accountants of choice at XYZ International and Megacorporation, Inc.

b. I plan to make my firm the mechanical, electrical, and plumbing engineers of choice at Misericordia, St. Elizabeth's, and Western General hospitals.

These goals can be achieved only if your firm does significant work for the named organizations. Achieving them requires fully understanding clients' business, organization, goals, and issues. The professional will also have to develop relationships with top executives and emerging stars.

- *Geographic Goals:* These are goals to build a base of business in a specific geographic market. Accomplishing this kind of goal can increase your firm's revenues from a market where it is underrepresented and get professionals who currently must travel frequently home at night to spend time with their families.

Examples

a. I plan to develop a practice that will support eight people serving clients in the Los Angeles area.

b. I plan to develop an office for the firm in Germany that will support five people.

Goals of this kind suggest that the professional will want to do some of the following: participate in the regional chapter meetings of specific trade associations, make cold calls on prospective clients in the area, over time develop relationships with people met in these ways, and seek referrals to prospective clients in the area from people his or her firm has served elsewhere.

- *Cross-marketing Goals:* These are goals to become the specialist of choice in a specific area for other consultants in the firm. This kind of goal is appropriate when a professional expects many leads to come from relationships that others in the firm develop.

Examples
a. I want to be seen as the Oracle [software systems] specialist of choice for other professionals in the firm.
b. I want to be seen as the deferred compensation specialist of choice for other professionals in the firm.

Achieving this kind of goal requires developing relationships with other key players throughout the firm. It also requires speaking and publishing to establish credentials that will make a professional easy to recommend to a client. It requires impeccable service to other people's clients.

One goal is plenty for many professionals. Some will want to take on two. But they should be discouraged from taking on too many at once because doing so will result in diffusion of effort. Three goals are too many for most people.

Management may want to provide broad directives about the kinds of goals that will be acceptable, but professionals should select their own goals. That helps ensure that they select goals that motivate them because they seem interesting and achievable.

Goals set by management may fail on these criteria. The rainmaker and founder of one firm I know set a goal of doubling the firm's size in three years and imposed it on his practice heads. A classic optimist, the founder felt it was achievable and stimulating. To others in the firm, it seemed impossible. Like all goals that seem impossible to achieve, it proved de-motivating. The founder might have been more successful if he had let people select their own goals and had asked that these goals be increased if they were achieved ahead of schedule.

3. *Ask for plans to achieve the goals.*

Each goal can be achieved only by action. Ask your professionals to list the actions required to accomplish them. One way to do this is to list major tasks required to accomplish a goal along with implementation steps required to accomplish each task. Each implementation step should be accompanied by a completion date.

Example

Goal: Become the best known consultant in the area of customer satisfaction in the insurance industry in North America.

> *Task One:* Speak on the subject at least three times per year for the next three years at trade association meetings.
>
>> *Implementation Step One:* Obtain information from major associations on meeting plans for coming year. To be completed by January 15.
>>
>> *Implementation Step Two:* Contact Lena Jones to see if she can help me obtain an opportunity at her association. To be completed by January 15.
>>
>> *Implementation Step Three:* Send letters to other associations offering to speak and mentioning possible topics. To be completed by January 31.
>
> *Task Two:* Assemble a contact list of people in the insurance industry concerned with customer satisfaction.
>
>> *Implementation Step One:* Review my business card file and select names for list. To be completed by January 31.

Each goal is likely to have ten to fifteen tasks associated with it.

Review the professional's plan to make sure it fits with the firm's objectives and is realistic in terms of the time requirement. If it does not include tasks that put a person in front of prospective contacts or third-party influencers soon, ask that it be modified to do so. To start, the plan should cover the first six months of activity required to achieve the goals.

4. *Apply revenue targets carefully.*

You will have to decide whether you want your professionals to include revenue targets among their goals. Of course, you want client development work to result in increased revenues, and revenue targets are appropriate for senior professionals experienced at client development. This is not so clearly true for professionals just beginning to develop business.

You need to motivate aspiring rainmakers with early success. Misapplied, revenue targets can be de-motivating. We have seen in Chapter 2 that early efforts at bringing in business are likely to have little noticeable effect though results grow more rapidly over time. This means that during the first six months to a year that someone works seriously at client development, input measures, such as the growth of the person's network, are more important than output measures in the form of sales. If you feel revenue targets are needed during this period, they should be kept low so that the aspiring rainmakers have a good chance of achieving them. Targets can be escalated in later years.

You will defeat your efforts to create rainmakers if you adopt the attitude that, for three hours of time spent on client development, you expect three hours' worth of results. This mindset is appropriate to managing client work, but cannot be applied successfully to client development, especially with people who are learning. One of the most successful efforts to develop rainmakers I am aware of was the brainchild of a partner at a big accounting firm. He established a marketing committee of aggressive young professionals, gave it a limited marketing budget, and provided small monetary rewards for effort rather than for results. Most of the people on the committee became rainmakers later in their careers. One eventually became the firm's chairman.

5. *Monitor performance against plan.*

Meet with your professionals monthly to review progress against plan. If your management of the rainmaking efforts of your people is inconsistent, so will be their rainmaking efforts. Monthly meetings to review performance against plan provide you the opportunity to coach, encourage, empathize, rehearse, celebrate, and nag.

6. *Cheer success and pick up after failure.*

In the hurly-burly of daily business activity, we sometimes miss the opportunities for these two forms of encouragement. Most firms will cheer a successful sale. Cheering a range of client development success sends a stronger cultural message. Someone gets a major speaking engagement; drop her a note. Someone gets a meeting for the firm with an important potential client; congratulate him. Professionals need to know that their successes, even small ones, are appreciated. This is especially true early in their careers, when returns on their time in the form of sales are likely to be few.

Picking up after failure is equally important. Selling is more of an emotional roller coaster than is client work. Professionals are often not prepared for its highs and lows. They need support after pursuing an opportunity for months and then seeing it go to a competitor or evaporate for reasons beyond their control. These things *will* happen because you have to pursue many to win a few. If lost opportunities are seen as failures, rather than as steps on the way to winning something else, a professional will find it hard to continue to work at selling. The appropriate response after most losses is, "That must be hard after all your work. What can we learn from this one that will help us win next time? What is the next opportunity?"

7. *Work on one issue at a time.*

Professionals learning how to develop business will do many things less than perfectly. You will be strongly tempted to correct shortcomings whenever you see them. This should be avoided because it is extremely damaging. We have seen how important optimism is to successful rainmaking. Many aspiring rainmakers will have to learn to be more optimistic about their chances of success. That will be hard to do if they are inundated with a stream of corrections on everything they do. They will learn best if they can focus on one thing at a time.

If someone is having difficulty making time for business development, focus on that issue until you see significant improvement. Then move to the next most serious issue. Always have something that you are working on with each professional, but focus on one thing at a time with each.

8. *Train and reinforce the training.*

Most professionals are expected to spend a number of hours each year in classes designed to keep them current on their profession. They also need training in various aspects of business development. How do you build a network? How do you handle a meeting with a prospective client? How can you make a competitive presentation? How do you write a proposal or a speech? How do you write and publish an article? Good training programs exist for all these topics.

Training will do little good, however, unless it is reinforced on the job. If you train someone in a skill, make sure he or she has an opportunity to apply it soon after the training is completed.

9. *Measure advances in commitment and in the development of skill.*

Because of the delay between the time when someone begins to develop business and the time when business actually starts to come in, it can be hard to tell whether your people are making progress or not. Early on you should measure progress in terms of their commitment to business development and the increase in their skill at it. If someone who made no phone calls before is consistently blocking half an hour three times a week for it now, she is making progress. If someone who was always consumed by client work in the past makes time to go to a trade association meeting and afterwards follows up with the people he met there, he is learning. Because selling is a numbers game, if your people consistently take action, eventually they are likely to start winning engagements.

You can also look at their skills. Are they getting noticeably better at making presentations? Are the marketing letters they are sending out improving in quality as well as increasing in quantity? When your people go to a trade show, do you see them actively working the room, when they used to huddle together? These are signs that they are making progress and will eventually succeed.

10. *Remember that market selection and luck play a part.*

If several of your people are learning to become rainmakers, some will win engagements sooner than others. Sometimes this will be because they worked harder and more skillfully than others did. Sometimes it will be because they were luckier or were working an easier market. Yes, these people should be cheered, but don't write off those whose success comes more slowly. Rather, continue to look for commitment and skill. If they are evident, be patient.

It is particularly important to have patience with people trying to develop new markets. Pioneering work generally shows much slower payoff than mining markets where the firm already has a strong presence.

Conclusion

Afirm that can consistently develop and retain rainmakers will have a strategic advantage over competitors. It will grow more rapidly, earn greater profits, win the best clients and most interesting engagements, attract the best young talent, and provide well for the retirement of its partners. All these ends are worth considerable investment. But professional firms have made relatively little investment in the production of rainmakers. A surprising number have made almost none.

I have one final caution for those who want to invest: Beware of piecemeal action. If you provide training without on-the-job reinforcement, your efforts will fail. If you ask people to develop business and then reward them only for billing, your plans will fail. If you generate leads, but have no people or systems in place to follow through on those leads, your plans will fail. Just as creating rain requires doing many things in a limited time, so does creating rainmakers. John Ferraro, one of the architects of Ernst & Young's stunning increase in sales over two years, states clearly that the firm had to put many things in place at once to effect the change. Doing it one piece at a time would not have worked.

Firms are increasingly willing to make the large effort required. Increased competition dictates that they must. The firms that take action first will capture the lion's share of advantage. They will be the ones that have rainmakers in the market winning new business against slower-footed competitors.

I hope that this book has eliminated the sense of magic about what rainmakers do without completely eliminating the wonder. I hope it has provided insight into how they can be created. Developing people is not only good for the firm; it can also be tremendously rewarding for those who do it. What finer heritage can the leadership of a firm leave behind than a team of rainmakers capable of ensuring the firm's success for the next generation?

Introduction to Appendices

Four appendices to this book address issues that others are more qualified to write about than I am. The first tells how to recruit a rainmaker should you have to. Though this book is primarily about turning professionals who are already members of your firm into rainmakers, sometimes that is not possible. Recruiting is then the only alternative. Appendix A was written by Terence Gallagher, President and Chief Operating Officer of Battalia Winston International, an executive search firm. Terry has recruited rainmakers for a number of professional firms, including Ernst & Young LLP and Deloitte & Touche LLP.

Appendix B addresses the issue of measuring and compensating business development. To a degree, people do what they are paid to do. If you want people to develop business, measuring their performance and compensating them for doing this right are essential. J. Mark Santiago wrote Appendix B. He is the president of the International CoSourcing Group ("ICG") located in New York City. ICG consults to law firms on strategic, administrative improvement, and cost reduction issues. Mr. Santiago has consulted to law firms for more than 25 years in the areas of partner compensation, profitability improvement, and strategy development. Though his remarks are addressed to law firms, they are applicable to other kinds of professional firms as well.

Appendix C explores the major issues in developing a centralized marketing function to support your rainmakers. Most rainmakers perform better when they receive the right kinds of support. Appendix C was written by John Bliss and Abigail Gouverneur, who are principals of Bliss, Gouverneur & Associates, Inc., a New York–based marketing communications firm that specializes in professional service clients. Their clients include national organizations such as Deloitte & Touche (accounting), Towers Perrin (consulting), Hunton & Williams (law), Lamalie Amrop (executive search), and Tillinghast (actuaries).

Appendix D looks at the issue of building presentation skills. As competition increases in the professions, winning work often requires winning competitive presentations, where we are judged as much on our abilities as speakers as on our professional expertise. Sims Wyeth of Syms Wyeth & Company, the author of Appendix D, has helped professionals at many firms build their skills in this area, including CSC, KPMG Peat Marwick, Parsons Brinckerhoff, White & Case, Hannoch Weismann, and McGladry & Pullen.

APPENDIX A

Recruiting Rainmakers

BY TERENCE GALLAGHER

The one alternative to developing rainmakers from existing employees is to recruit them from outside the firm. Firms sometimes do this when they want to add a new practice area in which there is little in-house expertise. It is also a way to raise the standard of revenue generation within the firm and to catalyze a culture change required to increase the market focus of the firm. In some cases, recruiting rainmakers on the outside has been the only solution available to a firm that doesn't have sufficient client developers in-house to rapidly increase revenue and profitability.

For instance, at our midsize executive search firm, a consulting partner recruited from a management consulting firm raised the standard of revenue generation significantly. He did so by bringing expertise in recruiting for senior-level partners at consulting firms, a high demand area. Work that he brought in increased the average consulting fees for the firm. He also opened a new office, broadening our geographic reach. Management practices he brought to the firm have helped other business developers increase their business development abilities, too.

Of course, there can be a downside to bringing in rainmakers from the outside. A dynamic player inserted into the firm can upset team dynamics as much as baseball superstar Darryl Strawberry did the Los Angeles Dodgers. All too frequently, professionals who have been highly successful client developers at one firm find their skills are not transferable to another. Rainmakers brought in from other firms can demand too many resources and upset support staff. Their large egos sometimes alienate the professionals they need to work with to be successful. The long-term firm employees, angered by the rainmaker's high compensation and arrogant manner, may cut him or her off from information on firm capabilities and past engagements that is needed to succeed. Under pressure to produce at the new firm, a hired rainmaker sometimes adopts a close-the-deal-at-any-cost mentality, which is destructive to the firm's reputation in the long run.

Given the risks, recruiting on the outside should be done only in situations that require it. These include:

- When a firm or practice is languishing and requires an injection of revenues or profits to survive;
- When the addition of new clients can help take a firm or practice to its next level of sophistication or critical mass;
- When a firm wants to expand to a new geographic area where it needs contacts and immediate stature with clients;
- When there is insufficient time to train someone on the existing staff to fill a rainmaking void;
- When the firm wants to expand into a new practice area to broaden the range of services it offers.

The clarity of a firm's vision about what it wants will have a big impact on how successful it will be at recruiting a rainmaker. First, firm management should assess its long-term, strategic goals and determine the key drivers for achieving them. For example, the firm's plan may call for expanding geographically by locating offices close to clients. In this case, hiring a rainmaker with extensive contacts at large companies in a city or region is key. Alternatively, a firm may want to broaden its services or develop new ones to increase the revenues it receives from its current clients. In such a case, a rainmaker who has a record of success in marketing and selling a portfolio of related professional services would be desirable. A firm may want to grow by acquiring key account managers to coordinate the delivery of many different services and assure the quality of their delivery to its largest international accounts. In this instance, any business developers the firm hires need to have track records in that kind of work with similar accounts.

Some firms adopt a different approach altogether. Instead of recruiting rainmakers, they recruit additional supporting professionals.

This frees up their current rainmakers' time so that they can bring in more business. A firm with a clear strategy, like one of these, will have the most success at recruiting a rainmaker.

If you are recruiting to expand, either geographically or by specialty, rather than change your firm's culture, you should evaluate your existing rainmakers to identify those attributes that make them successful. This will help avoid hiring a person who has been successful elsewhere but is not equipped to succeed within your culture. Some firms require selling in large teams. Others expect independent client development. Some practices depend on professionals who have deep relationships with a few large clients whom they sell services to year after year. Others are more interested in a rainmaker who can aggressively track down new clients each year. The attributes of the person you hire must fit the requirements of your firm.

The way different needs result in searches for different kinds of talent is illustrated by the case of one Big Six firm. The firm asked us to identify candidates for its information technology outsourcing practice. A new practice area, it needed an aggressive rainmaker with extensive contacts at senior levels in *Fortune* 500 companies who could sell outsourcing engagements ranging up to $3 billion and running up to three years in duration. Later, the firm retained us to recruit a consulting partner for one of its Midwestern offices. This person needed to have expertise in change management and reengineering in the consumer packaged goods industry. In this case, rather than an ability to obtain new clients, the company needed a person who had credibility in a specific industry from work he or she had done in the past. Different strategic needs result in searches for different kinds of people.

The attributes of the person who will succeed at your firm go beyond those required to make rain. Specific technical credentials may be essential in some firms for a rainmaker to gain peer respect. In others, broad business knowledge is valued more than deep specialization.

Always important, personality traits can be especially so when a firm is trying to challenge its culture. An absence of a sense of humor in times of high stress can be destructive. A person who focuses solely on his or her own success, even if successful at bringing in business, may create enough internal disruption to distract management from building the firm to deal with the problems he or she has created. In contrast, a sense of humor and a genuine caring for others can help bring people together. These attributes can also help your people tolerate the frictions that inevitably arise when a dynamic new force is brought into the firm.

In one case, a human resources consulting firm recruited a dynamic rainmaker to build a new practice. He was neurotic and self-centered by firm standards. As one of his colleagues put it, "There was a lot of 'I' in his talk." But he could also make people laugh and was willing to laugh at himself. Firm management acknowledges that these abilities may have made the difference between his acceptance and rejection. The firm is now well-established in the new practice area.

The attributes needed in the person you hire will not just depend on what you want this person to accomplish but when. Clearly delineating what you expect the person you hire to accomplish will help you select among candidates. Anyone you hire will require a ramp-up period, but some firms expect shorter ones than others. Some expect the rainmaker to manage the engagements he or she brings in and so are looking for a person with broad skills. Others want a client-getter who will be supported by dedicated project managers.

Some firms have hired a rainmaker with a strong track record only to find that, having achieved his or her personal objectives already, the rainmaker has lost the fire in the belly that management hoped would inspire others to greater achievement. Only careful interviewing and reference checks will determine if a candidate has the drive you require.

Preparing a Position Specification for the job you want to fill can help clarify your thinking about the attributes of the rainmaker you want to hire. Exhibit A.1 provides a sample Position Specification. Exhibit A.2 provides guidance on how to develop one for the position you need to fill.

Exhibit A.1
Sample Position Specification

Title	Partner, Information Technology Consulting — Consumer Goods Industry.
Client	A global professional services firm that is a leader in the information technology and reengineering consulting.
Reporting Relationship	The Partner, Information Technology Consulting — Consumer Goods Industry

reports directly to the Partner-in-Charge of the Detroit Information Technology Consulting Practice. He/she will manage a staff of professional information technology and performance improvement consultants on a project matrix basis.

Educational Requirements

An undergraduate degree is required.

Summary of Responsibilities

The Partner, Information Technology Consulting — Consumer Goods Industry will be responsible for building an information technology consulting practice in the consumer goods industry in the Detroit area as well as in the Great Lakes Region.

More precisely, the Partner, Information Technology Consulting — Consumer Goods Industry will:

- Prepare the strategic and operating practice development business plan for review and approval by the Partner-in-Charge of the Detroit Information Technology Consulting Practice.

- Develop and maintain high-quality, long-term business relationships with targeted key clients in the consumer goods industry in order to meet professional fee revenue and profitability objectives.

- Identify other management consulting needs for consumer industry clients, and cross-sell these services by introducing the appropriate Partner in the firm to assist the client.

- Work closely with the National Consumer Goods Industry Practice Leader to ensure a coordinated approach to practice development and client service within the practice.

- Take a proactive role in leadership positions with appropriate professional organizations, publish related articles, make public speeches, and network with charitable and civic organizations in order to enhance the presence of the firm and identify additional practice development opportunities.

- Maintain project management overview responsibility on the most significant consulting engagements, and ensure that all engagements are being managed properly so that clients' expectations regarding timeliness and quality of deliverables are met.

- Oversee consulting practice administration, including establishing standard fees, maximizing progress billings, selling add-on work to existing clients, collecting fees promptly, and avoiding bad debts, in order to meet profitability objectives.

- Hire, train, and develop Senior Managers, Managers, and Consultants in the department and provide them with learning opportunities and career counseling to enable them to meet their objectives and enhance their professional development.

- Maintain awareness of state-of-the-art information technology and performance improvement consulting practices within the consumer goods industry in order to be recognized by clients as an expert capable of applying this knowledge to their consulting needs and providing them with value-added advice.

Previous Experience and Abilities Required

Fully qualified candidates will possess the following attributes:

- A minimum of 15 years of related information technology and performance improvement management consulting experience for clients in the consumer goods industry.

- A demonstrated record of success in building and effectively managing an information technology consulting practice within the consumer goods industry for a major professional services consulting firm.

- A well-developed network of senior management executive contacts at consumer goods companies and a reputation for effectively providing solutions for these companies' information technology consulting needs.

- Demonstrated superior executive presentation skills in order to effectively market and sell information technology consulting services to new clients and enhance existing client relationships.

- Well-developed interpersonal and communications skills indicative of an ability to readily obtain client confidence, respect, and cooperation.

- Personal qualities, including a high energy level, creativity, self-confidence, initiative, and a passion for client service.

- Business maturity combined with sound business judgment and decision-making ability.

- The leadership ability to attract, motivate, and develop subordinates and provide them with timely counsel to enhance their professional development.

- Strong organizational and planning skills in order to manage many large consulting engagements simultaneously.

Location   Detroit, Michigan.

Compensation	A very attractive compensation package will be arranged for the successful candidate that will be based upon demonstrated capabilities. A comprehensive benefits package will also be provided. Relocation costs, if any, will be reimbursed in accordance with firm policy.

Exhibit A.2
Commentary on Sample Position Specification

Heading	*Comments*
Title	Be sure that the title you use is attractive to candidates, as well as being representative of the current organization structure. For instance, you may want to use a title like Director rather than Partner. This will give you the opportunity to evaluate candidates for their Partner potential based on performance on the job, rather than committing to a Partner position before you have had a chance to see them in action and before they produce results.
Client	Stress the positives of the firm in order to attract the best candidates. Typically, you will want to highlight such things as the firm's recent growth performance and probably use descriptives, such as high-growth and highly profitable. You should also identify the firm's geographic reach: global, national, regional, or local. If you are confidentially searching for a replacement for a current employee, then err on the side of caution so that you don't unintentionally reveal the search to the incumbent.
Reporting Relationship	In this section, identify who the position reports to, the number of direct reports, and the total number of staff reporting to the position. If a

near-term promotion is expected, state that here to enhance the attractiveness of the opportunity and to illustrate the firm's commitment to the advancement of the chosen candidate.

Educational Requirements

This is a culturally sensitive subject because, in some cases, firms make an advanced degree a prerequisite to being hired. Certainly, you will want to be sensitive toward precedents in hiring other rainmakers to the firm. However, keep in mind that the candidate that is most attractive and has the highest potential may be passed over because he or she lacks either an under-graduate or advanced degree. Small firms often waive a requirement for an undergraduate degree and place more emphasis on the candidate's proven track record of performance and results. But most large firms will require an undergraduate degree, and, in many cases, an advanced one.

Summary of Responsibilities

In this section, you typically want to provide a summary paragraph about the scope of responsibilities of the position. Then you can use bullets to highlight the most important responsibilities first, followed by the less important ones.

Previous Experience and Abilities Required

Specify the number of years of experience required for candidates, as well as any key skill sets needed to be successful in the job. As in the responsibility section, the requirements section should list the requisite skills and experience required in order of importance. Include both technical and functional skill sets, as well as soft skills, like interpersonal and listening skills, and personal traits, like a results-orientation or high energy level.

Location   Specify location of the position in this section. If
                        you can be flexible on the location, note that and
                        the alternatives that you would consider in order
                        to attract the best candidates. Some firms have
                        been flexible on both the location and start date
                        to attract the best candidate, whereas others have
                        not. In many cases, a firm requires the candidate
                        to be based in a specific location in order to be
                        able to work closely with other firm members.

Travel (optional)   You may want to share anticipated travel expec-
                        tations, especially for positions requiring the
                        professional to spend time at client locations.
                        The travel percentage range that you list should
                        be realistic and based upon actual travel percent-
                        ages of comparable positions in the firm.

Compensation   Most firms prefer to state that they will make the
                        successful candidate an attractive offer based on
                        proven capabilities. If there are any special bene-
                        fits or perks, they should be noted in this section
                        to increase the overall attractiveness of the posi-
                        tion. Likewise, if it is the firm's policy to reim-
                        burse all normal relocation costs, that should be
                        stated here, too.

After You Hire a Rainmaker

The cost and risk of hiring a rainmaker warrant planning carefully
to help him or her succeed once hired. A first step is often to mutually set goals that are realistic. Assigning a mentor, someone established
and respected in the firm, can also help smooth the rainmaker's transition and make him or her productive more quickly. Itemizing what
the rainmaker must learn about the firm and then determining how
you can help him or her learn those things will also help. This exercise will often result in the rapid assembly of useful materials, interviews with the right people in the firm, the opportunity to observe

others in selling situations, and the chance for you to observe him or her so that you can give early feedback.

One firm we know has been particularly successful at helping newly hired rainmakers transition into the firm. Before candidates are hired, they must be interviewed by all key members of the team that they will become a part of. Teams consist of either a consulting practice specialty or an industry group. From these interviews, the new partners get a more well-rounded and realistic understanding of the organization they will be entering. The interviews give the candidates a chance to start developing relationships with those they will be working with before they are hired. The interviews also allow a rainmaker to assess how he or she can introduce the team's strengths to clients.

When candidates accept the offer to become partners at the firm, they work with a senior partner as a mentor to create a list of goals and priorities to be measured against. By participating in this exercise, newly hired people feel ownership of goals and are motivated to achieve them. The firm uses this goal-setting exercise to identify resources the new partners will need to meet their objectives.

The new partners then work with their teams to develop client strategies. They are also teamed with more senior partners who introduce them to clients as experts in a specific field. The new partners also receive professional development and career counseling twice a year to help them with the transition into the firm. This process is structured to identify areas for individual development and to recognize the new partners' strengths.

Taking time to thoroughly orient newly hired rainmakers will help them succeed more quickly. It will help ensure that the firm receives a return on its recruiting expense.

Professional firms must recruit rainmakers when internal sources are inadequate. It is an approach that can be highly successful if the firm has a clear idea of what it is looking for and is willing to invest the time and effort to help a newcomer find a place in the organization.

Appendix B

Compensating Professionals for Making Rain

A Tale of Two Law Firms

BY J. MARK SANTIAGO

Not so very long ago, four law firms in a large U.S. city merged into two firms and became its third and fourth largest firms in that city. At the time, the two new firms were comparable in size, profitability, and, many said, future potential. One firm, Aggressive Growing & Profitable (AGP) has gone on to become the second largest firm in that city, and is now one of the 100 largest law firms in America. The second firm, Gentlemanly, Stagnant & Breakeven (GSB), has slipped to be the seventh largest firm in town with modest staff growth, slowly increasing fee income, and an uncertain future.

This appendix will explore how two firms that were comparable only a few years ago now face completely different futures. The discussions held by the respective management committees of the two firms on how to measure and reward performance have significantly affected these firms. Performance-based partner pay was not, of course, the only reason that these two firms' performances diverged, but it is one of the most important, and I hope to demonstrate why. Today, one firm appears poised to break into the ranks of the "National Law Firm Elite," whereas the other aspires (or hopes?) to become the local office of a "National Firm." How could this happen? What did one firm do right? And, more important, what did one firm do wrong? Are there lessons to be learned that will help you manage your own firm and ensure not only its survival, but its growth and profitability as well?

Be Careful. You Might Get What You Pay For.

Aggressive & Profitable was founded fifteen years before the merger. Bill Aggressive and Joe Profitable had been law school classmates and associates at the largest firm in town. Both were corporate attorneys of unquestioned brilliance and had a constant desire to achieve. They stunned both the firm and their friends, when, two months before their certain admission to partnership, they left to found Aggressive & Profitable (A&P). Very quickly, they established a solid reputation for outstanding work, innovative ideas, and top-notch client service. Eight years later, at the time of the merger, A&P had thirty-five lawyers and some of the biggest corporate clients in town. In addition, it represented several of the *Fortune* 500 in local matters.

Growing & Growing was founded almost fifty years before the merger. Within a few years of its founding, it had established a solid record of dependable, if not distinguished, client representation among a large roster of public companies. In addition to its corporate practice, the firm had developed strong tax and litigation departments and had a growing environmental practice. Although larger than A&P at the time of the merger, the Growing firm was clearly junior partner in the union. All the founding partners were gone, and the firm had failed to develop a talented second generation of leaders. As a result, the merger was viewed as "salvation" by many of the Growing & Growing partners.

At the time of the mergers, the firms had disparate management and pay structures. The newly merged Aggressive firm came to be dominated by Mr. Aggressive, the senior partner of the old Aggressive & Profitable firm. Upon the merger with Growing & Growing, Aggressive was elected Managing Partner and he has been reelected every two years for the last ten. Aggressive believed in building broad and deep client relationships, actively encouraged cross-marketing by every partner, and in 1992, engaged a professional marketing consultant to train every partner in the firm. The merger of the two firms allowed him to bring his style of practicing law to a much larger clientele.

Over the years, under Mr. Aggressive's leadership, AGP developed a distinct client service style. Major clients were served by a team of attorneys made up of partners and associates with a variety of skills and specialties. Annually, the entire team met to develop a Client Service Plan for major clients. The plans typically projected the baseline level of legal activity that they expected the client to generate as well as target areas to expand the scope of services that AGP provided. In addition, and as best they could, the team tried to crystal-ball any special situations that might arise that would result in a significant increase or decrease in legal services provided to the client. Periodically throughout the year, the team would meet to review and, if necessary, revise the plan. The sum of all the Client Service Plans provided firm management with a base-fee estimate that they could compare to the overall fee billing capacity of the firm. This variance analysis helped them quantify the approximate amount of new business the firm had to generate in the coming year.

Of course, some teams were more successful at projecting than others, and no one could accurately predict the next mega-merger or bet-the-firm litigation. But the exercise did quantify the aggregate amount of new business that the firm would need and established marketing goals at the firm, departmental, and ultimately, individual levels. As one result of this planning process, the firm could project its theoretical fee revenue. By applying a utilization factor to its theoretical fee revenue, it could estimate expected annual fee revenue. By comparing these figures, AGP could make strategic marketing investment decisions in people and programs. All this planning fed into the firm's goal-driven compensation system and rewarded desired partner behavior while allowing management to change goals if that supported the strategic direction of the firm.

AGP's compensation system had developed over the years. At the time of the merger, both Aggressive & Profitable and Growing & Growing had similar systems that rewarded all the partners within the same law school class the same number of participation points within the compensation pool. Over the years, the weaknesses inherent within such a pay structure became more and more apparent. The increase in competition as well as unwillingness of some partners to support less productive ones forced changes on the management committee. Increasingly, the management committee felt that it had little, if any, influence over partner behavior, and with the dramatic increase in competition for business, the old way of doing things had to change.

As a response to the increase in competition, the AGP management committee embarked upon an extensive partner training program. The program emphasized a collaborative approach to marketing legal services and recognized that the best source of additional business was existing clients. Soon after implementing the new approach, Mr. Aggressive and the rest of the management committee began to see both an upturn in partner collaboration and, as a result, new business opportunities. However, they also noted that not all partners participated in the initial team marketing efforts and that, after a flurry of activity, overall participation began to lag.

The management committee began to experience more and more resistance from the partners to the ideas contained in the training courses. And, although it was expressed in a variety of ways ranging from the amount of time required to coordinate and prepare a team of lawyers for a client marketing call to "my client doesn't need any other services but those that we currently provide it" (that is, my services), some digging by the committee members revealed other reasons. Most of the reasons involved the way AGP's partners were paid. Despite an elaborate document that itemized more than a dozen factors that the firm compensated, most partners believed that the only activities that were really compensated were individual billable hours and individual sales credits. In addition, AGP had no method for differentiating between fee billing and engagement management credits. It was assumed that if a partner billed a matter, he or she also managed it. The firm had no method of allocating sales and billing credits among two or more partners, and by custom, awarded all credits to the most senior partner on the marketing team. Despite all the appeals to firm loyalty and the best efforts of the management committee to jawbone partners into compliance, the majority soon figured out the system and either participated in team client development in a half-hearted, begrudging manner or did not participate at all.

The Gentlemanly, Whiteshoe & Corvat firm was one of the oldest in the city. It had a long distinguished history of serving the old money segments of the population. The Gentlemanly firm specialized in the practice of looking after all the needs of their clients and those clients' considerable wealth. In the words of W. Cody Troustman III, the Managing Partner, "We hatch them, match them and dispatch them." Over the years, the firm was governed by a five-member management committee that was ritually reelected every two years. Mr. Troustman, whose father had been Managing Partner in earlier years, had been involved with management for ten years at the time of the merger and was immediately elected chairman of the new firm. He has occupied that position ever since. The partners' compensation was decided by a subcommittee of the management committee and was based largely upon years of service with the firm.

Stagnant & Breakeven had a somewhat less blue-blood image than that of Gentlemanly, Whiteshoe & Corvat. The firm was the result of several previous mergers among small firms that appeared to have been made with little strategic thought. The firm was a collection of individual practitioners who shared office space. As a result, no real firm culture developed, and its style was open. The firm had few, if any, real rules and partners, even by law firm standards, enjoyed extraordinary freedom. The management committee of the Stagnant firm met quarterly ("After all, what's to manage in a law firm?"), and its most important activity was to decide on annual partner compensation. At the time of the merger, the Stagnant firm was in serious trouble. A series of bad investments in branch offices and new practice areas had left the firm short of cash and dispirited. When the merger was proposed, it seemed like a dream come true to many of the Stagnant partners.

After the merger, the new firm, Gentlemanly, Stagnant & Breakeven (GSB), benefited from economies of scale that their increased size provided. Revenues grew at the rate of 5 percent per year, and profits increased at an annual rate of 3 percent. However, on a per partner basis, revenues were declining and profits were flat. At the time of their merger, the management committee of both firms decided that the new firm would treat all partners in a fair and collegial way. In an abundance of caution, it was decided that partner compensation would be determined on a groupwide basis and that seniority would be the sole determinant of how many points were awarded to a partner. Despite some heated discussions at the annual partner meetings, the management committee refused to change this method of profit distribution.

There were a few attempts to cross-sell additional legal services between the old Gentlemanly and Stagnant clients. However, for the most part, despite a very successful integration of the two firms' various departments, departmental clients were departmental clients, and there was little attempt to introduce clients to the firm's other services.

On a fine spring morning, Mr. Troustman was confronted in his personal conference room by several key partners from the firm's Corporate Department. Distressed by slow revenue growth and little actual growth in income, they had decided to leave Gentlemanly, Stagnant & Breakeven and join the firm of Aggressive Growing &

Profitable. Shortly after the three corporate partners left, the entire GSB Capital City Office moved to new space and became the Capital City office of another firm. In very short order, the firm lost nearly 20 percent of the partnership. And though panic was an emotion that few Gentlemanly partners had previously been familiar with, it soon became a regular companion.

In response to the crisis, the management committee of GSB decided to revise the partner compensation system in order to encourage the partners to develop new business.

Two Solutions, Two Outcomes

Aggressive Growing & Profitable undertook an analysis of its situation and decided that there was a disconnect between the behaviors that the management committee wanted to foster (cross-marketing and team selling) and the partner compensation system. Analysis and interviews showed that the partners of the firm could not see, other than in the abstract sense, "what's in it for me." The firm compensation system was designed and administered to measure individual partner billable hours and individual partner fee billings. And the partners did as they were paid to do, to the long-term detriment of the firm. In response to this analysis, the management committee completely redesigned the system.

In a headline, it designed and instated a pay-for-performance partner compensation system. The heart of the system was its identification of those activities that would enhance the overall strategic objectives of the firm, realistic and measurable goals that supported those objectives, and a variety of roles in which partners could advance the interests of the firm. These "contribution roles" recognized that not all partners were equal in their ability to help the firm achieve its objectives, but that everyone could contribute, if in different ways. As an example, Technical Partners were expected to have far more billable hours than either Client Service or Engagement Managing Partners. And Engagement Managing Partners were expected to have more billable hours than Client Service Partners. Conversely, a Technical Partner was expected to have no client fee (sales) credits, whereas an Engagement Management Partner was. Client Service Partners had the highest amount of projected client fee credits, and it was the most important criterion that they were evaluated by.

The AGP system was designed to balance numerous ways that individual partners could advance the cause of the firm, depending on each one's abilities. However, no partner was given a free ride, and even

Technical Partners were expected to participate in marketing efforts. After Aggressive Growing & Profitable had identified the roles in which partners contributed to the firm, they established different measurement criteria for each one. So, although each partner was evaluated on the same criteria (billable hours, matter management, client management, professional development, and firm good citizenship), the relative importance of each evaluative criterion was different depending on the contribution role. At AGP, Client Service Partners were expected to develop $2 million of business each year. In addition, they were expected to bill 750 client hours, participate in several firm management initiatives, and assume a mentoring role with one or more Engagement Partners. Engagement Managing Partners were expected to have $1 million in new client business, at least 1,250 billable hours, and additional administrative and firm-enhancing activities.

AGP also wanted to promote team marketing and changed the way that fee credits were divided among members of a successful marketing team. Under the old system, the senior-most member of the team got all the sales credits. In the new system, teams were allowed to either divide sales credits equally among all participating partners or, on a client-by-client basis, divide sales credits based on how the team wanted to divide them.

The management committee was careful to identify and include a number of qualitative evaluative criteria for each of the partner contribution roles. They did this so that the partner evaluation process did not become just a numbers game and because there were many qualitative issues that the firm wanted to promote. The AGP management committee established a separate compensation committee that administered the new program and linked it to an annual partner evaluation process. The process had two purposes. First, it determined an individual partner's compensation, based upon the standard metrics of the partner contribution roles and individual objectives set by the partner in the prior year and contained in his or her development program. Second, for the coming year, it established qualitative objectives that the partner would be evaluated on. A natural result of this process was an assessment of the individual partner's strengths and weaknesses. The plan to enhance a partner's skills and thereby address any identified weaknesses was designated the Annual Partner Development Program and became a part of the next year's process.

The transition to the new system was not without its critics and had the kinds of implementation problems that one might expect.

However, within a year, AGP was achieving dramatic marketing results. Within two years, gross revenues rose by more than 30 percent with an even larger increase in per partner profits. The firm continues its rapid growth pattern and, as noted at the beginning of the chapter, is poised to enter the top tier of national practice law firms.

The Gentlemanly, Stagnant & Breakeven firm adopted a quite different approach. When the GSB management committee met, it was in a state of panic. Expenses had to be cut and quickly! The firm's once crowded offices were now quite open, much more expensive on a per attorney basis, and in the headquarters building of their largest client. The committee did not want to alarm the client in any way, so it decided that no overtures concerning a possible rent concession would be made. With that decision made, there were only two possible places to find the money necessary to keep the firm going: partner or associate compensation. The management committee quickly agreed that no partner would be dismissed, so the associates were the only remaining source of firm cash saving. In a very short time, GSB dismissed forty associates. Some had only recently joined the firm out of law school. Others had two or three years of experience.

The results of this mass dismissal are still being felt. Five years later, the firm still has more partners than associates, and what would be the sixth- through eighth-year associates (prime partner evaluation years) do not exist at the firm, with the exception of three lateral hires.

Of more significance is how the management committee changed the partner compensation system. The committee very quickly realized that it needed fees to survive. So they developed a new compensation structure that they believed would produce fees. The management committee decided that the allocation of profits among the partners was to be based primarily upon the number of hours that an individual partner worked. The formula that the committee adopted placed a premium on hours which provided a strong incentive to the partners themselves to bill as much time as possible. Which is exactly what they did.

The GSB partners were compensated according to the following formula: The total value of a partner's billed time was multiplied by eight and then added to the total amount of fees that a partner billed, multiplied by two, and the total value of the engagements that the partner managed, multiplied by one. These totals were calculated for all the partners, and then a percent of the overall total was calculated for each partner. This percent became a partner's share of the annual profits.

It soon became apparent to the partners that to invest additional time in selling more work than they could do themselves was of little use to them. So, over time, a curious thing happened. The partners began to work more than the associates. Indeed, five years after the mass partner walkout, the associates at GSB recorded 350 less billable hours than the partners! This in a firm with no leverage and little ability to charge a premium for partner time.

At this time, the GSB firm is slowly sinking into a morass. It cannot leverage its associates because there is not enough work for them to do. There is not enough work for them because the partners keep it for themselves in order to increase their own pay. The partners don't sell more work because they are fully utilized and to do so would not compensate them enough for the risks involved. Would you be surprised to learn that the firm is almost 33 percent below national survey averages for per partner profits in similar-sized law firms? Probably not.

These two cases demonstrate that approaches to partner compensation in law firms are changing dramatically. In addition, as extensive as the changes have been, I believe that far more substantive change is on the horizon. Increasing competition, the decline in firm loyalties, and the quest for a more balanced work life by some partners will drive the system to far greater changes than have occurred in the last ten years.

Shifting Loyalties

With few exceptions, law firms no longer command all of a large corporation's legal work. Gone are the days when a specific firm rendered day-to-day legal advice and handled everything from the lease on the Portland office to the purchase of a subsidiary and the issuance of new stocks and bonds. By and large, corporations are now shopping for service among groups of law firms to meet their diverse needs. These companies base their selections on a number of criteria, including perceived expertise in the required field, the cost and timeliness of the needed service, and the level of attention the firm's attorneys will be able to give the matter.

This situation is further complicated by the steady erosion of attorneys' loyalty to their law firms — and vice versa. In the past, it was not unusual for a law student to be hired as an intern for two summers and, ultimately, spend a forty-year career as an attorney at the same firm. At the same time, an unwritten but widely understood and accepted compact among lawyers required younger, more productive associates to defer income to the older partners. In return, associates were trained in the practice of law, and those associates who ultimately made partner received a stream of virtually guaranteed income until retirement. The fact that this income often exceeded the current value of their contributions to the firm made up for their lean years as associates. And the cycle was complete.

Today the situation is very different. Although many attorneys still spend their entire legal careers at the same firms, a growing number of partners can cite two, three, or even four previous firms on their resumes. Just as corporate clients shop around for legal services, partners are shopping around for career opportunities that will offer appropriate compensation and meet their work and lifestyle requirements. Firms contribute to this instability by actively recruiting partners and attorneys from rival firms to bolster certain practice areas.

Just as fewer attorneys are satisfied to stay with one firm their entire careers, firms are more aggressively evaluating performance at all levels. Partnership is no longer a guarantee of lifetime employment. Firms increasingly evaluate partners' performance and contributions based on absolute standards. And those who fail to meet the firm's criteria are frequently asked to leave — something that was unheard of several years ago. Firms are also more willing to lay off partners to clean house of ineffective colleagues, thereby improving the profit ratio per partner.

These weakened loyalties have made law firm compensation an increasingly complex and dangerous endeavor. Complex because of the myriad of compensable factors that firms now want to incorporate into their partner evaluation criteria. And dangerous because at no other time have firms been at such risk of losing key contributors to rival firms.

There are also other variables to consider — globalization and mergers and acquisitions among them. After all, what worked for ten partners in a single office with similar backgrounds and long work histories together simply will not work for a firm with hundreds of partners with diverse backgrounds, spread throughout the world who have been brought together by plan, merger, or happenstance.

Compensating the Rain Dancers

It is no longer appropriate to determine partners' compensation by asking, "Who was the chief rainmaker?" or "Who founded the firm?" The founders usually are long gone, and the very definition of "rainmaker" is being challenged. In many cases, it is difficult, if not impossible, to credit any individual attorney for a client relationship. Managing a client relationship is a convoluted process, involving the work of attorneys throughout the firm. In addition, with firm–client ties more tenuous than ever, the traditional rainmaker who persuades a client to sign on with the firm, but never has any real contact with the client again, may actually hinder the firm's ability to maintain that client. Increasingly, firms are realizing that a partner's contribution does not begin and end with billable hours and client billings. In turn, the firm's compensation system must reflect these new priorities.

Increasingly, firms want to go beyond these financial factors and recognize and reward nonfinancial contributions that partners make to the firm. Some of the most common nonfinancial factors include:

- Client tending, which includes maintaining superior ongoing client relationships and forging multiple contacts at different levels;

- Attorney development, including personal legal skill improvement, as well as enhancing the technical legal, marketing, and presentation skills among junior partners and associates;

- Practice development by increasing the public's awareness of the firm's expertise or specialty areas;

- Administrative management at the department, practice, office, and firm level.

As the number of compensable factors increases, formally documenting the compensation system and ensuring that all partners understand how it works become increasingly important. On more than one occasion, we have heard a partner say, "I used to know what was important around here — now I am not sure." As firms broaden their evaluative criteria, many struggle with how much emphasis to give the various factors. But once the weighting has been determined, it must be applied evenly between offices and among the departments within those offices.

As the compensation system grows more complex, the demand for accurate, timely, and detailed data to support compensation decisions also increases. Often a firm's existing, antiquated off-the-shelf accounting software does not even capture the correct data that the firm needs to manage its compensation program. These systems were designed, purchased, and installed when the only important information to capture and report was billable hours and fee credits. Few can handle multiple partner origination credits, and fewer still can be modified to distinguish between responsibility for supervising a matter and client management. Any firm that is contemplating a change in its billing and accounting systems should review its quantifiable compensable factors and ensure that data on them will be readily available from the new system.

Building Trust in the System

The declining loyalty of attorneys to their firms exacerbates the inherent dangers of implementing any changes in the compensation system. Partners must be able to understand and trust the decisions made using the system. If partners feel they have been wronged by a new compensation system, they may appeal to a management committee to review their case. But, just as likely, they may dial up a friendly headhunter or accept the long-offered lunch invitation from the managing partner of a crosstown firm. In addition to losing a key partner, the firm may also lose several promising associates and several million dollars in billings.

To simplify the process and minimize the dangers of changing compensation systems, it is important that a partnership compensation system contain the following key elements:

1. A clearly defined and broadly supported firm vision and a strategy for achieving that vision;

2. Defined roles for partners within the partnership with explicit expectations and a clear definition of success in each role;

3. A structured goal-setting and evaluation process that provides partners frequent constructive feedback;

4. Wide availability of substantive data that will allow partners to personally validate compensation decisions using available guidelines and criteria.

Vision and Strategy Development

Vision and strategy development are the logical starting points for a firm's partner compensation program. After all, if a firm does not know where it is going, how can it direct and reward the actions that will make it succeed? Although strategy development can be a long and arduous process, it can be addressed as logical answers to a series of questions, such as the following:

1. How does the firm want to build its competitive advantage?
2. What is the firm's culture?
3. What behavior does the firm want or need to change?
4. What is the firm unwilling to change?
5. What does the firm do well?
6. Who "owns" the firm's clients?
7. What aspects of the firm's culture are very important to partners?
8. What does the firm need to reward?

This list is by no means exhaustive, but it demonstrates the breadth of issues that a strategy and its supporting compensation system must address. A firm's responses to these questions will also help define partners' roles — that is to say, what success is in each of the roles. In turn, these roles provide a standard or benchmark against which all partners will be evaluated in the future.

The importance of a firm's strategic vision cannot be overemphasized. The recent breakup of one major New York City law firm can be attributed to many factors, including a flawed strategy of growth for growth's sake. The firm's partner compensation system also lacked meaningful links with either a partner's individual contributions or support of the firm's vision.

Individual Partner Goal Setting

This phase has two distinct steps. First, each partner develops an individual plan outlining how he or she will contribute to the firm's overall success. These plans are developed late in the year in connection with the firm's business planning cycle for the coming year. These plans are based on clearly defined and differential role models — client manager, engagement manager, working attorney, administrative manager — conceived during the vision and strategy development phase. The strategic plans should also include specific milestones that, when achieved, produce identifiable results to help achieve the firm's overall strategy.

For example, partners Smith and Jones are in the same law school class. Partner Jones is a truly great litigator who attracts, and usually wins, major cases. On the other hand, partner Smith is a brilliant technician with an ability to manage and remember hundreds of individual facts and circumstances. The best use of these individuals is quite different. Partner Jones's role in the firm would be that of an individual contributor, whereas partner Smith might be called upon to be a case manager. The partners' plans would recognize their areas of expertise and, in light of their different roles, establish different objectives and evaluative criteria. Partner Jones, as an individual contributor, might be evaluated on the quality of his work, the complexity of the litigation he handles, and his responsiveness to clients. As a case manager, partner Smith is evaluated on the selection and management of the attorneys performing the assignment, identification of potential engagement expansion opportunities, and of course, the quality of work performed.

The second step of this phase occurs late in the firm's business year and requires each partner to submit a written self-assessment to the firm's management. This assessment compares the year's goals from the partners' individual strategic plans to their actual achievements. The assessment also allows the partners to notify management of other noteworthy accomplishments for the year that were not in the original strategic plan.

Assessment and Evaluation

At the end of the year, the assessment process begins. Individual partners meet with their evaluator — department head, office manager, compensation committee member, or managing partner — to review their prior year's achievements. This conversation is based on the individual partners' strategic plans and the year's results. Individual partner performance data — his or her numbers — are still a major topic of discussion, but performance in more subjective areas, such as attorney development, practice enhancement, and firm management is also included.

At the conclusion of the individual meetings, the evaluators get together and, based upon the firm's overall strategy and needs, evaluate the partners relative to each other. This process groups partners into various hierarchical levels and allows for a firmwide "equity" evaluation.

Before beginning the evaluation process, some firms establish expected distribution percentages. For example, "Relative to our firm's standards, we expect 5 percent to substantially exceed expectations, 10 percent to exceed expectations, 75 percent to meet expectations (with gradations in the 'meet' category), and 10 percent to fail to meet expectations." Such a distribution ranks partners and helps the firm and the individuals involved make long-term career-planning decisions. But the ultimate outcome of this phase is, of course, pay and bonus decisions.

It is important that a partner be able to independently confirm his or her performance evaluation periodically and, at the end of the year, validate the firm's pay decisions. Therefore, whatever criteria a firm uses to evaluate its partners — client development, management, billing, collections — the firm's management information system must provide a ready means for individual partners to assess their performance. If partners are measured on something, appropriate information should be available so that they can keep score.

Communicating Pay Decisions

The final phase of any compensation program — and the one most frequently overlooked — is communicating final results to the individual partners. Firms that downplay the importance of effective communication squander one of their best opportunities to direct partner behavior and affect firm performance.

An appropriate member of the firm — department head, office manager, executive committee member — and the affected partner should discuss individual partner pay and bonus decisions. These discussions should clearly and directly link the pay and bonus decisions to the partner's actual performance, compared with the goals set in their individual strategic plans and previously defined roles with the firm. This is an opportunity to explain "why you got what you got," and to discuss how individual partners' strengths can be leveraged and what weaknesses need to be addressed. It may be an appropriate time to discuss a partner's long-term career goals and opportunities at the firm and that individual's role in the firm.

Although all partner compensation systems differ, many lack functionality. Many of the problems that a partnership encounters from its pay decisions are rooted in the system itself. For example, many systems have individual components that are poorly documented and misunderstood by those involved. In addition, the linkages between the various components are unclear to firm management and to individual partners, or are simply not there.

The Partnership Compensation System

A complete partnership compensation system can be broken into four key phases, as illustrated in Exhibit B.1.

Exhibit B.1

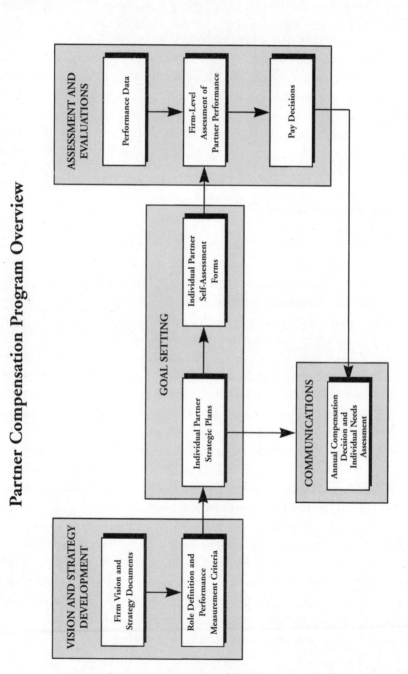

Partner Compensation Program Overview

This annual review is also the starting point for the following year's compensation cycle when partners prepare their individual strategic plans for the coming year, based on these discussions.

Closing the Loop

By closing the compensation loop, the compensation system becomes an effective mechanism for directing partner behavior and achieving the firm's strategy. As firms adapt to succeed in their changing environment, the compensation system can help individual partners appreciate the integral part they play in their firm's long-term success. As in all change, the most difficult step is the first. Before embarking on a major overhaul of its compensation system, a firm needs the following four components:

1. A clear, broadly shared, articulated vision of where the firm is going;

2. A management group that is committed to undertaking the substantial changes required to achieve the firm's vision;

3. A managing partner with both the patience and the drive to take day-to-day responsibility for implementing and managing the necessary changes;

4. A partnership that understands and supports the firm's vision and strategy, as well as the behavioral changes required to achieve the firm's goals.

Revising a compensation system in a partnership is a long and arduous process. It strikes at the foundations of the firm, and a revision has as much potential for ill as for good effects on a firm. Change should be undertaken neither lightly nor with the expectation that any fix to the compensation system is permanent. Compensation systems need annual reviews and periodic adjustments to ensure that they correctly reflect the firm's current thinking about its strategy and how best to achieve success.

A complete overhaul of a partner compensation system can consume the better part of a year and substantial amounts of the firm management's time. But those firms that stay the course and commit the necessary resources reap substantial benefits.

Appendix C

Three Legs of a Stool

The Decisions That Shape the Marketing Function

BY Abigail J. Gouverneur and John Bliss

M ost of the chapters of this book have dealt with the most visible aspect of rainmaking: sales. Yet there is another, equally important, aspect of rainmaking: marketing. In effect, by identifying and cultivating potential clients, marketing is seeding the clouds. Let's look a little closer at this area.

Successful rainmakers are wondrous people, whether born or self-made, but there are clearly never enough of them. That's true for firms of all sizes, and that's why most organizations must sooner or later address the question "How do we organize (institutionalize) the marketing function?"

The trigger for this decision often results from a situation like the following. The firm (or the practice unit) has enjoyed years of steady growth because of the rainmaking talents of founder Pat Smith. Pat promotes the firm (markets) and Pat sells; the other partners implement. But nothing is forever, and wishing it won't make it so. Eventually, Pat decides to (pick one): retire, join another firm, take two years off to hike the Himalayas. Pat's rainmaking days are over.

From a marketing standpoint, the firm's partners can choose to (1) hire a Pat clone, (2) perform that role themselves, or (3) develop the marketing function. The first course can be extraordinarily expensive, and the second is likely to be difficult for people without marketing experience. Only the third can create an infrastructure that outlasts individuals and stands the test of time. But where to start?

The Marketing Department Philosophy

Fast forward to the future: Let's say that you just accepted the position as the senior marketing officer for a major international professional service organization. The search was competitive; the headhunter interviewed more than twenty-five candidates, the search committee dined with a dozen, and you are the lucky recipient of the offer and the signing bonus. After the champagne, what next? What philosophy do you bring to the assignment? How will you organize and manage the function? What will be your first task? What objectives will you set?

Few of us have the luxury of wiping the slate clean and starting from scratch. But in our experience of fifteen plus years in counseling professional service firms, it is clear that each marketing department we encounter has a philosophy — sometimes explicit, sometimes assumed — about "how we do things here." There are, in our opinion, three fundamental junctures where this philosophy becomes visible as the standard operating procedure of the marketing department.

These three junctures relate to (1) the brand, (2) the organization structure, and (3) the fundamental role of the marketing staff. Each juncture requires hard choices that define the marketing posture of the firm. What follows are the opinions of senior marketing professionals who think about these choices. Most were interviewed by the authors; footnotes reference other published sources. Each of these professionals has an articulate point of view, as well as experience in making the model work within a large organization.

The Marketing System

The marketing communications function does not live in a vacuum. It exists as part of an overall system that identifies clients, generates leads, and sells and performs the work. The best schematic of this system we've seen was developed for this book and has already appeared as Exhibit 4.1.

Unfortunately for professional service marketers, many of their clients — the professionals — do not understand this system. They see the marketing department as something "other," hanging out in space, there only to pump out brochures and maintain the mailing lists. Ideally, of course, the marketing team and the selling/performing team should work closely together. It's their joint responsibility to generate relevant market information, target potential clients, identify pertinent business issues, create intellectual capital around those issues, and develop tools to advance and maintain relationships.

To quote Rob Duboff of Mercer Management Consulting, "Internal 'disconnects' — senior partner attitudes that can hinder the marketing team's effectiveness — are typical. First priority is given to sales and client service, with marketing often playing a secondary role."[1] In other words, line managers and practitioners give lots of attention and emphasis to the right side of Exhibit 4.1 and feel less ownership for the left side. A lack of interaction and feedback between the two roles can throw off the marketer's ability to add value to the practitioner in a timely, relevant way.

Whether the organization sees the marketing department as integral to the success of its business or as a printing and production services arm is more a matter of persistence and influence than command and control. According to Gary Gerard, National Director of Marketing & Communications for Deloitte & Touche:

> On any given day in a consensus-driven, flat matrix organization, no one has to listen to one word from the marketing communications department. For the communicator focused on control, this is definitely the wrong kind of environment in which to maintain a rewarding career. Gaining respect and trying to manage perceptions of the role of the communicator is a daily effort. Persuasion and logic play a big part in this. The power of the idea will always win the day.[2]

Market the Practices vs. Market the Brand

So, what do you — the new senior marketer — turn to first? Probably the initial question will be "market the practices or market the brand?" There's a constant tension between meeting the needs of the practitioners, who are working to sell services across the client's desk, and meeting the needs of the firm's global identity, which adds credibility and identity to all practitioners. Where do you put your emphasis?

We select this as "Job #1" because it drives so many resource allocation decisions. The people who put their eggs in the branding basket will begin their work by conducting an up-to-date positioning study, putting huge chunks of the total budget into national advertising, centralized graphic design standards, and an overarching public relations image campaign. The people who sit on the "practices" side of the teeter-totter will be more likely to fly around the country to meet with local office marketing staff; sit in on practice group or industry meetings; train industry spokespeople; help practices define their products and markets; and train their staffs to provide practice level plans, strategies, and tactics.

You might think that where the weight falls on the teeter-totter would depend on the inherent strength of the brand. For example, if you don't yet have a national brand name, you focus on marketing the practices until the overall brand begins to build of its own accord. Conversely, marketers for large, well-known professional service brands would focus all of their time on managing those brands. That's not what we found.

Even among a tight group of national brand name service organizations — the Big Six accounting firms — we find differences of opinion. Each marketing professional has a strong point of view on the matter, and each believes his or her way is the "right way." First, let's hear from the "build the practices" school of thought. Mary Ellen Bianco, of Coopers & Lybrand, says, "I think professional services are not really brandable in a way that is sufficiently discreet to do marketing." Robert Moulthrop, currently from Scudder but previously a marketing executive at KPMG Peat Marwick, notes:

> The glory days of Big Six television advertising tell the tale. Andersen is still where they were and, while their ads were excellent, that's not the reason. The others spent magnificent sums for Super Bowl ads (and other stuff), and it really didn't help. The growth is in the practices, and the practices are driven by individuals who know their growth depends on *their* products.

Frank Ruotolo, CEO of The Futures Group, a management consulting firm that specializes in business intelligence and scenario planning services, comments, "the strength of the people in selling is more important than all of the above [branding, practice building] put together. You can have the best marketing program in the world, yet if the troops aren't aggressive about sales, it will fail."

From the front lines of branding, we hear this from Adrian J. R. Smith, Arthur Andersen's managing partner worldwide for marketing and communications: "Performance and reputation are inextricable, and one has to drive both. You can't rely on performance to lead image without having the right performance, and you can't rely on image if the performance isn't right." Yet he knows what he's responsible for: "What I'm marketing is Arthur Andersen. And it's the building of the brand equity, and the measuring of the brand equity from year to year, and the enhancing of that brand equity, which is so much of my responsibility today."[3]

Sam Hill, former head of marketing for Booz-Allen & Hamilton and now head of Worldwide Strategic Planning and Business Development for D'Arcy Masius Benton & Bowles, has this to say: "Andersen and McKinsey have proved that brands are important even in a relationship marketing business. Andersen has shown that even in a sophisticated, complex service business, clients are susceptible to advertising." In his mind, the move to branding may drive professional services into a two-tier industry model:

> You're either a billion-dollar-plus firm, or you have a prof-itable 100-person-or-under firm. Anything else in between is a train station on your way to one or the other extreme. That's because big firms can support the brand with major dollars, while smaller firms can compete in clear niches.

Randy Lindel, an advertising executive with Arnold Communications in Boston, agrees:

> If there's no brand, there's no marketplace leverage for individual products and practices. A brand can provide recognition, quality standards, and a positive value set for any business unit under its umbrella. For new businesses or practices, this is particularly valuable. Established practices contribute to the value of the brand with their success.

With Mary Ellen Bianco's point, that service businesses are difficult to differentiate sufficiently, Lindel disagrees. "Service firms really do differ greatly. They are aggressive, conservative, cutting edge, traditional, intellectual, practical, etc." Yet, on the other side of the argument, when Smith is asked what the brand equity of the name Arthur Andersen is, he replies, "smart, creative, and innovative people who can improve their client's business performance."[4] To us, that positioning could apply to almost any services firm we know.

Our bottom line: We're concerned that while national and international services firms will continue in the direction of major eight-figure branding campaigns, they might lose sight of the importance of their ideas, the work being done in the trenches. That's where firms truly differentiate themselves, not in thirty-second advertising spots.

Centralize or Decentralize?

The next critical question addresses the issue of where marketing activities are actually performed. This is another dilemma that influences resource deployment as much as the branding decision.

Deloitte & Touche, one of the Big Six accounting firms, found this out in 1990 when Deloitte, Haskins & Sells merged with Touche Ross. Deloitte had traditionally operated a well-staffed, centralized marketing operation that performed market research, identified national opportunities, created marketing plans around those opportunities, and then fed them to the local offices. Offices were not constrained to follow their advice, but most of them did. At that time, National Marketing was vertically integrated, from strategy through advertising and video, through printing and production.

On the other hand, Touche Ross had operated from a "bottom-up" paradigm, almost diametrically opposite to Deloitte. Its emphasis was on local office support; any national resources were used as if they were contractors — preparing a bid for work requested by the local office. When these two firms merged, the two styles clashed. The coincident recession of 1990–1991 blunted the clash because the firm cut back on marketing expenditures severely. When the merged firm came out of the recession, it adopted a balanced approach — more complete resources at the local level, with flatter and less didactic direction from National. It's a combination that seems to work well. According to Marketing Director Gerard, "We centralize the approach but not the responsibility. Today, national marketers need to be great internal consultants and worry a lot less about tactical matters related to delivering communications."[5]

In our interviews, we found again that there's clearly a choice to be made, with pluses and minuses on both sides. If, for example, one centralizes marketing, one risks building a costly, high-overhead empire that might not stay close enough to the real market. Referring to Exhibit 4.1, this approach risks breaking the feedback loop because the information has so far to travel to get back to decision makers. Yet how else can one ensure quality and optimize the brand and its positioning?

There's a large gathering in the "centralized" camp. The new KPMG CEO Stephen Butler "plans to take basic support functions —

such as marketing, hiring and financial control — away from partners and managers and centralize those tasks." The move, he insists, will free people to spend more time on client business. It won't be easy, he admits. "If you take away something that gives people power and control, they don't like it," he said. "But the real power of a $2.5 billion organization is in leveraging shared knowledge."[6]

Coopers' Mary Ellen Bianco agrees: "Centralize the functions," she says, "to take advantage of technology and compete in both a global marketplace and a truly national marketplace. You can't do it either effectively or efficiently if it's decentralized." Jerry Walsh, President of Walsh Communications and a specialist in professional services media, feels some functions are better kept decentralized. "I find that it's essential to centralize national public relations, especially media relations, but that many marketing functions, excluding advertising, work best when they're close to the local offices and regions."

To Sam Hill, late of Booz-Allen & Hamilton, there's no current "best way," simply a life cycle that firms go through. First, large firms do "amateur marketing," where they let everyone do what they want. Then, they centralize markets to get more control over messages and budgets — but these centralized departments eventually break down, for a handful of reasons, namely:

- There's a limit to how much you can control centrally anyway, especially with desktop publishing. When Booz-Allen audited itself in 1996, it found twenty-one paper-based newsletters as well as several Internet-based newsletters. As Sam Hill said, "God only knows what companies we market to by accident."

- The department must exist within expense control parameters. "Only one firm I know of has ever shown the discipline not to touch the marketing budget, and that's McKinsey."

- It's difficult to stay fresh if you're not on the front line of the market. If you have a large enough staff to perform all the marketing disciplines, then they get distant from the market. If there are six people in National Marketing, then they're still speaking to journalists, line people, public relations counsel. "If you have thirty or forty people, they talk to each other," he says.

- People inherently want to buck the system. "If you centralize graphic design, newsletter production, and Web sites, you may be able to clean it up once, but the next time they won't even tell you they've taken the initiative."

To some degree, what a professional believes about the importance of the brand will influence how he or she feels about the locus of power for marketing communications. As Randy Lindel comments, "As with financial services, professional service firms need to develop a top-down marketing strategy if they are to have any chance at creating a distinctive 'brand.'" He believes, as do many of his forward-thinking colleagues, that the marketing strategy must be an integral part of the firm's business plan, and responsibility for it should reside with a chief marketing officer (CMO) who is a member of top management.

On the subject of execution, however, Lindel stops short:

> Execution of the marketing strategy should reside within individual business units. Unit marketing directors should have a strong dotted-line relationship to the CMO for plan development and executional consistency, but day-to-day marketing work should be accomplished in the business unit.

Robert Moulthrop agrees:

> Any firm with more than one office needs a strong, single vision from the top about what the firm is, what its priorities are, and what its long- and short-range goals are. At the same time, the firm's current and prospective clients aren't really interested in 'the firm'; they're interested in the partner, the kind of work performed, quality, timeliness, and cost. Virtually all implementation strategies and tactics need to be decentralized down to the lowest possible place in the organization — preferably with a professional marketing person who knows the business, knows the partners, knows the market, and can develop a realistic program that will deliver potential clients and enhance existing relationships.

Our bottom line: Two priorities emerge — first, make sure that local offices have more than adequate information gathering, proposal writing, and other feedback to make a stellar sales effort, coupled with strong in-market visibility. Then, deliver a clear, well-conceived national umbrella program from National Marketing, centralizing the headquarters marketing functions (like national publicity) and anything else that can be done more efficiently from one spot. As for proliferation of newsletters and Web sites and bad design, we'd rather see professionals encourage target-specific marketing than squash it, even if it means suffering some bad execution.

The Role of the Marketing Staff

Put more bluntly, this section would be called, "to outsource or not to outsource," and it's a particularly thorny question for people who inherit full-blown departments. It has to do with what you expect from your internal staff: (1) expertise in a particular marketing communications discipline, such as speech writing or media relations; (2) playing the role of content specialist for a particular practice; (3) generalist/account executive, acting as a marketing advisor to any area that requires counsel.

This is the one leg of the stool where most of the professionals we interviewed agreed: building complete in-house capabilities for marketing communications services doesn't by definition get the work done better, faster, or cheaper in the long run. In-house staffs over time grow to accommodate the peak workload, not the base level. Frank Ruotolo, of The Futures Group, summarizes the thinking of many of our panel: "I believe in developing a core team, sufficient to handle the lowest ebb you can expect, while outsourcing to accommodate growth."

In the past, many marketing staffs operated on the "waitress model": when the phone rang with a partner or practice request, the marketing professional was responsible for getting the job done — whether it was a brochure, a PR plan, some advertising, or a newsletter. In the current environment, marketing staffs have had to move to the "nutritionist" model, where the marketer develops a recommendation based on a market analysis, specifying what's needed, and execution is, in some ways, less of a critical subject. The trend seems to be to hire internally a cadre of strategists and generalists who can help the professionals develop intellectual capital, and to outsource most communications functions, such as media relations and collateral development, to external specialists.

As providers of outside services, we clearly have a bias. However, we don't believe that an outside firm can be all things to a client — one outside firm can't and shouldn't provide all communications services to a large firm. That would rob the firm of the biggest benefit of using an outside firm: focus. In the words of Randy Lindel:

> People know a third party will generally pay more attention to the work, get it done well, on time and on budget. Firms need a small number of inside people who can strategize, plan, and direct firmwide and practice-level marketing. Professional service marketing people should be strategists and planners, not managers of departments.

Deloitte & Touche, LLP works with twenty or so outside service providers. According to Gary Gerard:

> Managing multiple vendors is a challenge. It's a lot like sailing — constantly trimming and tacking. Keeping the right mix requires constant review and getting the right measurements of performance. You also need someone inside the practice — staff or a consulting partner — to manage relations with the outside expert. And outside firms need to turn working relationships into partnerships by coming up with ideas and always staying in touch."[7]

Regarding the question of whether to outsource or build internal resources, Robert Moulthrop advises:

> Don't build more than you have to; don't buy more than you should. These days, a couple of professionals, a computer, and a realistic budget can go a long way. I also think a small firm that knows the needs of professional service marketing can provide a lot of help. The subject should be approached almost on a project-by-project basis.

Our opinion is that content managers will be the model for the next decade. We are hearing about more and more firms who want to hire "information managers" who will track an industry or a function on a daily basis, feeding the relevant information to the practice people on an as-needed basis. If we take a final look at the system illustrated in Exhibit 4.1, we can see why: Management information generation is the link between the marketing and sales effort and, as information becomes increasingly demand-driven, rather than supply-driven, professionals need an extra set of eyes and ears to help them be good marketers.

The New Paradigm

So, what does all this mean? When a service firm institutionalizes the marketing function, it's an indication that it has matured as a business and is no longer solely dependent on the work of a few rainmakers. In early 1997, Bliss, Gouverneur performed a benchmarking assignment for one of our clients to determine how they should capture marketplace information. Based on this study, and the interviews we completed, we can confidently assert that the wave of the future in marketing professional services includes:

- A centralized, top-down strategy;
- An increased emphasis on brand management and development;
- Additional outsourcing of functional capabilities;
- Decentralized (practice- or geography-based) implementation;
- Specific, assigned responsibility for information capture and dissemination;
- Penalties for line professionals who don't share marketplace information;
- Reliance on new media to share information, but not to the extent that it replaces face-to-face meetings between colleagues.

As Sam Hill noted, "The definition of a brand is a relationship that goes beyond the transaction or the individual, a multistep process between awareness and purchase intention." Did we ever use to talk like that? We have all witnessed a huge increase in marketing sophistication in the service business in the past decade, and we expect to match it in the decade to come.

Appendix D

Creating Presenters

BY SIMS WYETH

Mark Twain once saw a lawyer speaking with his hands in his pockets, and commented on the rarity of such a sight, a lawyer with his hands in his *own* pockets. Lawyers are no different from other professionals: They all want to be paid for the full value of their services, and they don't know what to do with their hands when talking to a group. Actually, professionals' ignorance of speaking doesn't stop there. Having devoted years to acquiring their technical skills, most have not developed themselves as speakers to any great extent. Their education has not taught them the skill (as it used to), and their training as young professionals has focused on technical subjects. Although lawyers can be expected to be more rhetorically skilled than, say, civil engineers, in general the need for sales and presentation training is evident in all the professions. Professionals don't know what to do with their hands. They also struggle with the fundamentals of sales and persuasion: Know your audience, define your objective, and structure your remarks accordingly. This ignorance of persuasive speaking dumbs them down at moments of high visibility, and being a dumb professional in a sales situation is a problem.

It's a problem for several reasons. First, it's hard to get business if your people act dumb up in front of the room. They may be smart and know everything about the subject at hand, but if someone comes across better than they do, they lose. Clients make judgments based on their perceptions, and if your people can't speak with conviction, clarity, and color about their area of expertise, someone who can will beat them out. Second, it's incredibly draining to be a bad speaker — draining for the speaker, his or her staff, and the resources of the firm. People who have developed the knack for speaking effectively can prepare rather quickly. People who haven't waste their own time and their companies'. Compounding that, they don't get good return on the time they invest in preparing because their speaking is not colorful, compelling, and memorable.

There is a school of thought that says the marketing of professional services *is* the delivery of those services. In other words, the professional service business is a performance business. The product is a performance. If that is true (and it is at least partly true), presentations become a key iconic element in the clients' perception of your capabilities. How you present demonstrates how you will do the work. In fact, some firms admit that in certain "beauty contests" there is no perceptible difference in technical capabilities. All firms in the running can do the work more or less equally well. So the client judges you not on your technical abilities, but on the perceived quality of your presentation. And if they're hiring a litigator, they will want to be impressed when the litigator speaks.

Given the importance of this fundamental skill, how can a manager ensure that the skill is being developed and nurtured throughout the organization?

Creating the Right Values

One important way is to make sure the skill is valued. Although it may seem obvious to some that technical expertise is only as good as the firm's ability to communicate it, many professionals harbor a negative attitude about sales and sales presenting. They may not admit it, but they associate sales with something distasteful, and will scorn the sales process for being "manipulative" and "phony." You may hear such things as "I don't want to be a used-car salesperson," or "I don't want to sound like a late night infomercial." These sentiments are the sounds of someone clinging to an image that a professional is someone who has mastered a body of knowledge and who is valued by the world for his or her thoroughly reasoned expertise. The sales process is simply a necessary evil to them, one that is best left to the guys who can't cut it technically, the semiretired, and the slicksters on staff who are a mile wide and an inch deep.

One way of combating this attitude is to ensure that firmwide initiatives in sales presentation training are (1) well conceived for the particular challenges that the firm faces, and (2) led by internal people who have credibility with technical experts and senior management. Your people must see that the training does not attempt to turn skilled, experienced introverts into back-slapping enthusiasts. The program must make it plain as day that there are many ways to be successful as a sales presenter. This article will address the particular competencies individuals should be able to demonstrate later on, but people are most effective as presenters when they are simply and fully themselves. Someone who is extremely thorough, attentive to customer issues, and deliberate in style and pace can be extremely effective. People who are logical and fact-based in their arguments do not have to come across like Mr. Spock — flat, emotionless, and dull. They, too, can be substantive and stylish in their own way.

In fact, that false duality is the pernicious core of the problem — the belief that you're either substantive and boring or shallow and entertaining. In the pursuit of excellence in sales presenting, that false reasoning should be rooted out of the firm. Management should reward and recognize all those who bridge that gap, and should insist that technical competence is only a fraction of the battle. After all, they should say, what good is the competence if we can't get the work?

Underlying these dismissive attitudes toward sales and presentation skills is the fear of presenting. Public speaking has appeared on many surveys as the number-one fear in America. Death is number seven on the list, which means that some on your professional staff would rather die than make a presentation. Jerry Seinfeld commented on this by observing that when we go to a funeral, we'd rather be in the box than deliver the eulogy. Presenting to strangers is often easier than presenting to our colleagues, so the idea of a training process is even more threatening. For these reasons, it is important that the method for exposing people to training and coaching in presentation skills is sensitive to these fears.

Managing the Process

On a more concrete plane, there are several ways to begin to build the competence into your organization. One way is to hire an outside consultant who can conduct both curriculum-based training and advise individual professionals and presentation teams on specific sales presentations. The combination is a good one-two punch because what gets taught in the training room gets reinforced in the real world.

Another method is to hire an outside consultant to develop a corps of internal trainers and coaches who can run training and advise on specific presentations. This can also work, but only if the internal people have credibility with the professionals and the backing of senior management. Management should select the internal people for this responsibility based on their ability to contribute in different geographic and functional areas of the firm. The individual's credibility with technical experts and senior management should be the overriding criterion for selection.

The outside consultant needed to launch such a training initiative will have to develop a curriculum for your training program, teach the curriculum to your internal trainers, and coach them on how to deliver it. The outside consultant will also have to counsel the internal people on how to be coaches and coordinators for important sales presentations.

The internal trainers and coaches will face a special challenge when interacting with senior members of the firm who outrank them. Preparing and rehearsing a major sales presentation can be a high-stress activity, and chances are that the senior member will feel the need to take over. In their role as presentation experts, your internal consultants will become "servant leaders" who must learn to use sophisticated interpersonal communication skills in coaching their bosses in high-stress moments.

In this instance, the internal consultant can point out to the senior member pulling rank that the world is more competitive than it was, that the old-boy network doesn't work as efficiently as it used to, and that competitors are employing more sophisticated sales approaches than they did in the past. They are gathering more information, devoting more people to the marketing effort, developing more sophisticated written materials, and using computers and videos in their presentations. Not only that: They are having their presenters trained and rehearsed by professional consultants who specialize in corporate sales presentations.

Any initiative to develop sales presentation skills should have as its goal an improved win-rate and a cost–benefit ratio. Management will want to know:

- The current percentage of sales presentations that result in revenue-producing assignments for the firm;
- The cost of preparing for an average sales presentation;
- The cost of the training to develop both your professional staff and, if applicable, your internal trainers;
- The percentage of wins once the new training and coaching program is up and running.

To be successful, a training initiative in sales presentation skills, whether run by internal or external trainers and coaches, will require short-term good word of mouth, and long-term proof of its contribution to the bottom line. If possible, senior members of the firm should attend and participate in the program, and afterwards honestly endorse it if they can. The big challenge will be getting partners and other busy professionals to attend. Good word of mouth and senior management endorsement will help get them to the door. After that, it will be up to the course design and the trainer to keep them engaged.

Running training during billable hours is almost impossible in some professional firms. The training can take place on Friday night and Saturday, or it can take place on consecutive evenings. However, people can always find even more reasons not to attend at such times, and the momentum and reputation of the training initiative can falter if sparsely attended. Requiring attendance is probably possible in some firms, but not all. Managing professionals is like herding cats. Getting them in the seats is one goal. Getting them to speak well of their experience is another. Getting the desired results is the ultimate indication that the effort has paid off.

Any training course in sales presentation skills should include videotaped exercises that allow your professionals to see themselves as others see them. The experience is often a powerful motivator for change, and people can make significant adjustments to the way they approach a presentation. But the improvements will be lost if the firm does not develop a systematic approach for preparing for sales presentations for it is there, in the real world, that the skills will take root. Someone must be in charge of coordinating the effort to design and rehearse the presentation so that the process does not depend on a committee. Designing and rehearsing a presentation is a creative process, and doing anything creative by committee is an invitation to mediocrity. Creative ideas are often squelched for one or two reasons: (1) people don't share their ideas for fear of being ridiculed or for fear of hurting somebody else's feelings, or (2) they criticize other people's ideas because they can't abide someone gaining more recognition than themselves, and so good ideas get dragged down and trampled in the mud of personal rivalry. For these reasons, presentation design should be handled by a trained, skilled, experienced individual who has license and credibility to call the shots. This means that once the strategy for the talk is set, it must be communicated to all who will be part of the presentation, and they must come to rehearsal having prepared themselves accordingly.

The rehearsal process must also be protected in the same way. No one will want to attend a rehearsal if all the good work they did to prepare is going to be torn apart by a pack of hyenas. The designated coordinator must maintain control of the rehearsal process, demand that presenters be prepared and attentive, and supervise the editing and feedback that will occur on the fly. It will be very much like running a contentious meeting. Again, the credibility and expertise of the individual running the meeting will be crucial to its success.

The following is a sample checklist to be used by a presentation coordinator for design and rehearsal. You will note that the task is not a simple one, especially if the person in charge is directing his or her superiors in the firm:

- Identify presenters.
- Distribute proposal to team members.
- Contact client to preview room and establish rules of presentation.
- Identify technical support team (graphics, and so on).
- Arrange kick-off meeting (consider videoconferencing).
- Brainstorm with professional in charge on strategy and tactics (including strengths and weaknesses of your firm and competition).
- Outline or "storyboard" presentation.
- Develop outline for each presenter (or have them submit one).
- Coordinate the creation of visual aids.
- Schedule rehearsals (sooner rather than later).
- Schedule equipment needed for rehearsal.
- Make sure people are prepared for rehearsal.
- Force people to use rehearsal as part of the editing process.

- Work with problem presenters in private.
- Prepare leave-behind document.
- Invite internal audience for dress rehearsal and Q&A drill (early enough to make changes if necessary).

Building Competence

Finally, what about the particular presentation competencies that the firm is seeking to develop in its professional staff? Like many soft skills, they're hard to define, but you know them when you see them. The ancient Greeks gave this some thought, and they claimed that the most important skill is simply a presenter's ability to project who he is, allowing the audience to know him and like him. They called this *ethos*. We might call it personality, style, presence, or charisma. It's hard, if not impossible, to teach, but it can be encouraged if management approaches this developmental undertaking in the right spirit.

That said, one universal characteristic of good sales presenters is enthusiasm. If a speaker demonstrates in her own way that she is enthusiastic about the subject, the occasion, and her firm, she stands a much better chance of being heard and liked. For some dry souls, this is a challenge. And yet people can project this quality in a variety of ways. Expressive people will use voice, gestures, and facial expressions to communicate their enthusiasm. Less expressive people will say things such as, "This research we did turned up some really neat information," and the client will be just as intrigued, not so much by the heat of the enthusiasm as by the quiet intensity of the light. We must remember that the greatest presentation material in the world is useless if the presenter is a bore. Good presentations are marriages of heat and light, emotional energy and intellectual distinctions. The audience listens and watches on both channels at once. If the speaker isn't enthusiastic about the topic, the audience gets the message that the topic is not worth getting excited about. Emotions are contagious. Your presenters should make sure that theirs are worth catching.

It is said in the theater that casting is nine-tenths of directing. This means that if you choose the right people for the job, your job as boss is easy. Chief Ben American Horse of the Oglala Sioux said the same thing in a different way: "Be careful with your immigration policies," he warned. "We were careless with ours." This is one way of approaching the challenge of building a corps of world-class presenters: Choose people who are naturally gifted at it. But few people are truly skilled at sales presenting. They may be gifted raconteurs, but that skill can get them in trouble as often as it can win them business. They often don't prepare well because they believe they can successfully wing it. They are not good role models for others whose personalities are less colorful; they don't make good coaches because they tend to operate from instinct; and they are not consistent winners for themselves or the firm, primarily because there are other competencies aside from personality that are required for excellence in sales presenting that they have not felt the need to study and develop.

One such competency is the ability to see the situation from the clients' perspective and structure the presentation to their point of view. For example, an engineer may want to explain to the municipal selection committee exactly how he's going to build the bridge, whereas the committee is much more interested in how the engineer is going to manage the disruption in traffic patterns during construction. An astute sales presenter must structure her presentations based on the audiences' desire to know, not her desire to talk.

This is true for all of us who consider ourselves subject matter experts. We love to talk about what we know. The golden rule of sales presenting is to talk about what the audience wants to hear. Uncovering what they want to hear, their worries and issues, is another competency that should be built into the sales presentation process. It's better if the issues are uncovered earlier, in the proposal process, but the skill is relevant to our discussion here. Your professionals are only as good in the sales presentation arena as they are at asking clients and potential clients questions long before they put the presentation together. To that end, firms should have a checklist, or a process, that encourages people to ask potential clients questions that illuminate the issues and concerns that should be addressed in the proposal and the presentation. Without this skill of questioning, your firm's ability to focus sales presentations on client interests is severely compromised.

The ability to make complex ideas easy to understand is another skill to be addressed, and one that requires effective use of language and storytelling. First, language. Professionals have their own vocabularies. You know how difficult it is to speak with doctors about personal medical issues: They use Latin words when a plain old English word would do. Your presenters must make sure their language is audience friendly. According to one survey, the primary reason why clients express dissatisfaction with their consultants is language usage. Consultants speak a foreign language of their own that isn't easily understood by the client.

Your firm may be deeply attached to its lingo and be able to justify why it's necessary to use it. But teach your people to keep it simple. Tell them to speak English.

Storytelling is an integral element of successful sales presentations. No audience has the stomach or the patience for sustained fact reporting and abstract discussion. They want to hear concrete "for instances." The best communicators are often the best storytellers, and stories are a great way of making a point that would otherwise be lost. Of course, stories must support a point, and they should be accompanied by factual, or data-driven, support as well. But all of your professionals should be encouraged to collect anecdotes and war stories that are short, pithy, and to the point.

Simplicity is also important in visual aids. If your firm also owns stock in a binocular company, then have your presenters compose their slides with small, dense fonts detailing inscrutable and arcane facts. However, if you want your clients to understand and remember what you've said, keep your slides big and simple. Visual aids are meant to have visual impact in the presentation arena. Often, consulting firms will saddle their presentation document with two irreconcilable tasks: (1) being an interesting presentation document, designed for the ear and the distant eyes of the audience, and (2) being a written document to be left behind for the reading eye, 20 inches from the page. Consulting firms do this to save time, but they could save themselves and their clients much agony if they created big and simple visuals for the presentation and a separate written document with more detail that the client could depart with.

There will always be people whose personal mannerisms undermine their expertise and therefore their ability to contribute. They may speak in a monotonous voice. They may say "er" and "uhm" more than they should. They may spend a good deal of their time in front of clients speaking to the tops of their shoes or to the visual aids. They may pace nervously, gesture awkwardly, and speak in endless, serpentine sentences. More important, they may insist on speaking about their expertise, rather than on how their expertise is going to solve the client's problem. And they may talk for hours and fail to ask for the business.

These problems can be erased, and should be erased, with a well-designed approach to developing sales presentation skills. Management can boost productivity and grow the bottom line by systematically supporting the values and practices needed for effective sales presenting.

Endnotes

Introduction

1. Marc Galanter and Thomas Palay, professors at the University of Wisconsin, have traced the first appearance of the term in reference to lawyers to 1978. Prior to that time, the term *business-getter* was often used. See Galanter, Marc, and Thomas Palay, *Tournament of Lawyers, The Transformation of the Big Law Firms* (Chicago: The University of Chicago Press, 1991), p. 53.

Chapter I

1. Wolf, William B., *Management and Consulting: An Introduction to James O. McKinsey* (Ithaca, N.Y.: Cornell University, 1978), p. 16.

2. Maister, David H., *Managing the Professional Service Firm* (New York: The Free Press, 1993), p. 122. The three categories are: The First Team (including small seminars, speeches, article writing, and proprietary research), The Second String (including community/civic activities, networking, and newsletters), and Clutching at Straws (including publicity, brochures, large seminars, direct mail, video brochures, advertising, and cold calls).

3. Weiss, Alan, *Million Dollar Consulting, The Professional's Guide to Growing a Practice* (New York: McGraw-Hill, 1992), p. 38.

4. Connor, Richard A. Jr., and Jeffrey P. Davidson, *Getting New Clients* (New York: John Wiley & Sons, 1987).

5. Schiffman, Stephan, *The Consultant's Handbook: How to Start & Develop Your Own Practice* (Holbrook, Mass.: Bob Adams, 1988).

6. Weitzul, James B., *Personality Traits in Professional Services Marketing* (Westport, Conn.: Quorum Books, 1994).

7. Seligman, Martin E. P., *Learned Optimism: How to Change Your Mind and Your Life* (New York: Pocket Books, 1990).

8. Wolf, *Management and Consulting: An Introduction to James O. McKinsey,* p. 15.

9. O'Brian, Bridget, and Gabriella Stern, "Nonstop Schmoozing Propels an Accountant into the Big Leagues," *The Wall Street Journal,* March 19, 1997, p. A1.

Chapter 2

1. This relationship is known as Metcalfe's law.

2. Dörner, Dietrich, *The Logic of Failure: Why Things Go Wrong and What We Can Do to Make Them Right* (New York: Metropolitan Books, 1996), pp. 110–114.

3. For a description of these studies, see Gould, Stephen Jay, *Bully for Brontosaurus: Reflections in Natural History* (New York: W. W. Norton, 1991), pp. 463–472. Also see, Paulos, John Allen, *A Mathematician Reads the Newspaper* (New York: Anchor Books, 1995), pp. 181–183.

4. Rucker, Rudy, *Mind Tools, The Five Levels of Mathematical Reality* (Boston: Houghton Mifflin, 1987), p. 47.

5. Ibid., pp. 48–49.

Chapter 3

1. Smith, Donald G., *The Joy of Negative Thinking: How to Face Life with a Good Negative Attitude* (Philadelphia: Delancy Press, 1995).

2. Seligman, Martin E. P., *Learned Optimism: How to Change Your Mind and Your Life* (New York: Pocket Books, 1990), p. 165.

3. Ibid, pp. 43–52.

4. In addition to Seligman's book, I would recommend Burns, David D., *Feeling Good, The New Mood Therapy* (New York: Avon Books, 1980). Many professionals, who must learn a certain amount of cynicism to do their jobs well, may be put off by the title. I hope they can get past it.

Chapter 5

1. "McKinsey & Company *(A): 1956,*" Case Study 9-393-066 (Boston: Harvard Business School Press, 1992), p. 16.

2. Ibid., p. 9.

3. Linowitz, Sol M., with Martin Mayer, *The Betrayed Profession, Lawyering at the End of the Twentieth Century* (Baltimore: The Johns Hopkins University Press, 1994), p. 102.

4. Ibid., pp. 22–23.

5. Wolf, William B., *Management and Consulting: An Introduction to James O. McKinsey* (Ithaca, N.Y.: Cornell University, 1978), p.42.

6. Linowitz, *The Betrayed Profession, Lawyering at the End of the Twentieth Century*, p. 59.

7. A few rainmakers in the survey escaped antisolicitation tyranny, at least in part, through mentoring from a successful rainmaker. For example, both Gene Kohn, of Kohn Pedersen Fox Associates, and Tom Bathgate, of PWI Engineering, mentioned the mentoring they received from architect Vincent Kling, a highly dramatic and successful rainmaker.

8. *1979 Statistical Abstract of the United States* (Washington, D.C.: U.S. Government Printing Office, 1979), p. 416, and *1995 Statistical Abstract of the United States* (Washington, D.C.: U.S. Government Printing Office, 1995), pp. 411 and 414.

9. Wolf, *Management and Consulting: An Introduction to James O. McKinsey*, p. 43.

10. Luckman, Charles, *Twice in a Lifetime: From Soap to Skyscrapers* (New York: W. W. Norton & Company, 1988).

11. See endnotes to Chapter 10 for references.

Chapter 7

1. Stewart, Thomas A., "Your Company's Most Valuable Asset: Intellectual Capital," *Fortune*, October 3, 1994, pp. 68–73; Stewart, Thomas A., "Mapping Corporate Brainpower," *Fortune*, October 30, 1995, pp. 209–211; Quinn, James Brian, Philip Anderson, and Sydney Finkelstein, "Managing Professional Intellect: Making the Most of the Best," *Harvard Business Review*, March–April, 1996, pp. 71–80.

2. For a concise summary of Drucker's contribution, see Micklethwait, John, and Adrian Woodridge, *The Witch Doctors: Making Sense of the Management Gurus* (New York: Times Books, 1996), pp. 63–78.

3. Pine, Joseph P. II, *Mass Customization: The New Frontier in Business Competition* (Boston: Harvard Business School Press, 1991).

4. McKinsey, James O., *Budgetary Control* (New York: Ronald Press, 1922). For a description of the importance of this work, see Wolf, *Management and Consulting: An Introduction to James O. McKinsey*, pp. 4–5.

5. Manganelli, Raymond L., and Mark M. Klein, *The Reengineering Handbook, A Step-by-Step Guide to Business Transformation* (New York: American Management Association, 1994).

6. Maister, David H., *Managing the Professional Service Firm* (New York: The Free Press, 1993), pp. 123–128.

7. Ingrassia, Paul, and Joseph B. White, *Comeback: The Fall and Rise of the American Automobile Industry* (New York: Simon & Schuster, 1994), p. 40.

8. For an elaboration of the timeliness of consulting concepts, see Stalk, George, and Thomas M. Hout, *Competing Against Time* (New York: The Free Press, 1990), pp. 4–28. This book was written by consultants from Boston Consulting Group, a firm that, under the leadership of Bruce Henderson, has been particularly sensitive to the importance of timing in the introduction of ideas. See also Harding, Ford, "Where's the Gravy?" in *Management Consultant International,* issue 66, February 1995, p. 11.

9. Hammer, Michael, "Reengineering Work: Don't Automate, Obliterate," *Harvard Business Review,* July–August 1990.

10. Hammer, Michael, and James Champy, *Reengineering the Corporation* (New York: Harper Business, 1993).

11. Crosby, Philip B., *Quality Is Free* (New York: McGraw-Hill, 1979).

12. Ingrassia and White, *Comeback: The Fall and Rise of the American Automobile Industry,* p. 140.

13. Peters, Thomas J., and Robert H. Waterman Jr., *In Search of Excellence: Lessons from America's Best-Run Companies* (New York: Harper & Row, 1982).

Chapter 8

1. Wittreich, Warren J., "How to Buy/Sell Professional Services," *Harvard Business Review,* March–April 1966, p. 129.

2. Shenson, Howard L., *Shenson on Consulting: Success Strategies from the Consultant's Consultant* (New York: John Wiley & Sons in association with University Associates, Inc., 1990).

3. Holtz, Herman, *The Consultant's Guide to Winning Clients* (New York: John Wiley & Sons, 1988).

4. Ibid., p. 49.

5. Maister, David H., *Managing the Professional Service Firm* (New York: The Free Press, 1993).

6. Schiffman, Stephan, *The Consultant's Handbook: How to Start & Develop Your Own Practice* (Holbrook, Mass.: Bob Adams, 1988).

7. Harding, Ford, *Rain Making: The Professional's Guide to Attracting New Clients* (Holbrook, Mass.: Bob Adams, 1994), pp. 19–132.

8. Donald, David Herbert, *Lincoln* (New York: Simon & Schuster, 1995), p. 389.

Chapter 9

1. Axelrod, Robert, *The Evolution of Cooperation* (New York: Basic Books, 1984).

2. Wolf, William B., *Management and Consulting: An Introduction to James O. McKinsey* (Ithaca, N.Y.: Cornell University, 1978), p. 42.

3. Axelrod, *The Evolution of Cooperation,* pp. 129–130.

4. Burt, Ronald S., "The Social Structure of Competition," in *Networks and Organizations: Structure, Form, and Action,* ed., Nitin Nohria and Robert G. Eccles (Boston: Harvard Business School Press, 1992), pp. 72–73.

5. O'Brian, Bridget, and Gabriella Stern, "Nonstop Schmoozing Propels an Accountant into the Big Leagues," *The Wall Street Journal,* March 19, 1997, p. A1.

Chapter 10

1. Harding, Ford, *Rain Making: The Professional's Guide to Attracting New Clients* (Holbrook, Mass.: Bob Adams, 1994), pp. 133–182; Miller, Robert B. and Stephen E. Heiman with Tad Tuleja, *Strategic Selling* (New York: Warner Books, 1985); Rackham, Neil, *SPIN Selling* (New York: McGraw-Hill, 1988).

2. Ibid., *SPIN Selling.*

3. Wolf, William B., *Management and Consulting: An Introduction to James O. McKinsey* (Ithaca, N.Y.: Cornell University, 1978), p. 43.

4. James O. McKinsey used an approach similar to this one, as will be seen in Chapter 12.

5. The Rodent, *Explaining the Inexplicable: The Rodent's Guide to Lawyers* (New York: Pocket Books, 1995), p. 117.

Chapter 11

1. Wittreich, Warren J., "How to Buy/Sell Professional Services," *Harvard Business Review,* March–April 1966, p. 132.

2. Neuhauser, Peg C., *Corporate Legends and Lore: The Power of Storytelling as a Management Tool* (New York: McGraw-Hill, Inc., 1993), p. 6.

3. Wittreich, "How to Buy/Sell Professional Services," p. 133.

4. Neuhauser, *Corporate Legends and Lore: The Power of Storytelling as a Management Tool,* pp. 33–35.

5. For a discussion of the variations normally found in oral literature and the effects of writing on them, see Lord, Alfred, *The Singer of Tales* (New York: Atheneum, 1965).

Chapter 12

1. Guzzardi, Walter, "Wisdom from the Giants of Business," *Fortune,* July 3, 1989, p. 81.

2. Wolf, William B., *Management and Consulting: An Introduction to James B. McKinsey* (Ithaca, N.Y.: Cornell University, 1978), pp. 44–45.

3. Anonymous, "Confessions of an Ex-Consultant," *Fortune,* October 14, 1996, p. 110.

4. Kelly, Michael J., *Lives of Lawyers: Journeys in the Organizations of Practice* (Ann Arbor: The University of Michigan Press, 1994), p. 152.

5. Bok, Sissela, *Lying: Moral Choice in Public and Private Life* (New York: Vintage Books, 1989), p. 13.

6. Carr, Albert Z., "Is Business Bluffing Ethical?" *Harvard Business Review,* 46(1), 1968, pp. 143–150.

7. Huff, Darrel, *How to Lie with Statistics* (New York: W. W. Norton, 1993). First published in 1954.

8. Nash, Laura L., *Good Intentions Aside: A Manager's Guide to Resolving Ethical Problems* (Boston: Harvard Business School Press, 1990).

9. Luckman, Charles, *Twice in a Lifetime: From Soap to Skyscrapers* (New York: W. W. Norton, 1988), pp. 289–290.

10. Bok, *Lying: Moral Choice in Public and Private Life,* p. 25.

11. Courtis, John, *Bluff Your Way in Accountancy* (Horsham, West Sussex: Ravette Books Ltd., 1987) and Viney, Nigel, *Bluff Your Way in Consulting* (Horsham, West Sussex: Ravette Books, Ltd., 1986).

12. The Rodent, *Explaining the Inexplicable: The Rodent's Guide to Lawyers* (New York: Pocket Books, 1995).

Chapter 13

1. Almost all the rainmakers in the survey stated explicitly that providing good service to their clients was critical to their success at obtaining new business. This is hardly surprising. I find it more surprising that there were any exceptions at all. For the record, here is an example of one:

He tended to burn through clients. He was very smart and had little patience for those who were less so, and clients soon sensed this and became uncomfortable working with him. So, every year, he would go out and find $3 million in business from new ones. [a management consultant]

Most of us would agree that this is the hard way to build a practice.

Appendix C

1. Speech by Robert Duboff to the Public Relations Society of America, Professional Services Section, June 4, 1996.

2. Speech by Gary Gerard to the Public Relations Society of America, Professional Services Section, June 4, 1996.

3. Telberg, Rick, "Behind Arthur Andersen's Brand Name Strategy" in *Accounting Today*, October 21, 1996, p. 5.

4. Ibid.

5. Speech by Gary Gerard to the Public Relations Society of America, Professional Services Section, June 4, 1996.

6. Messina, Judith, "KPMG's Day of Reckoning" in *Crain's New York Business*, December 2, 1996.

7. Speech by Gary Gerard to the Public Relations Society of America, Professional Services Section, June 4, 1996.

Index